Construction and Design Manual
School Buildings

Natascha Meuser
Born 1967, architect and interior architect. Studied at the *Illinois Institute of Technology* in Chicago and the *University of Applied Sciences Rosenheim*. From 2000 to 2005 she was research assistant at the *Berlin Technical University*. Architecture firm with international projects and publishing business.

Hans Wolfgang Hoffmann
Born 1970, Architecture studies at the *Berlin Technical University* with a focus on urban sociology, the history of architecture and typology of buildings. Editorial work and publications in trade magazines and daily newspapers, author of architectural guides (including for Berlin and Warsaw).

Thomas Müller
Born 1947, degree in the Technology of Wood and Plastic at the *Rosenheim University of Applied Sciences*, followed by Promotion at the *Berlin Technical University*. Professor for materials handling and logistics at the *Hamburg University of Applied Sciences*. DIN delegate for European school furniture standardization. Founder of a Museum of Education (1990). Managing director of the *VS Vereinigte Spezialmöbelfabriken* in Tauberbischofsheim.

Jochem Schneider
Born 1964, co-founder of *bueroschneidermeyer*, an architecture firm in Cologne. Many years of experience with the architectural and municipal planning assistance of local school construction projects and publications on the subject (for instance *Empfehlung für einen zukunftsfähigen Schulbau in Baden-Württemberg, Schulen planen und bauen*).

Construction and Design Manual
School Buildings

Edited by Natascha Meuser

With essays by Hans Wolfgang Hoffmann,
Thomas Müller and Jochem Schneider

Contents

Preface

6	Learning and Design	*Natascha Meuser*

1

Theory and History

10	5,500 Years of Detention	*Hans Wolfgang Hoffmann*
34	From Classroom to Learning Landscape	*Thomas Müller*
46	Learning from School Buildings	*Jochem Schneider*
56	Selected Literature	

2

Primary Schools

60	Hardenberg · Holland	*Marlies Rohmer*
68	London · United Kingdom	*Building Design Partnership*
76	Schulzendorf · Germany	*zanderroth architekten with Guido Neubeck*
84	Rudrapur · Bangladesh	*Anna Heringer, Elke Roswag*
92	Cressy · Switzerland	*Devanthéry & Lamunière Architectes*
100	Rolle · Switzerland	*Devanthéry & Lamunière Architectes*
108	Hamburg · Germany	*Spengler · Wiescholek*
116	Leusden · Holland	*RAU Architects*
126	Chemnitz · Germany	*bhss Architekten*
136	Siegertsbrunn · Germany	*Fischer Architekten*
144	Berlin · Germany	*Numrich Albrecht Klumpp*
150	Grono · Switzerland	*Raphael Zuber*

Secondary Schools

162	Copenhagen · Denmark	*3XN*
172	Slough · United Kingdom	*Foster + Partners*
182	Nijkerk · Holland	*Broekbakema*
190	Zutphen · Holland	*RAU Architects*
198	Cape Town · South Africa	*Sonja Petrus Spamer, Noero Wolff*
206	Melbourne · Australia	*John Wardle Architects*
214	Schleswig · Germany	*C. F. Møller Architects*
224	Vienna · Austria	*Atelier Heiss*
232	Gjerdrum · Norway	*Kristin Jarmund Arkitekter*
238	La Orotava · Spain	*AMP arquitectos*
246	Deutsch-Wagram · Austria	*franz Architekten*
256	Mosfellsbær · Island	*a2f arkitektar*
266	Eidsvoll · Norway	*Kristin Jarmund Arkitekter*
274	Dinkelsbühl · Germany	*Fischer Architekten*
284	Berlin · Germany	*Numrich Albrecht Klumpp*

Special Schools

292	Bogotá · Columbia	*Giancarlo Mazzanti*
300	Zurich · Switzerland	*Christian Kerez*
312	Lausanne · Switzerland	*Geninasca & Delefortrie*
320	Chemnitz · Germany	*bhss Architekten*
330	Regensburg · Germany	*Georg · Scheel · Wetzel Architekten*

Ten Design Parameters

340	Introduction
344	Space Allocation Program
350	Safety and Security
356	Access
360	Teaching Rooms
370	Meeting Rooms
372	Library
374	Staff Rooms
376	Toilets and Washrooms
380	Cafeteria and School Kitchen
384	Open Areas and Gyms
388	Index
390	Illustration Credits

Learning and Design
The Purpose of this Manual

Natascha Meuser

This book is about school buildings. They are presently going through a process of transformation like very few other building types. While other building types simply touch up their exteriors and forms, the school building of today is marked by completely new learning and use concepts. Only office buildings have gone through a similar process in the last decades.

A school building, regardless of the form, is the second most common type of building after the residential building. In the life story of every human being, next to the family home, the school, at least in most parts of the world, is the building which is consciously perceived as an architectural space by children and youth who spend a large part of their lives there. Everyone can remember the architecture and the spatial peculiarities of his or her school. Schools are usually public buildings where individuals truly learn for the first time to find their place and act as a member of society outside the family home. Schools are the places where interactions of the individual and society become architecturally concrete.

If the spatial demands and architectural standards of a school have changed significantly, this is above all the result of changed goals, methods and the instruments of knowledge transfer. This transformation was also implemented architecturally: from the front facing classroom with blackboard, to the work place with digital network.

Office buildings and school buildings have many similarities in this regard. The isolation of workplaces predicted with the introduction of digital media gave way to the team idea and group formation. While setting up a workplace with a chair was considered progress at the end of the 18th century, desks for working, archiving, or writing desks are no longer needed. Tablets are now desks and filing drawers in one. Mobile workplaces can be carried everywhere and have become a space-condensing decentralized work and learning medium.

Digitalization has liberated learning from fixed locations and schematic learning processes, with a direct effect on the architecture. Almost any location and room shape can be converted into a space for teaching and learning. As in modern offices, desks and rooms are shared. Intermediate areas which until now were hardly used are being integrated in everyday school life. Students and teachers meet here to work together, depending on the objective goals or subject being taught. Learning requires a reorganization of the tools and objects, which in turn place new demands on the use of space. Students today must no longer sit at the same place in order to concentrate on inner, order creating and mental processes.

School construction is usually a state activity. It is often the construction task which represents the first large commission for a young architect, which therefore involves a great deal of experimentation. When they are commissioned as a result of a competition, school buildings usually exhibit exceptional architectural quality. School construction is thereby a typology that influences the style for entire architectural epochs, from the monumental school houses of the industrial revolution to the landscape-emphasizing pavilion architecture of the Modern, to the digital knowledge factory of today. Especially in the western societies with their dwindling levels of population quantity is no longer so important, and the school is distinguished by the level of teaching. In this context the notion that high quality architectural space can create a successful learning atmosphere has been established. This development can be seen in new construction and expansions as well as space optimization in the framework of renovation.

The school construction planning today is more complicated than it has been in the past decades. In addition to handicap accessibility and safety, the social background and cultural environment are now the priorities, which means increased admission control, threshold free entrances and interreligious common areas in the performance specifications.

This book asks to what extent school buildings react to contemporary forms of teaching and learning, because changed pedagogical concepts always have brought spatial changes with them. What is the form of the space that corresponds to the form of knowledge to be transmitted? Will schools begin to be individualized like apartment buildings or hotels? Should the floor plans and spaces be flexible in order to be able to respond to future pedagogical concepts of even more democratized school architecture? The digital media transformation revolutionizing the school construction typology or learning in the 21st century is a process which we are now in the middle of and which we will be able to evaluate in ten or twenty years. Above all the architects must bear in mind that they must be conscious of their social responsibility and their cultural architectural contribution.

Three authors portray school construction typologies from ancient times to the 21st century in this manual.

Hans Wolfgang Hoffmann's essay asks what homework does the school still have to offer – a cultural and architectural historical genesis from the discovery of the school to the coming designs. In eight lessons he takes us on a trip around the world through more than 5,000 years of human history. Hoffmann presents the protagonists and historical and contemporary learning concepts and acutely analyses which spatial changes have accompanied and will accompany school construction.

Thomas Müller defines the design task of school construction as the focus on the reciprocal relationship between architecture and the human being. On the way from the classroom to the learning landscape his essay explains why the design of classrooms exerts a significant influence on the performance, wellbeing and development of children and youth. Müller examines functional schematics and relevant factors of influence for the design of school buildings in societies undergoing change and locates them in terms of architectural history. He presents modern learning landscapes, for instance the various aspects of a flexible use of space, work ergonomics, and the standardization of furniture and work devices.

Jochem Schneider presents an expanded and reworked version of the study on *Typologien and räumliche Organizationsmodelle* (Typologies and Spatial Organization Models), which the author produced in 2012 on behalf of and together with the Montag Stiftung Urbane Räume in the framework of the project *Leitlinien für leistungsfähige Schulbauten* (Guidelines for Efficient School Buildings). He shows current concepts for learning locations, teachers' areas and community rooms, and by explaining them on the basis of easy to understand organizational models, creates a reference framework for quality criteria.

In the practical part of the book, the richly illustrated planning and design aid, more than 30 international new buildings and expansions as well as renovations for primary and secondary school are presented. Another section is devoted to special schools. Every school construction, organized according to the number of pupils, is exhaustively presented with informative photos and the project data.

Ten design parameters round out this compendium of school construction. The practice-generated experience is prepared for working architects and is intended to function as a practical aid in order to implement creative ideas in the project.

Theory and History

5,500 Years of Detention	10
From Classroom to Learning Landscape	34
Learning from School Buildings	46
Selected Literature	56

5,500 Years of Detention
Which Homework does the School still have to Offer?

Hans Wolfgang Hoffmann

Who would want to underestimate the importance of education? "We don't need no education!" – our parents may have howled the Pink Floyd song with glee but that kind of appeal to ignorance is no longer in vogue. The opinion looks differently today: no school is a no-win situation. Unfilled or vacant posts in the schools generate negative headlines immediately. It is already a point of honour for the youngest students to have a packed curriculum and no politician will get elected who doesn't call for the extension of education. So architects don't have a choice: they may refuse to design a defence facility, traffic lanes or tower blocks, but no architect can turn down a school assignment in good conscience. Conversely school construction can become a veritable hornet's nest of expectation. Educational facilities are crammed full with the most varied types of rooms. In general we can say that the school that makes us what we are, is no longer good enough! The door is then opened for unconventional approaches to planning, most of which are contained in this book. Even the absolutely newest educational models can make a go of it with children as guinea pigs. There has to be something more than the tried and true and no one is worried about too much!

If nothing else the effect of the school can be explosive. The report card that simply watches from the side lines doesn't exist. The most garden variety of scientific evaluation is critical. The problem is about as old as the Pink Floyd song but is still relevant and won't go away. It was first published in 1979 in *The Limits and Possibilities of Schooling*. In it the American sociologist Christopher Hurn compared the influences of the parental home, the society and school with the later social status of their charges. Science confirmed what experience already knew, namely that the diploma was crucial for the first job. However Hurn could not point to the school as the main factor in the path taken from there. Subsequent studies in fact show that origin and environment are the dominant factors. The school has lost in influence, despite the good grades!

In light of this contradiction, it cannot hurt to widen the point of view. For the first time homework will be examined from an historical overview: from the discovery of the school to the not yet built designs of today we will travel around the world. During this arduous journey there is much to encounter that seems to cry out for implementation but which actually has been tried long ago and rejected! Interestingly enough it was often the schools which sooner or later made themselves obsolete. There are only a handful of lessons to be learned today. Each of them can be recognized as an original archetype which can be derived from a very particular interplay among society, didactics and architectural form. It is even more amazing how the focus wanders from epoch to epoch:

In the Temple of Knowledge the focus of education shifts from academics to the ignorant. All in all, a clear line of development can be seen, which is inescapable. If you run through the

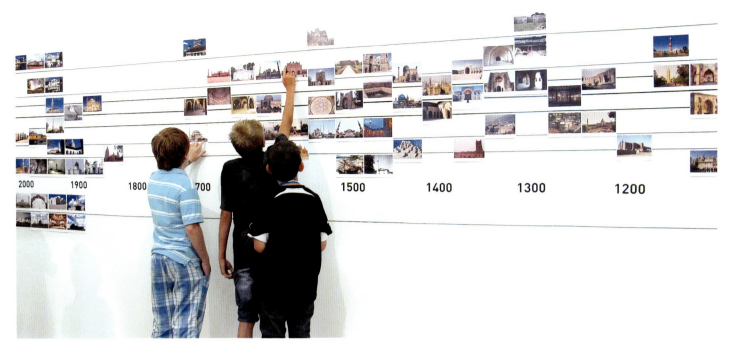

The school as institution has a long history: knowledge was being transferred 5,500 years ago all over the world.

ancestral line in fast forward you inevitably end up in the school of tomorrow!

First lesson: The Temple of Knowledge

The first school was in Upper Egypt at the end of the pre-dynastic Period. Instruction began in front of a library, which was tucked into an alcove in the temple. From the beginning in all ancient cultures the central role the school played inside the main building is always the same: this is where the political-religious leaders trained the civil servants. The fact that the pupils had a place right next to the library is a giveaway that the discovery was a direct consequence of another innovation: The school used the medium of writing. A short time beforehand, the clay tablet and paper had replaced the stone tablet to transmit information. At the same time abstract symbols begin to enrich the simple pictorial language. The hieroglyphics are easier to use but are not as self-evident. Simply looking at the pictures, like the parents or the masters did when they slowly worked through a comic book, was no longer enough. For the new medium to be able to transmit knowledge, a school was needed as a general guarantee for the validity of the written word. That is why the school was already an institution 5,500 years ago. From that point on no advanced civilization could do with it. In Asia, America or Europe the homework was the same: The school was there to ease the entry into society. And the target group which the school took under its wing was always the same: the school welcomed those who were no longer small children and said good-bye to them on the threshold of adulthood. The side effects were no less noticeable: the parents took a back seat because an educational facility had been placed at their disposal where they could just send their children and be done with them. As a consequence the powers that be were strengthened: the school gave the community a live cell therapy, coupled with individual development. The archetype was established: the school became a special place between home and the world, a germ cell to be approximated in the cultural sphere.

But that was not enough. More than just the product of its environment the school had to work creatively. The calculation is easy. The school, which cashes in on the maximum growth in vitality of the human being, is where the Homo sapiens fiddles away the first half of his biological highpoint. Later on the school will demand more entertainment from his dwindling energy. Only a surplus value can compensate for the unavoidable loss of vitality as a benefit for the world of the adults, which in turn means that the homework increases. Put another way, the school implies its own change! A world improving machine as perpetuum mobile? The prototype began modestly enough.

Education (*Bildung*) means reproduction (*Abbildung*) in the scribal school. The hand and the eye copy the existing document. In the process the student learns to read and write. It can even happen that what has been written down becomes planted in the

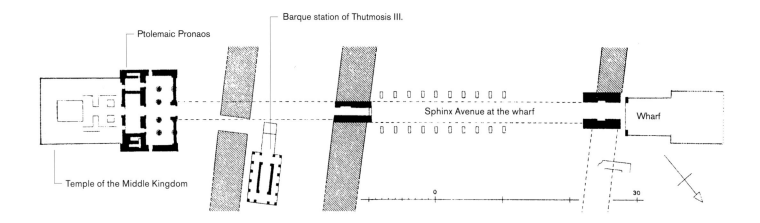

Month Temple, El-Tod, 2000 B.C.
In ancient Egypt instruction is conducted in a niche of the library. However education, including learning to write, mathematics, geography, history, astronomy, sculpture, painting and sports is a privilege reserved for the wealthy.

young mind. But above all what counts is the copy of the information itself! For that you need a person who can compare the original and the copy, namely the teacher. The teacher's main concern is the integrity of the content. It is more practical when several students sit together. The mechanical didactic makes hardly any demands on the architecture. Writing desks should be put next to each other. But the scriptorium is always located in the shadow of the library which is the heart of the endeavour. The scribal school is a pure Temple of Knowledge. Today contemporary documents only show how the first specimens looked. Architectural artefacts like the Month-temple, founded around 2000 B.C. in El-Tod, show the fully developed plan.

At first the Temple of Knowledge is very successful. With the support of the scribal school information spreads quicker, further and with fewer errors. Thanks to its preliminary work an administration is established which deals with problems. Egypt goes through a change in epochs and is unified for the first time under a dynasty and the pyramids immediately celebrate their premiere. Meanwhile the scribal school on the Euphrates and Tigris expand, where very similar enabling technologies are developed in their own buildings, the so-called tablet houses, named after the clay tablets used there as storage media and which were part of the palace city recognize teachers and school directors as distinct professions. Starting from the Nile and Mesopotamia, the networks of temple, scriptorium and library spread through North Africa and half of Asia and Europe. Because of the fidelity to the original which the copy embodies, the archetype is at home where there are only a few eternal truths, especially in monastery schools. The onset of the high Middle Ages marked the beginning of the end for the institution. Thanks to the invention of printing the scriptorium became obsolete, just as new media have recently made the library dispensable. The (physical) posture from the Temple of Knowledge survived: if you can write, you're right …

Second Lesson: The Temple of Education

A more enduring influence was the recognition that education required a modicum of mobility. The ancient Egyptians already found an alternative. At the beginning of the second millennium B.C. the local community had become so puffed up that it was bursting at the seams. So the temple did a re-boot. The scribal school stepped back a bit from the executive and sanctuary. It was now closely associated with the hospital ward.

From the viewpoint of the pupils this arrangement may not seem to make sense, but from the standpoint of the professionals who were liberated by the move, the advantage was obvious. The teachers and the doctors were working hand in hand on

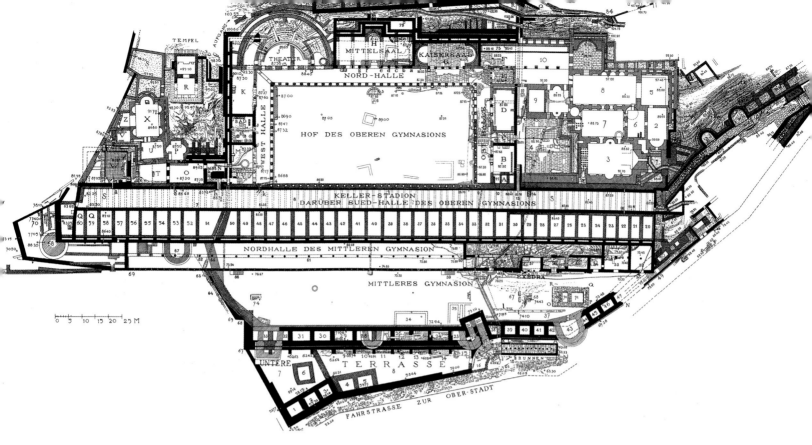

Gymnasion Pergamon, 200 B.C.
Mental and physical health is taught in in ancient Greece. A pillar enclosed courtyard (palastra) adjoins the teaching rooms. It was used as a training centre for sports until the 6th century B.C., and later served as a facility for mental and physical health.

the integration of the high performers in the society. The joint home was called the so-called *per-ankh*, the best surviving example of which is located in Achet-Aton – the new Nile capital which Pharao Echnaton dedicated exclusively to the sun god in 1345 B.C. This *House of Life* implied – the floor plan may also indicate parallel worlds – a completely different understanding of education. From now on healthy bodies resided together with healthy minds! This educational idea brought movement in the true sense of the word into the schools and bestowed it with a new archetype 500 years later. The Greeks perfected it because it was a question of survival for them: they settled in city-states which were in constant conflict with each other so that physical and mental and fitness spelled the difference between war and peace. They aimed for a safe connection between the two and looked for a suitable space to exercise. The temporary solution was the Olympic Games. No sooner were they invented, than the same pedagogical principle solidified in a more lasting variant: the gymnasion, whose most striking attribute is the palestra, a courtyard framed by pillars.

In the centre of this so-called wrestling school is an open space where the boys were comprehensively educated in sports, militarily, artistically, and even in sex. Movement shapes the body, rules of play tame the spirit. Socially the pupil is here more than ever a neutral entity and therefore naked. That meant that training halls, baths, cloakrooms and promenades enclosed the grass covered square completely, which is what the special space *school* represented in a pure form.

The gymnasion was first tested in Sparta. It was realized in its most exemplary form by Sparta's potent adversary Athens, around 550 B.C. Up until the dawn of the Christian era dozens of such learning locations are established. Every larger city in the Greek antiquity built one. The body-building movement actually misses the mark. This kind of education at best promotes inner peace, but exacerbates the conflict externally. As the city state expanded into empires, the schools took on a life of their own. The best evidence for that was around 220 B.C. in the Roman partner province of Pergamon. It was a virtually post-modern collage of wrestling ring, thermal bath, temple and theatre. Under the hegemony of Imperial Rome, which no Greek gymnasion could stop, this development came to an end. Bread and circus without the pretence of education was offered.

The state withdrew from education until Rome was finally overrun by migration. Still, body building has survived as a special form of instruction and the sports field and gymnasium still augment education today. The spatial arrangement is also articulated on a European basis: the post-antiquity cultivates the monastery and nowadays the classroom school features a public square.

The Library of Alexandria, 305–282 B.C.
The drawing (O. von Corven) shows the inside of the library according to a modern concept. The Roman inscription from the 1st century A.D. refers to the existence of the Egyptian library.

Where the art of fighting dominates the curriculum the whole gymnasion is still resistant to change.

Third Lesson: The Temple of the Academics

Physical education was truly not the only tic of antiquity, and the intellectual sphere was not neglected. So much knowledge piled up that the library required its own building contract but in spite of how many impressions one may gather, one never makes it through the mounds of books and comprehends the world as it is. The only possible aid to memory is presence of mind. The search for system makes thinking a thing in itself. The oral path immediately takes on new momentum as a didactic method. The spoken word represents the actual situation in contrast to text; the art of speech allows for confirmation that counts for the moment. As the land of democracy, where rhetoric decided the fate of the community, Greece was especially keen on that point. The school is not affected at first. After all, the pupils understand speech differently than writing. But they at least have to listen to the teacher, as opposed to the time when each student could copy on his own. Instead of a scriptorium an auditorium was now considered appropriate. But these things take time. The motor of the change in school opinion is the teacher. His knowledge of relationships elevated him to academic status, and his critical attitude made him an advice-dispensing, public figure so that philosophers like Socrates or Plato exert considerable influence and enjoy prominence in ancient Athens.

In terms of buildings there was no appreciable difference; Socrates held forth more often at the market than in the school and the hallowed grove of Plato's Academy (academia), was hardly a building. Of course the gymnasion – as the Pergamon project already indicates – soon became more loquacious, by absorbing foreign archetypes like porticos and amphitheatres. But as Vitruvius analysed shortly before the change in era in his *Ten Books on Architecture*, these were at best adjuncts. The Mediterranean antiquity never understood the auditorium as a focal point. During the Regnum Romanum (Roman Empire) the school of the philosophers became a strictly private matter.

It was the Chinese who derived an archetype from the academic lecture, if they didn't in fact invent it! According to the legend, the ball started rolling already in the 23rd century B.C. in what is today the province of Shangxi. The rumours converge at a point mid-course in the Yellow River and the imperial capital of Puban. The putative capital city was also supposed to have provided boarding schools for deserving civil servants. Shun, the last emperor, was said to have sent his young civil servants there to learn from the elderly. If it happened at all, the sudden exchange of experience began orally.

If one believes the narrative afterward, within two dynasties and one and a half millennia five different school types emerged. The thoroughly compartmentalized educational system was even supposed to have provided instruction for field workers …

Confucius Sinarum Philosophus, 1687
The essay *Principis Confucii Vita* describes the life of the namesake of the School of Academics. He envisioned education as the path to harmony and equilibrium.

Of course to date there are no contemporary witnesses. Reading has a higher logic for that. In contrast to all other ancient advanced civilizations China recognized no idols. The Middle Kingdom only had a real existence to take care of; it was a solitary offspring of itself. The community and its leaders shouldered responsibility alone: natural catastrophes were nothing more than natural catastrophes. As a consequence the Middle Kingdom needed ancestors as examples. Conscientious emulation was the first responsibility. Conversely, he who wasted his inheritance lost face. The supposed exchange of experience was in that case the least one could expect.

The authority of the academics is established by the end of the last millennium before Christ. New agricultural methods reorganize the earth and make China's antiquated slave holding society obsolete. Politics has nothing more to offer in the way of wisdom and the Zhou Dynasty collapses. In the middle of the collapse in 551 B.C. Kong Qui, who is known in the west as Confucius, became famous. He made a career as a building and justice minister, but was driven into exile several times. In the face of wide-spread chaos, Confucius preached a love of order. Followers, who travel with him and hang on his every word, attribute his belief to education. As he becomes old he prefers to stay home and teach. When he dies in 479 B.C., his disciples turn his family seat in Qufu into a school of scholars. In the year of his death they honour the Master with a temple expansion, whose completion is personally attended by the local duke.

The facility rapidly becomes a campus. The teaching spreads throughout the country to such an extent that the time of the warring kingdoms has become known as the period of the hundred schools. Their intellectual output was the basis of the new empire which became a feudal society. After the founder of the Han Dynasty visited Qufu around 200 B.C., thousands of temples (schools) are established, also outside the Chinese domain of influence. Their spirit spread over half the world, its form of instruction and campus the whole world over. Wherever education operates as an substitute religion, there is no better blueprint. Until the end of the 19th century the school of the scholars stood for heavenly peace in the Middle Kingdom. It represented nothing less than the reason of state.

The basis of the success was in no little part due to the universality of the archetype. Since the world in the Middle Kingdom is everything, the architecture emulated that in the small. The school, which began in the residential district, resembled the original form of the Chinese house, the jian. It was based on a square which replicated the location. The roof embodied the settling of the firmament. Mostly made of wood, it is always stable. It needs no walls to stand, just supports. They can be located anywhere, but not in the middle. A hall is formed in between, which can accommodate at least twelve people. To be clear about it: the original Chinese home is already the ideal auditorium!

Confucius Temple, Qufu, 480 B.C.
At the beginning of the 20th century, as a photographer and architect, Ernst Boerschmann was the first European to explore the Chinese pagoda and temple art.

The same principle is valid for the overall facility. The order that was passed down, which Confucius incorporated, is absolutely essential. Just as the emperor had to set himself apart as the mightiest in the empire, the scholar had to occupy the most sublime position within the school. The space behind was reserved for the otherworldly, while up front things became more mundane. Hierarchy was also the rule in breadth. Key functions occupy the first row, while the profane observed the appropriate distance. In its pure form the principle was that of the neo-Confucian Namgye or Piram Seowons, which originated in 1552 and 1590 on the southern Korean peninsula. The temple arises behind the auditorium, in front of it and across the way were accommodations, with the library and farm buildings in the background. The highpoint of the Chinese school is of course in the capital. In 1784 Guozijian University is bestowed with its *Piyong (royal instruction halls – added by the translator)*. Hundreds of listeners could congregate in the Auditorium Maximum of the royal university. At the same time the central building symbolized something else than a "final truth". The library, which was always modest, was also a plus. The knowledge portal was never more than an exhibition hall. Everything is done in such way to underscore precisely the imitation.

To put it simply: the Temple of Scholars was the perfection of the epigones! The eternal rehashing caused an increasing calcification in the Middle Kingdom. In the final phase the school and the feudal society were founded on behalf of each other. When the communists took them over, that meant the irreversible Cultural Revolution …

Fourth Lesson: The Temple of Indoctrination

When the battle cry of "education for everyone" resounded through China, the appropriate school had long been developed and built ten thousand times. It first saw light in Europe, where in the High Middle Ages one out of five could read and write. On the surface the situation at the time was similar to that in Asia. It was usual for the students to live there and at least the teacher is at home there. He almost always teaches in one single large room, with all students present at the same time. The sanctuary is never far away.

Only the context cannot be compared. European scholars are prohibited the quasi-religious rank of a Confucius from the beginning: idols have been around here a long time. Belief has trickled down into a contingently formulated "God". In the light of this monotheism the school can at best represent a second opinion. Plato & Co. perfect this role by emphasizing ignorance and by striving for knowledge, cast everything in doubt. As a mainstay of the community the schools were no help, which is why Imperial Rome had no interest in them. The school became even more a loose cannon on deck. The Christians were the first to recognize that fact. Although they took over Rome in a surprise attack, they were more concerned with their pressing need to execute everyone in the name of the One and Only. So the fellow Christians recruited the schools for their mission and lead them in turn through the chaos of the great migration. Already in the seventh century the first monastery schools were liberated and

All Souls College, Oxford, 1443
Founded by Heinrich IV and Henry Chichele, today the college is above all a research centre for trained academics.

became universities. Later examples like New College (1380) and All Souls College (1438), both in Oxford, follow the early Italian models of Montecassino or Squillace (Vivarium). From the outside their one metre thick walls guarantee security, while providing the ultimate shelter inside. The explosive power slumbering in this bunker spirit surfaced between 751 and 785. The first step was an arbitration award issued by the papal think-tank elevating the ex-monastery pupil Pippin the Small from custodian to King of France. His son went even further. He turned his own royal seat into a school, founded new schools outside the purview of the monasteries and was finally crowned as the Emperor Charlemagne. And that broke the building monopoly of the church! From then on the rules governing schools developed more freely than in Asia. The claim to leadership peters out. The omnipresent sanctuary is reduced to a schoolhouse altar and then to a crucifix, coat of arms or portrait of the leader. In the best case the monastery form survives as a courtyard. First the school was created near a place of worship or a royal seat, and then it was built on its own. The accommodations which had penetrated the learning in the monastery were now assigned their own wings, if they were not immediately removed to another location. The schools differed very much from each other according to their own rules, like curriculum and level of performance. The class distinctions begin to disappear and competence increasingly determines the attendance in school. The Benedictines, who established the first monastery schools, educate regardless of standing, as long as one is willing to learn. Some members of the nobility also suspected that education was not God-given at all.

All in all the school that Plato & Co. had dreamed about became a fact. Of course, that kind of pure Temple of Freedom was hardly ever built. Examples like the Old School which the Hanseatic city of Wismar built around 1300 in the Gothic quarter, or the Queen Elisabeth Grammar School in Ashbourne, which was built in the wake of the English secularization in 1585, are the great exceptions. Fewer than one out of five Europeans could read and write during the high Middle Ages. The Temple of Enlightenment remained an unrealized obsession.

Reality first conquered the new school as a Temple of Indoctrination. The opening salvo was fired by Martin Luther, who was concerned about the understanding of his bible. Since 1520 the father of the Reformation had relentlessly demanded that the councillors of all German cities "send children to school. In plain language: literacy should become the law! A good reputation is followed at first only by the strokes of a pen, which declare the mental attitude as public domain. The first to take a step in this direction was the Dukedom of Württemberg, whose agenda of 1559 initially was limited to religious instruction for boys. Soon after many of the small reform princes delegated compulsory education. When the all year daily school becomes law in the great power of Prussia in 1763 the era of the enlightenment is already the talk of the land. Education had become a must for every child. Now, the obligatory school itself is not new. Plato had argued for it; the ancient Aztecs and Hebrews had it, without creating an archetype for it. That became necessary in Europe where literacy and urbanization were on the

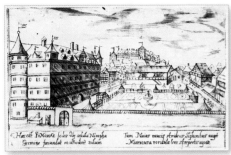
Park grounds of the fencing hall courtyard

Inner courtyard

Gymnastics hall 1

Dining room

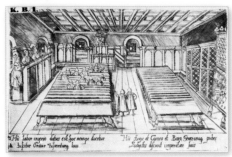
Auditorium

Gymnastics hall 2

Collegium Illustre, Tübingen, 1588
The building where young noblemen were once prepared for civil service later became a university. The copper plates from 1606 show the variegated spatial program.

rise like nowhere else. The exponentially increasing school density cannot be accomplished by building alone: technically optimized model school houses, with no reference to the old archetype, are possible at best in the settlement of the virgin estates in East Prussia. Other than that, the furniture offered possibilities to expand the capacities. Benches like those which welded together the faithful in the churches are deployed. First in a U-shape, then rising in rows.

The British pedagogue Joseph Lancaster crafted the most clever arrangement around 1800. In his London classroom up to 1,000 pupils could be instructed at one time! Half of them were seated in long rows. The dumbest sat up front in the middle in order to learn from their bench mates. The smartest listened to the lesson at separate tables or in galleries, sometimes standing and in any case on the outskirts of the room. The idea was that knowledge would spread by rotation. The prototype went through tests dozens of times, especially in Great Britain and the USA. One of the last attempts was in 1847 in New York in Public School No. 17. The experience is everywhere the same: the Lancaster School worked like the children's game *Chinese Whispers*, and the results are just as abstruse! In the mid-19th century it had to be admitted that education for everyone is not to be reconciled with the one room schoolhouse! Only the pedagogical principle that the pupils learned from the pupils survived later as an inspiration. Meanwhile the Auditorium Maximum has degenerated into an assembly hall for special occasions ...

The more fruitful approach was to multiply the tried and true unit of instruction. The challenge meant dividing up the pupils. After the separation by sex, which originally was the only barrier to education, fell victim to the Enlightenment, the only criteria were age and the level of performance. The effect on the archetype can already be seen in isolated experiments in the Middle Ages. The St. Gallen monastery plan from 820 envisioned an abbey school for external pupils that was divided by a folding screen. A clearer case was the knights' academy which Georg Beer built in reaction to the Reformation in Tubingen in Württemberg. The Collegium Illustre placed classrooms sideways, lengthwise and transversely, and on top of each other.

More quantum jumps were made by the Paris College de Sorbonne, which Jacques Lemercier 1635 touched up on behalf of absolutism, or the Karls School in Stuttgart, which moved into a barracks in 1775 behind the Württemberg royal seat. In both cases stairways and corridors connect dozens of classrooms!

The uniform is no accident: a bureaucracy was set up here which the barracks as the most mass oriented structure could only dream of! What the institutions of higher learning had individually sketched out in preliminqary form, fanned out quickly in all directions after the French Revolution: the class(warfare) defines the school and the nation itself. Beginning in 1805, Denmark systematically adapted her stock in educational buildings, like the Katedralskole (Christian Jensen Mørup) in Aarhus. Less

Karls School, Stuttgart, 1775
Coloured steel engraving based on a drawing by Karl Philipp Conz. The military and art academy founded by Duke Karl Eugen was designated a university in 1781 by Joseph II.

than a quarter century later Great Britain shifted over. One example is the Grammar School which non-conformists built in the London suburb of Mill Hills. The triumphal march of the classes is unstoppable there, where the Auditorium Maximum had been the measure of all things.

Whoever wants literacy for all cannot do without standard instruction units. There is no alternative to this school model which can be expanded as needed, where as a consequence of the industrial revolution population and cities were exploding. The blueprint was copied one hundred thousand times. The world wide spread provided another advantage: the uniform is per se neutral, so it offers the society an ideal projection surface.

Absolutists like to celebrate their enlightenment with their school castles and economies can cloak themselves in modern efficiency, like the Fritz Schumacher double elementary school in 1930 in Meerschweinstraße in Hamburg shows. And the egalitarian people's democracies, in the former GDR or in the Soviet Union deploy prefabricated rectangular solids with universal grid façades, where the entryway proclaims: Welcome, we shall indoctrinate you all equally!

There was more conflict in the inner life. The school had not basically changed in more than two thousand years. The teacher ruled over the instruction and the space, even if a profane professional held forth from the lectern in place of the sublime gurus. Now of course frontal instruction under compulsory education and selection according to cleverness still took place. Statisticians pick up the first mavericks, whose learning performance triumphs over origin. The little steps forward that are made can be seen most clearly in the system of repeating a class for those who can't keep up. In the normal case everyone progresses so that the majority creeps forward. Those who have the top pupil stuff can even jump ahead a year or two! In brief: the Temple of Enlightenment rewards the know-it-alls! It should be self-evident that this kind of pushiness quickly strikes back at the system …

Dorotheen-Lyzeum, Berlin-Köpenick, 1929
Well-equipped specialty rooms are needed in the so-called progressive schools for the teaching of handicrafts.

Fifth Lesson: Temple of the Teachers

The store of knowledge was now exploding, just like the population had before. Especially the technical disciplines descend upon day-to-day life, with a wealth of invention that can hardly be expressed in words. The trusted lecture pedagogy drew even more clearly on a subject that had only attained to university status in the middle of the 19th century, namely psychology. It is based on the wilful development of the individual, whereby the student had always been the craven client of the academic. That in itself posed a lesson for the teaching profession, and the old school felt directly discredited. Just when the millennium task of *education* had been answered with a general "yes", a whole generation of reform pedagogues wrestled with the question: "which one, actually?"

The academic banter exacerbates social distortions. As a consequence of general enlightenment the middle class had reached the point that it no longer wished to be indoctrinated and classified. Education policy makers appear on the scene, opinions about schools compete with each other like national rivalries. Parents who feel robbed of the last right of co-determination by compulsory education, now become fixated on where their children are instructed, what they get from the official school plan, and watch out! The teaching profession is now in the eye of the storm. Looking around for help, they reach for the only straw they can find, the form of instruction. Within decades the teachers start more school experiments than had been started in the previous millennia. To list all the cock-eyed courses is almost impossible, but a few will be mentioned here, whose pedagogy depended on the space, that is, on the following criteria of selection: which approach has at least the potential to become an archetype?

Class 5A: Professional Learning

The first approach updates the form of instruction analogue to the knowledge. Since the 13th century the subjects become more and more distinct from each other, especially the applied arts and sciences. They quickly design their very own blocks of instruction in their autonomous bastions. An early example is the Polytechnical Institute, built by Josef Schemerl in 1817 in Vienna. Collections of natural specimens congregate in the lecture halls. Display tables and later test workshops, where only the blackboard remains from the old auditorium, take the place of the speaker's pulpit. Karl Friedrich Schinkel's Berlin Bauakademie register additional milestones as well as Felix Duban's Paris École des Beaux-Arts, both of which are founded at the end of the 1830s. Their galleries and communal studios make the most of light and acoustics. Even the philologists joined in and installed language labs. The various disciplines put it to the test: education is now plastic, bland theory is now something that can be experienced. Beginning in the middle of the 19th century specially equipped classrooms are now required for the mainstream schools. An early example is the Municipal Preparatory High School in Liegnitz, which went into operation in 1867 in Silesia.

When Walter Gropius' Bauhaus began training designers in 1926 in Dessau, professionalized learning received an aesthetic touch. Functionalism was a good fit with the autonomous aspirations of the various subjects, which tried to find a form for their specific demands. Now there was to be no single subject specific classroom. The school was the sum of several subjects. It became in any case larger, because the specialist rooms ate up space and only paid off when there were more pupils. It was also abundantly clear what the prominent position was within the school building. Subject specific learning was located where it was guaranteed to be noticed. In the best case it should be located right on the sidewalk, where the non-school pedestrians could see it too. Something is going on here! Nuborgh College is a good example for that. The latest benchmark has been established by the Usasazo Secondary School, which Noero Wolff Architects put directly in a traffic artery in Cape Town. The wood, hair, leather and automobile workshops turn up in the local shops in the vicinity. Actually, the student body, in workshops for the blind or incarcerated, takes care of the needs of the whole community. In return the community directly finances the training.

Even more archetypal is the grouping of kindred spirits and the campus, which keeps the faculties together. Ideally, professional learning leads to the university. Especially in the USA the subject has taken on a life of its own. The college is not the only

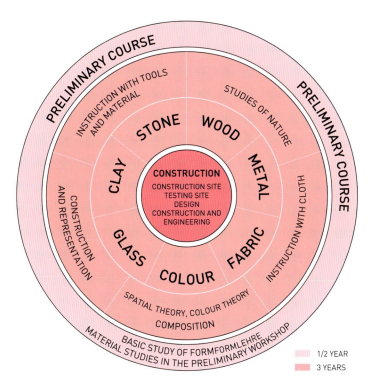

Bauhaus Curriculum, 1922
The Bauhaus teaching of Walter Gropius is based on the principle of three pillars, the core of which are the workshops with their optional subjects.

level to experience the breakthrough. The teenagers all attend preparatory high schools, which are almost all organized – nomen est omen – like universities.

A representative school is the New Trier West High School, which was built by The Architects Collaborative (Walter Gropius, Norman Fletcher, Jean B. Fletcher, John C. Harkness et al.) in 1965 near Chicago. Instead of the hereditary classrooms the lockers take over the role of the home room. The student body migrates on the hour to their classes without returning to a home room. The individual is classified more according to learning content and preference than age and performance. Every school can be specialized, in astronomy, fashion, home economics and so on. Everyone has something to gain. The graduate gravitates towards the specialist, who can attend to his vocation semi-professionally. The society at large receives exactly what it is missing. Above all professional understanding benefits and it is no accident that the Anglo-Saxon educational system registers the greatest number of Nobel prizes.

There is another side to the coin. Wherever there is hard work, education, the community and general education are literally left out. Over the long run the subject itself does itself a disservice. Just as information technology is leaving behind the computer labs, know-how is constantly progressing faster than its specialist routes. In addition, sooner or later every branch and biography needs an interdisciplinary infusion and fresh blood which specialist milieus explicitly keep out. No one will become a laptop artist or environmental activist, if the stretches between the sources of knowledge are too great to span and colleagues get left behind.

To exaggerate a bit: specialist classrooms can be especially idiotic! That is why in the mainstream school specialist classrooms are on the way out, at least in Europe. For instance, the Crestwood School, built by the buildings department of the Hampshire County Councils in 1982 in Eastleigh in England, was still subdivided in specialist classrooms, but they are almost indistinguishable from each other. In the case of the Heimdalsgades Skole, which Kant Arkitekter built in 2001 near Copenhagen, the faculties are seamlessly fit together. For the day-to-day work visual aids that are brought into universal teaching rooms are enough. Now and then a trip to a science centre provides a good diversion. The specialist paths only chart the way at the end of the learning trajectory. Researchers and greenhorn professionals offer built-in large scale tests invaluable assistance. In the universities and technical schools specific professional learning is still required. The circle returns to the status quo and the Temple of Knowledge is updated but nothing new has been discovered.

Class 5B: Natural Learning

The reform pedagogues do their homework more philosophically than pragmatically. They jointly assume that everyone can learn everything by nature! The school can at best remove roadblocks, and ideally it needs the institution as little as it does the building. This attitude goes back to Jean-Jacques Rousseau who earlier promulgated the noble savage. As an idea it was first put to the test by the Swiss Johann Heinrich Pestalozzi, who operated farmsteads around 1800 with orphans. A little while later Adolpf Diesterweg characterized these experiments as "natural education". The site of learning became all the more potent when the Pestalozzi student Friedrich Frobel forged The "kindergarten" ("children garden"), exactly what the word describes, in Blankenburg in Thuringia in 1840! Natural education had its moment of glory when the exploding populations of Europe's cities turned into breeding grounds for epidemics (Diesterweg died from cholera). For reasons of hygiene, mainstream school construction looked for refuge outside the city limits. An early example which still refers to the antiquated archetypes is the Valdemarskole built by the Dane Anton Haustrup on the tranquil outskirts of Ringsted in 1912. The school is a square of little schoolhouses surrounding a central grass area, where sports were practiced and taught. A little later the old continent began modernizing all the antique columned halls into open-air classrooms. In 1928 an experimental pavilion planned by Bruno Taut in the Berlin working class district of Neukölln was built with a retractable all-glass front. At the same time Jan Duiker and Bernhard Bijvoed in Amsterdam experiment with an open-air-school, with stacks of classrooms and open-air-spaces! And two years later Ernst May did the same at the Friedrich Ebert Progressive School in Frankfurt on the Main in a row house configuration. In 1956 the Munkegaard Skole near Copenhagen (Arne Jacobsen) expanded into a housing estate. The free space was unveiled as a fruitful element of the kindergarten: the schoolyard designed as garden becomes the norm!

Les écoles en plein air …

Les écoles en plein air …
Drawing by Adolf Bayer (1948) based on
a design by Marcel Lods (1934) for the
open-air school in Suresnes in France.

Right: Orphanage in Berlin-Dahlem, 1930
Beginning in 1907, many schools around the world follow
the model pedagogical concept of Maria Montessori with
the motto: Children educate themselves!

Open-air-classrooms and pavilion schools are only an option in the warmer latitudes of developing countries. Beyond that the architecture of natural learning is just a means to an end. Most of the time the decision was made on the basis of urban development, whose possibilities were increasing considerably. That is how the BDP (Building Design Partnership) 2003 commandeered an open space in a London intersection in order to build the Hampden Gurney Primary School. And since the Kokusai Academy and its student body were growing continuously, building the housing estate naturally occurred to C+A Kojima-Uno-Akamatsu at the same time. However on its central field of battle Natural Learning makes little headway. It most often fails because of the weather. The open-air-classroom is anyway a didactic concept and instruction under a blue sky is no different than instruction indoors. Since there is more space to play, the smaller children have the most to gain and therefore the open-air-classroom benefits the pre-schoolers. In the final analysis what remains of the kindergarten is the kindergarten!

Class 5C: Individual Learning

The school didactic approximates that of the Italian reform pedagogue Maria Montessori. As a psychiatrist she noticed that the only given in nature is curiosity. The rest can be actively acquired, although not all learn at the same speed or in the same way. The teaching staff and household have their role to play to "do it for yourself". By mixing age groups and using freely structured work Maria Montessori circumvents the mainstream school. In her system age is not a qualification and each student receives an individual curriculum to work through. In order to do that she uses toys for learning which appeal to different senses. The Casa dei Bambini, which Montessori opened in 1907 in the Roman working class district of San Lorenzo, resembled a large apartment consisting only of children's rooms. All doors were always open. The building was divided into experience stations which the children worked through at their own pace. At the end of the instruction the ego always emerged triumphant!

The Montessori method spread rapidly, especially in Holland, the adopted country of the founder. The pure spatial form fell on fruitful ground in the Anglo-Saxon countries, where initiative is encouraged from the youngest age. These kinds of building concepts have become standard for primary education in the Pacific territories, as the Woonara Park Primary School in Dandenong North shows, which was converted according to plans by Mary Featherston in 2005 in Victoria, Australia. Nevertheless the design possibilities for individual learning are as little exhausted as its possibilities and limits are concretely outlined. The only thing that is certain is that it can never be the norm, which would only be a contradiction. The educational method itself adds additional fuel. Montessori does not recognize a purpose in the community which founds the school. Instead she supports without reservation the ego, in order to resist what is foreign to that.

That becomes a problem at the latest with the onset of puberty. When Montessori approaches young juveniles, who are in the best position to go their own way, with an "Erdkinderplan" or a "cosmic education", she comes on like Goethe's sorcerer's apprentice. The approach is all the more inveterate where it extends the educational facility into the child's room (and not the other way around). After basic skills have been individually acquired, we are all the winners. Ideally the Montessori method prepares the school, as a "pre-school"!

Class 5D: Experimental Learning

Whether in kindergartens, pre-schools or universities, all reform experiments were restricted to peripheral areas. An all-encompassing alternative first appears when the experimenting takes on a life of its own and the reform pedagogues start looking for professionally appropriate milieus for themselves. In 1844 Karl Volkmar Stoy at the University of Jena assembled theoreticians, teachers-in-training and normal students. This pedagogic workshop is perfected a half century later by the American John Dewey, whom the world came to know from his motto "Learning by Doing". He founded the Experimental School, which was open to all age groups, at the then recently established University of Chicago. What was required in order to modify different forms of instruction and maintain an overview of the results quickly becomes obvious: flexible blackboards, partitions, platforms and lots of space. Since traditional school buildings could not offer all that, unconventional archetypes were recruited.

Especially the commercial building branch donated workshops and open-plan offices. The first result were mediation processes which anchored the experiment per se. With team-teaching several teachers work together; project instruction presents the student body as a whole with problem complexes, while individuals look for their personal approach, workplace and contact person. Schools required more flexibility from professionals as well as from amateurs than any other school before. In the mid-1960s the experimental school had progressed to such an extent that it was autonomously established without serving primarily as a facility for training teachers. Whether it was the Disney Magnet School, built according to a design by Perkins + Will in 1970 in Chicago, or the East-Harlem Pre-School by Hammel, Green and Abrahamson in New York, they all observed the open-plan-principle and in terms of appearance made an extremely reduced impression. The approach also found abundant echo outside the USA. In 1974 Hartmut von Hentig conceptualized a 1:1 knock-off of the pedagogical workshop. He systematically enlarged the open floor plan of his experimental school in Bielefeld with galleries. In German-speaking Europe, in contrast to the USA, where the architectural form never went beyond the simple classroom, the process took a quantum jump. Learning complexes are created like the Easterburken Comprehensive School, built according to plans by Bassenge, Puhan-Schulz

Crow Island School, Winnetka, 1945
The workroom for projects combines the classroom with the garden courtyard.

and Schreck in 1967 near Karlsruhe, or the Zofingen Education Centre, which was completed ten years later in the vicinity of Luzern according to a design by Metron architecture AG. These mega-buildings accommodate the needs of more than 1,000 students at one time. Air-conditioning, artificial light and instability accompany them through their learning career. The large experimental schools do not survive this acid test. As often as not a lesson unit is abandoned before its fitness can be determined. Concentration and learning success provably deteriorate in the artificial milieus, which can be hazardous to the health. Constant turmoil is the rule in the experimental school, with an effect that extends beyond the school. The overwhelming din cannot be completely tamed even with maximum room acoustic countermeasures. The permanent noise is especially aggravating for the faculty, but the pedagogues continue with the experiment, and only want to alter the set-up of the experiment. The experimental school continues to develop in analogue to office construction. Individual reference points which pre-determine the floor plan prevail. The Bexley Business Academy, which has been offering training since 2003 near London, represents the typical example. Norman Foster stacked class cubicles around the work atriums, which were missing at least one wall. The Hellerup Primary School in Gentofte, built two years before according to a design by Bjarne Bach (Arkitema) in the vicinity of Copenhagen, still provided the teachers with closed conference areas. Like islands of quiet these refuges also order the teaching floors which have no walls. In addition, at the entrance to the school the students are required to take off their shoes. These kinds of tricks bear witness to the gist of the experimental school. It provides more openness than is normally available in the community. In the end society only allows one experiment, namely project work. This is conducted in circled off zones in the middle of the classrooms. They keep the self-experimentation in check from the beginning.

Class 5E: Learning From One Another

The rapid growth draws attention to the size of the school. The parents long for the small circle, which of course focusses on their own children. This perspective also suits the teachers. They constantly inspire teacher-student communes, substitute families which are by their nature much more fragile than their models. In fact child abuse is a not infrequent occurrence in these live-in schools and this educational model has aroused suspicion. At best those boarding schools are tolerated, where students live alone in the communal living situation. The mini-group still has the best individual learning success today. The Boston School of Girls from 1870 proves that as does the monastery school of St. Gallen, which was founded one thousand years before that. Both institutions organize the number of students in groups of one hundred. Only those deserving of support are allowed in the study rooms, and that is not many today. When individuals can be taught and tested in peace the mini-group gains in momentum. In Massachusetts Francis Wayland Parker

Experimental school in Bielefeld, 1974
The open-plan office for children offers open floor plans. There are no classrooms here.

produces student newspapers as part of the curriculum. He needs at least a handful of pupils, but much more than a dozen is hardly practicable. So, Parker sets up teams. The German girls' pedagogue Hugo Gaudig summarizes this advantage a little later. A division of labour is created which brings with it emancipation! The individual can only develop to the advantage of the rest in a smaller group. The students learn from each other because of their differences, and not in spite of them! Teamwork first becomes a subject of architecture when totalitarian types provoked two world wars. At the beginning of the 1960s in Italy the Reggio pedagogue Loris Malaguzzi initiated a series of self-help projects in areas of retreat, which are rapidly realized in day-care and pre-school construction. In West Germany private booths are even augmenting schools of higher learning. In the Geschwister Scholl Preparatory High School built by Hans Scharoun in 1962 in Lünen in Westphalia the group dynamic can be seen in the design of the building. Leftover space for wardrobes, storage and teaching preparation will soon be bundled into separate seminar rooms throughout the Federal Republic of Germany. One of the most recent examples for this is the expansion of the Bugenhagen School by the architectural office Stölken + Schmidt in 2000. It has since then become standard practice in Anglo-Saxon primary education for two classes to share a group area. In other locations special learning zones have been demarcated. The classical school room is divided into galleries, landings or winter gardens. For the Vestre Skole in Svendborg which was built in 2004, the Danish architects Per Olsen and Michael Holst use all the tricks at once. The variable partition is even more widespread. All these artifices are designed to furnish the team formation with temporary nooks. The result is cooperation, but in no case smaller classes. Those are pedagogically desirable but exorbitantly expensive. The dying out of village schools and private tutoring dispels any doubt about that.

Sixth Lesson: Temple of Learning

In their pure form none of these experiments can prevail, but they are not in vain. Their failure reveals the character of the school, which pardons failure more than the world outside. In addition they consolidate the central role of the teaching staff for the school. The experiments also establish new educational archetypes. Some forms of instruction have become so indispensable that there is no older building that can be used without the relevant changes being made. A new school archetype is in the beginning the sum of all the experiments. Post-modern education explicitly compels such interaction, because it wants everything all at once. According to the opinion of teachers today, for instance in the interdisciplinary formulation of Gerold Becker, the small group has subsumed the key tasks of the classical class structure. But autodidactic learning and partner work also have their place. Open project presentations and concentrated lectures require even more space. And there is no school community that can exist without extracurricular activities, like sports or art festivals.

School Herning, 1970
The Jørn Utzons design combines several spatial modules into an education campus. A prototype of the school in Herning in Denmark (picture on the right) was built in 1976.

From an architectural standpoint a public square is needed, some workshops and auditoriums, many galleries and even more alcoves. Of course the wish list doesn't say how these individual elements should be put together, which is why in the beginning they are assembled one at a time. In 1970 Jørn Utzon designed a whole catalogue of room modules for the Danish town of Herning which have never made it beyond the experimental stage. Twenty years later Rafferty Rafferty Tollefson Lindeke Architects had even less success, when they changed the spatial arrangement from adjacent to on top of. In order to outfit a former museum in St. Paul, Minnesota for the Saturn School, they distributed the smallest units on the top floors and the largest on the bottom. The museum may have been a fitting location for a nice idea, but the school was lost in the shuffle. That should make it clear: forms of instruction cannot simply be added up. They become pedagogically valuable when they are mixed. The mixing possibilities are manifold. For instance the Kokusai Academy of C+A Kojima-Uno-Akamatsu combines components of natural and experimental learning. In a dense housing project-like layout, the classes open to the outside as well as to the inside. In 2002 Herti Enzmann + Fischer in 2002 weave together airshafts, terraces and partitions in the design for a Swiss school. The patchwork is especially conducive to teamwork; partner work as well as larger projects can progress separately and cooperate at the same time. The most constructive combination was in the Råholt School built in 2005 in Eidsvoll in Norway, with a design by Kristin Jarmund. The university and the experimental school merge here. Everything that must be compact and closed, auditoriums, staff rooms, wet rooms, workshops and even shelves, is stand-alone. The individual components form the backbone of the entire school, organizing as room dividers the per se open educational floor plan, and as agenda items they bolster the time-plan. Corlaer College in Nijkerk in Holland shows that everything can fit together. The firm of Broekbakema mixed a cocktail in 2006 in which every component had its own internal logic. Wild combinations like that have now become the norm in Northern Europe. A top notch report card underscores the fact that these regions are in the lead in the United Nations PISA tests: the school was never so learning-friendly than in these hybrids! That is no wonder: all the archetypes that don't fit have been weeded out. Only the original forms of instruction have been retained.

The Temples of Learning have an even more emblematic effect which recycles the ideal city planning of the Renaissance or the architecture of the French Revolution and radically sorts out the space allocation program. On a small scale Jan Verhoeven demonstrates the idea with his design for the Montessori school in Leusden in Holland in 1980. Norman Foster bends it even more in the Thomas Deacon Academy in Peterborough in England in 2007. At the same time Marlies Rohmer tries to square the circle in the Brede School de Matrix in Hardenberg in Holland. If some of these schools are as unlikely to survive the everyday reading matter as the idealistic plans, they even more interestingly underscore the basic idea of the Temple of Learning. The circular schematic puts the partnership between the students and the teachers in the midpoint! The teachers were bumped from the lecterns so that both parties could be on the same level.

In addition the fortress-like staff rooms, for which the entire main floor was reserved in the past, become history. At the most individual offices distributed throughout the building are retained. Both construction measures bring the teachers and students closer together. Instead of the pole star of wisdom the students now have a personal guide along the path of knowledge. The same is true for the school building. The architecture abstains from every aesthetic end in itself. The buildings often practice an almost abstinence from design. The temple aspires to be an instrument of support. It picks up the students where they are and custom fits every unit of instruction to the level of their performance. Those who were stuck in the same place for years now change their position often, sometimes within the same class period. The school building is not just a learning facilitator. It much more imparts an agility to the next generation which accelerates future development. The learning partnership is often evaluated as the expression of school democracy. This educational structure actually works as a catalyser but in no way as the spearhead of social change. Above all, the Temple of Learning resists everything that lies outside curriculum and social responsibility. The fine tuning of its organization limits the leeway to the pre-established path of progress. The students are taken by the hand and the teaching staff sharpens their glance for them. Windows between the instruction units and their access ensure ubiquity to the supervisors. They are even there during the breaks. That kind of radial lay-out does not need more than one teacher. The teachers only tweak their workplaces, turning the school into mirrors of themselves. There is noting more to expect from reformers, who live from this process.

Seventh Lesson: The Temple of Students

Breakthroughs happen when people learn on their own. The power that this phenomenon embodies can best be seen in the astonishment of those big mouth professionals, who were at best tolerated. Teachers describe the process, which had already done its work long before the school, as informal learning. They define its ubiquity in the exclusion procedure. Informal learning actually defines its existence neither formlessly nor independent of the main school. The Greeks were the ones who laid the mental cornerstone. School and muse are same word in their language. Therefore, as in Pergamon, thermal baths and theatre are part of the gymnasion. And that pre-programs the archetype of informal learning: When the daily work is done, recreation buildings are the places of choice to visit. Of course the feats of strength at the time were anything but childish. The whole society is based on slaves, and every student had at least one at his side. The aesthete enjoys his privilege at the expense of the many who are not educated. Consequently the Modern rediscovered educational freedom. The first space encompassing rendezvous occurred in the course of the general enlightenment. In order to defend their knowledge advantage citizens saturated with refinement founded literary salons. The real subversives hollow out absolutism from the inside and infiltrate the Parisian noble palaces. The French Revolution is worked out ahead of time in a casual tête-à-tête! The salon culture immediately goes public and sets up the first club houses in England. Typical examples are the Athenaum, founded in 1797 in Liverpool or its London branch, built according to plans by Decimus Burton in 1823. Architecturally they are akin to coffee houses which have been expanded to include bookstores. Hundreds of such Gentlemen's Clubs are set up throughout the whole Empire. They lend a practical shape to the dreams of colonists on the threshold of the New World. The Industrial Revolution liberates even more of the pioneering spirit. It demands a life of learning from ever expanding circles. Day to day life changed so dramatically that post-school educational building had to be built to keep up. The working class was the most affected. Their night class schools were elevated to the status of palaces of culture. A perfect example is the Mechanics' Institute in Leeds, for which Cuthbert Broderick combined a veritable theatre with classrooms and club rooms in 1867. The sister project of the New Swindon Improvement Company, the Swindon Mechanic Institute planned by Edward Robert, evolved from 1853 to 1893 into an urban palace which ruled over the whole working class district.

When patrons or philanthropists give something a push, it quickly becomes self-propelled. When Union Homes are established in the USA, they become social forces to be reckoned with in Germany. The golden age of adult education was in the 1920s, when the proletariat assumed power in Russia. The revolutionaries could only slowly reform the Tsarist educational heritage. The vanguard of the new soviet citizens is organized primarily in workers' clubs, consisting of little more than lecture theatres and foyers. Konstantin Melnikow and his colleagues implement the reduced spatial program just as austerely. They build avant-garde buildings by the dozens, which present the school as a world-improvement-machine for the first time. At the same time with their constructivist icons the Modern celebrated their world premier as the social lounges. From that point on the evening school as a public square was the place to be!

Class 7A: Community School

Their popularity is self-evident. They beautify free time, give meaning to and encourage those who are already mid-stream in life. There was therefore no doubt that adult education would benefit the young just as well. The question was: "how?" The first idea which was already making the rounds in the 19th century is as obvious as it is ambitious: the Community School, where the grown-ups learn with the children, where they share a building and experiences. The Volkshaus Jena just brought in the youth. In addition to the Technical Museum and reading room, the Festsaal completed in 1900 also included an art and trade school. The architect Arwed Rosbach shaped a city in miniature from all these ingredients. The central location reflected the close connection of the community to the school. The augury changes under the influence of the Russian Revolution. The school becomes the germ cell of arts centre projects. The step to serial production is made in the Anglo-Saxon motherlands of democracy, informal learning and community schools. Dozens of so-called Junior, City and Village Colleges, some of which are public, are founded in the USA and Great Britain.

Burevestnik Club, Moscow, 1933
Konstantin Melnikov designed this club for workers (culture house for continuing education, conferences and cultural events). The glazed tower features recital rooms and reading areas.

Zuev Workers Club, Moscow, 1929
The former culture house for workers and employees of a nearby streetcar depot in Moscow is used today for light drama. It was designed by Ilya Golosov.

Walter Gropius and Maxwell Fry attend an hour of instruction on the eve of World War II in Impington. The usual teaching paraphernalia was grafted onto an adult format and open to the public. The school library becomes a city library, the auditorium graduates to a festival theatre, and the gymnasium goes off in the direction of an arena. It is just these kinds of leisure time facilities which may imply an informal use. Of course the old school reacts: The village sized school grounds are not half as modern as Gropius' Bauhaus built fifteen years before. These discrepancies disappear after World War II, as a result of which the Community School celebrates its most striking moments. The Holocaust and the H-bomb decimate the basic trust in progress and authority in general. At the same time, especially in the West, the standard of living and freedom are on the rise, enabling individuals to enjoy an autonomy they never knew before. The first to reject their schoolbooks are the students. Their rioting gives the signal for the post-Modern. Their protagonists no longer attempt to present anything that can be generally understood because they are only interested in refuting and relativizing. In 1966 Robert Venturi shows how it works with *Complexity and Contradiction in Architecture.* In order to survive contradictions buildings are needed that behave just as contradictorily. Formally speaking, the principle can be applied to the city, village or farmstead, where confusion with trusted platitudes is ruled out from the beginning. In practice the solution is called, Anything Goes! The ease of use especially encourages the growth of the niches between the practical constraints.

Entrances, stairways and corridors now appear as squares, parks, boulevards or malls and are planted or furnished accordingly. The fact that everyone can just stop anywhere they want to has an autarchic quality. Education understands itself very much in the sense of the post-Modern as a self-sufficient habitat. The Community School is especially interested in the construction plan which implies integration. It imagines that one can just as well learn to read from buildings as from teachers.

The École de la Sourderie, which Leon Krier envisioned in 1977 for a Ville Nouvelle near Versailles especially embodied this hope. His sketches magnify the leisure area into the most important part of the school. Krier's blueprint actually becomes an international standard. The Warsaw Community High School in the state of Indiana in the USA which is built by Perkins + Will 1990 with Odle, Mc Guire & Shook, is only one example from many. The planning principle becomes inveterate for large projects. Post-Modern building blocks are generally welcome in the melting pot. It also helps England get over its loss of empire. In its emigration society, where this system was used in two out three schools, the situation was certainly more peaceful than in France, where that kind of education had almost no chance to be implemented. Integration is still the basic quality of the Community School. It owes its success explicitly to the adult volunteers who are attracted to the school by the leisure time activities. They increase the motivation and sense for reality just by walking by, creating a counterpoint to regular curriculum.

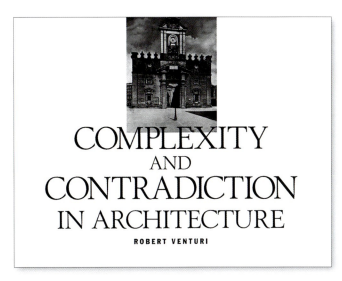

Complexity and Contradiction ..., 1966
The manifest of Robert Venturi, the American architect and one of the most significant representatives of the post-Modern, makes the point with the functional solution: Anything goes!

Competition model, Muri / Bern, 1971
The project submitted by the *ARB-Arbeitsgruppe für rationelles Bauen* in the framework of a secondary school competition shows the required polyvalence of post-Modern school buildings.

And they provide the school with its best rating, namely that the Community School is the centre of gravity of the community. The flip-side of this new career is that the homework has been turned upside down. Schooling the society is now the priority, although basically the complete opposite is the case. When it comes to capturing the great big world, architecture cannot afford to start with the small. The logical consequence is childish design which ultimately prevents development. After all, the parti-coloured park bench in front of the classroom is not necessarily the better park bench.

Class 7B: School Community

What the Community School starts, gets turned upside down by the School Communities. They compel the children to stay together after the summer vacation. The first example is the summer camps, which are established in the USA in the mid-19th century. The tent camps are supported by the working parents who have an income, but not so much vacation that they can afford to take over the counsellor role of the teacher. The older children now supervise the younger ones. This curious middle-class invention sets up camp everywhere. The first archetypes are created where full employment is compulsory. Around 1960 the Pioneer Palaces make their debut in the Soviet Union. These are hobby landscapes which are distinguished above all by their furnishings. The equipment is so child-appropriate, that contents which are foreign to instruction like ballet, space travel

or war are self-conveyed. A casual visit becomes the daily routine for everyone a little bit later, after the first youth leisure centres evolve into all day schools in Northern Europe. They have many advantages. For one, the day ends where it begins for the children. In addition a minimum of personnel is required. While more and more of youth is spent in the school, the adults withdraw more and more, with home and the world receding in the background. The architecture is sole contact for the pupils. The homework is becoming truly dramatic: helping the student body now means relying on oneself!

It is as simple as it sounds. The target group is small and needs less space than adults, which is why the school as a whole remains compact. It doesn't need separate areas for free time. It prefers to mingle in the classroom and strengthen every community, which then keeps an eye on itself. This kind of pure form of School Community is especially prevalent in Denmark. The Ega Preparatory High School in Arhus is a good example. Built according to a design by the architectural firm of CUBO 2006, it looks like a cathedral of child development. Erick van Egeraat goes one step further with the Metzo College in Doentinchem in Holland two years before, where he stacks a park, gym and café in a school pyramid. Ramps, split levels and galleries run between all the chambers. Wherever the students congregate, they feel like sun-gods. One of the few examples from outside Europe was built in Fairfield Connecticut, USA in 2004, the Burr Street Elementary School. The architectural firm of

Skidmore, Owings & Merrill whipped up specialist and leisure time areas together in a concoction which is brimming with the joy of discovery. It becomes clear that in addition to formal aspects the functional is also addressed. The purely functional orientation has no point, where a high level of performance is yet to be produced. If the building is occupied anyway, the expensively furnished recreation room is not needed. Just combine them! The cafeteria is more a lounge than a company canteen, the library, which does not have to observe the silence of the dead, boldly announces group work. The festival theatre can do without a scenery storage room, dividable stage or its own entrance – which is how the auditorium is elevated to a foyer for the whole school. The sports field, as is the case with the De Matrix Community School, is also a playground. Simplification on a large scale allows for refinement in the small. No one is more addicted to this love of detail than Herman Hertzberger. The Dutch architect has been designing learning environments for almost three decades. His studio designs at least one school per year. The Montessori College Oost, built in 1999 in Amsterdam, is an often copied masterpiece.

He upgrades parapets to secretaries, and stairs to bleachers. The more recent Hertzberger buildings are an even richer kaleidoscope: in the De Salamander Brede School, which was inaugurated in 2009 in Arnheim, there is hardly one necessary building element that does not morph into a cavern, snuggle corner or seat step. In the Stedelijk Preparatory High School in Leiden the group work tables are like banquet tables. These kinds of artistic touches are officially encouraged in Northern Europe. Individual new buildings already rely on them completely. In addition the approach is standard when interior decorators renovate existing schools. The Temples of Students are there where self-help is at work. The advantages are obvious. Leisure time and instruction flow together. Learning is a constantly playful endeavour. Spontaneous action alliances are created among the students. Sometimes knowledge is created which is not at all part of the curriculum.

With all the anarchy it is of course difficult to determine the social effects of the Temple of Students. It is even more notable that the form of learning matured before globalization and computer communication break ground according to the same pattern (it also occurs in the grey zones beyond the guidelines of the community). In a certain sense the Temple of Students anticipates the large scale phenomena of the present. One thing is certain: when it makes an offer to the autodidact, it calls up the do-it-yourselfer!

Eighth Lesson: The Temple of the Autodidacts

The mega-trends in school construction continue. The optional courses for autodidacts which is only offered in the Temple of Students as fillers, is now required in the curriculum, because in the wake of the globalization the world has become a giant pool of labour. Today there is no doubt that the mother tongue is not enough and many professions require overseas experience.

Left page
De Matrix Community School, Hardenberg, 2007
The school building designed by Marlies Rohmer consisting of five cubes in Hardenberg in Holland is more than just a teaching facility. Whole day supervision including advice for the parents is provided for children from birth to twelve years of age.

Left
School Complex, Kronberg / Taunus, 1974
The specialized classes of the two storey building, planned by the architects Fesel / von Torne, are on the first floor with outside access, with classrooms for general teaching located above them.

In the future what will be needed are less but more universal skills for understanding. Apart from that, highly specialized, world class service will be provided on an international basis. That is something the autodidact can provide, but not the old school. The old school may try to adapt its curriculum by offering more foreign languages. But as a cosmopolitan entity it doesn't have much to offer. On the one hand, the school cannot educate the children to become world citizens by taking them from home prematurely. On the other hand the employer puts on the pressure. Every school continues to be subject to the authority of a defined community and the limits of very real customs. International performance comparisons make clear this problem but show no way out. At the best they whip up competition among the educational systems and some may be more successful than others. But the rankings do not lie: no one possesses the philosopher's stone. Everyone must find their own way to education for themselves off the beaten path.

Computer technology claims to solve the education problem of globalization by making information more available than ever before. The school thereby goes over a similar elementary bump as it did when writing was invented. It really no longer must be a Temple of Knowledge. It simply has to teach how to learn, from others or per se. However in contrast to the Temple of Students instead of a process in itself, this activity is a means to an end defined by minimum results. Naked data will continue to be structured, evaluated and finally processed. That will have to proceed far more efficiently than before because the overstimulation has vastly exceeded human capacity to absorb it and the new technology permits the linking of facts via mouse click, a capability which was previously inconceivable. More school may be needed, but certainly more training. What is crucial is that the school is always there for the pupils, not for those who do the teaching. Sometimes it could be the parents, sometimes fellow students or interactive learning programs which are exclusively addressed to the autodidacts. All sources of assistance are relevant. The self-motivated learners, who with the aid of modern communication technology connect with their personal network of advisers, and drink from several fountains of education at once, are the only invariables the architects have. The school itself disappears and theoretically it could be possible to design it completely virtually and simulate it with software.

The first examples already reveal how education looks when students and school do not necessarily have to be at the same location. They will all be reborn as universities. In the mid-19th century the University of London summoned only a majority of students for exams. After World War II correspondence courses, or open universities as such were conceptualized. As with the Toulouse Le Mirail University, the "campus" of which was planned by George Candilis in the 1960s, they are based on administrative archetypes whose public clientele comes and goes in postal envelopes. By the time that model reached the youth three decades later, the transmission technology had already advanced. Learning now happens on the monitor and schools like the Open Training & Education Network (OTEN),

Corlaer College, Nijkerk, 2006
In the school house planned by Broekbakema, the stairway is used as a meeting point and common break room.

which opened shop in 1995 in Strathfield in Australia according to plans by Philip Cox, look like television studios. The live presentation is now the exception. The compensation these institutions all offer is that at a minimal expense they can reach a maximum of human beings, who otherwise have no access to learning. OTEN services approximately 50,000 students who live scattered throughout the outback, who now can attend class without having to fly in by airplane. The AllamaIqbal Open University in Islamabad founded in 1974, one of the largest open universities in the world, is attended by more than a million human beings, a fraction of which are pursuing their studies as full time students. The new media is also changing live school attendance, to the extent it becomes interactive. If this is the case, the built school will become a virtual learning labyrinth, with WLAN holding the network together. Teachers and students communicate permanently via email. Those who are not there can be instructed using podcasts and blogs. Learning videos can be individually repeated and even in exams the laptop can generate answers without learning beforehand. The doors in the media branch are open for all students who begin their careers at these kinds of virtual preparatory high schools, whereby most of them have already distinguished themselves before school has begun. Some of those schools which have already switched over to the virtual system are criticized, especially for the insufficient structure of the day to day learning. The students spend more than half their time in front of a monitor. School has become a calculating operation!

The deficient IT skills of the pedagogues, who often have to teach themselves the necessary computer knowledge, is a point of criticism. In contrast architecture is hardly mentioned in any teaching log, as if it can be simply neglected. The prototypes which have already been built run the danger of all virtual schools, namely the feeling of responsibility is absent! Where do we go from here? How will the school archetype of tomorrow look? Bearing in mind the whole pre-history, there can only be one answer. After the school has emancipated itself to a great degree from the parental home and the society and its inner life no longer revolves around knowledge or the teaching staff that conveys that knowledge, there is only one choice. In addition to their education, the students will also be responsible for the location of their education. The Temple of the Autodidacts can offer pointers here. The pupils can run the same operation that has shrunk to an internet cafe! Schools under the trusteeship of the students are currently being propagated in countless TV series for youth. It is the inescapable consequence of 5,500 years of detention. And now the Pink Floyd song makes sense: We don't need no education? Absolutely! Teachers, leave them kids alone? Please!

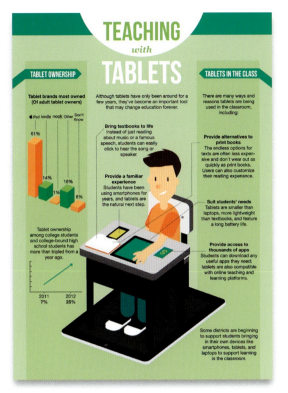

Learning takes place in the monitor!
Computer supported teaching and learning methods transform the classroom. The space allocation program and furniture must be coordinated.

Learning follows technology!
Monitors, a so-called white board and a beamer belong more often than not to the basic equipment of a contemporary classroom.

Literature

Brubaker, Charles William: *Planning and Designing Schools*, New York 1998.
Encyclopædia Britannica: *History of Education*, London 2007.
Undervisningsministeriet (Ed.):
Rum, form, function i folkeskolen, Copenhagen 2000.
Undervisningsministeriet (Ed.): *Inspirationskatalog til renovering og byggeri af daginstitutioner og folkeskolen*, Copenhagen 2009.

From Classroom to Learning Landscape
Teaching Rooms in the Era of Information Technology

Thomas Müller

"We give shape to our buildings, and they, in turn, shape us." Winston Churchill described the design task of architecture and its effect on us as a mutual interaction. We register this effect on different levels. With reference to the school these are:

- The urban developmental integration,
- The building itself,
- The interior (especially the classrooms), and
- The furnishings.

As a rule, from the pedagogical standpoint, the functional requirements of school construction can be well described quantitatively and qualitatively. But the future users are not always included in the planning because the builder, most often a local authority, can operate independently. However in addition to purely quantitative considerations the design challenge facing the architects can by no means be overlooked. In the final analysis the realization of the desired functions together with the quality of the design determine the value estimate of a school. This estimate becomes reality when the students and their teachers actually identify with their schools. However there has never been a lack of examples of the contrary. Extensive construction programs accompanied the founding of the German Empire in 1871 for the first time. Especially in the large cites, school buildings several storeys high were built, replete with monumental, expensive façades to represent the authoritarian state, while offering little more than long, dark corridors flanked by barracks-like classrooms. They replaced the idyllic school from the beginning of the 19th century.

Beginning in 1890, progressive schools emerge which as so-called work schools promote the principle of self-initiative of the students based on the insights of the philosopher and pedagogue John Dewey. Maria Montessori developed further the principle of self-reliant learning. Her approach was based on the desire of the students in reference to the teacher: "help me to do it myself", together with a conducive environment. This environment includes the Montessori teaching material as well as spatial design appropriate for a child and for learning outdoors.

After World War I and the establishment of the democratic Weimar Republic, the pavilion school emerged as a new school type, mostly on the outskirts of the cities. These schools were intended to realize the demands of the youth movement for fresh air, light, sun and nature. The one storey class pavilions usually have window fronts which can be opened, an access to the garden, illumination from two sides and transverse ventilation. Square floor plans facilitate roomy furnishing. A good example is the Bruno Taut School Dammweg in Berlin and the Ringplan School of Richard Neutra. The Bruderholz School by Hermann Baur and the Crow Island School by Eero Saarinen with Perkins + Will have become internationally significant. But it was in the 1950s that pavilion schools in greater numbers were first built, like the Munkegaard School by Arne Jacobsen in Gentofte. Back in 1929 Jan Duiker provided open terraces for gymnastics and sports in order to take advantage of as much fresh air and natural light as possible in school buildings several storeys high in the inner cities. A contemporary interpretation of these ideas can be found in the primary school in Regensburg, Germany by Twoo Architekten. It features room high windows and expansive roof terraces; raised flower beds and skylights provide seating on the roof.

The classroom has great significance within the school building. According to Johann Heinrich Pestalozzi's formulation, it should be a "sitting room" where the student and the teacher

1823

1904

1926

1928

1929

1935

1939

1948

1954

2012

Fig. 1
The development of the learning spaces:
From class room to learning landscape

- **1823** The School, drawing by Johann M. Voltz
- **1904** Eppendorfer Middle School, Hamburg
- **1926** Ringplan School, Richard Neutra
- **1928** Bruno Taut School, Bruno Taut, Berlin
- **1929** Open Air School, Jan Duiker, Amsterdam
- **1935** Bruderholz School, Hermann Baur, Basel
- **1939** Crow Island School, Eero Saarinen with Perkins + Will, Chicago
- **1948** Montessori Primary School, Berlin
- **1954** Munkegaard School, Arne Jacobsen, Gentofte
- **2012** Primary School, Twoo Architekten, Regensburg

From Classroom to Learning Landscape 35

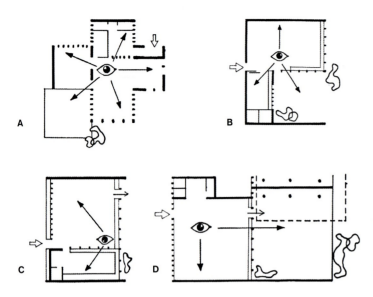

A Kindergarten: Internal transparency aids the work in groups.
B Classes unified with teaching rooms, work niches and a gardening room
C Classes unified with staff rooms and work room, exit to open area
D Classes unified with large teaching room (9 × 9 Meter), partially covered terrace

Fig. 2

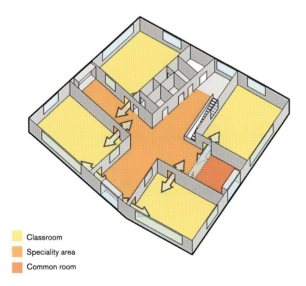

- Classroom
- Speciality area
- Common room

Fig. 3

Fig. 2
Basic classroom types according to Alfred Roth (1950)

Fig. 3
Functional lay-out of the Welsberg Primary School by Klaus Hellweger (2009)

Fig. 4
Overall plan of the Girls' School in Lünen by Hans Scharoun (1962)

Fig. 5
Different "class domiciles" of the Girls' School in Lünen

Fig. 6
Six form secondary school *Auf dem Schäfersfeld* by Günter Behnisch in Lorch (1973)

feel at home. In addition, Maria Montessori specified that the design should reflect the respective proportions of the school children. Over the long term boundary conditions including illumination, ventilation, acoustics and colour scheme influence the quality and the measurable results.[1]

In 1950, in *Das neue Schulhaus*[2] (Fig. 2), in reference to the different pedagogical concepts, Alfred Roth defined some of the basic classroom types which are still valid today. In the wake of the ongoing social change today pedagogy and schools have more tasks to perform:

- All-day care,
- Integration of children from immigrant families,
- Consideration of handicaps,
- Competence orientation, in the context of knowledge transfer,
- Classes spanning several age groups to offset smaller numbers of students.

The Büro Schneidermeyer developed a school construction typology based on those parameters for the Montag Stiftung. A good example of the result is the Welsberg Primary School in South Tirol – with a classroom, differentiation area and group room (Fig. 3).

1 OWP/P Architects, VS Furniture, B. M. Design: *The Third Teacher,* New York 2010. Compare Breithecker, Dieter: *Bewegte Schule. Vom statischen Sitzen zum lebendigen Lernen,* Wiesbaden 1998.
2 Roth, Alfred: *Das Neue Schulhaus,* Zurich 1950.

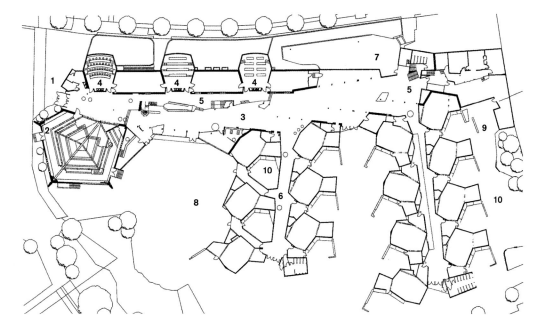

1	Main entrance
2	Assembly hall
3	Recreation hall
4	Auditorium
5	Staircase to "class domiciles"
6	Hallways to "class domiciles"
7	Side entrance
8	Central playground
9	Staff area
10	Class garden

Fig. 4

The school also needs a central meeting point for all students, like a market place, as a place and opportunity for encounter which enhances the feeling of us among students and teachers. (Fig. 4 and 5) This meeting point has been ideally realized in three phases from 1956 to 1962 by Hans Scharoun in the Girls' School in Lünen, which was recently completely renovated and declared a listed building.

Fig. 5

In 1973 the sixth form secondary school *Auf dem Schäfersfeld* in Lorch was built. The architect Günter Behnisch also took a position regarding the consolidation of several schools into so-called comprehensive schools from different localities or city districts: "By relocating the school away from this village, the locality or city district, one loses the opportunity to use this school to solve other non-school problems. [...] the school should bear the stamp of the area [...]."[3] Instead of an accumulative spatial organization in Lorch, Behnisch conceptualized a light-suffused school, which was also focussed on a spatial midpoint. The central hall, which also absorbs part of the intramural traffic, is the hub of the school life.

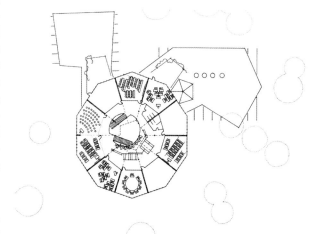

Fig. 6

From today's standpoint the spatial concepts of Alfred Roth, Hans Scharoun and Günter Behnisch have been validated, enabling them to be transferred in a way that will be appropriate for school construction in the 21st century. It should however be noted that the equipment of the classrooms and the additional learning locations in the building have already changed and will continue to do so in the future.

---

[3] *Unbehagen am Schulbau der Gegenwart* (Anxiety About Current School Architecture). Interview by Max Fengler with Günter Behnisch, in: Architektur and Wohnwelt 5/1975.

Fig. 7

Fig. 7
Flexible classroom arrangement allows for different teaching methods like teacher-up-front (see figure above), or group work (see figure in the middle) or team work at individual tables (see figure below).

Fig. 8
School desks with free form desk tops are ideal for the transformable classroom. Because they are uncomplicated, quick to arrange and do not require much space, they can be arranged in circular groups or arranged in rows for team work.

Fig. 8

Fig. 9–11

Fig. 12–14

Some of the significant factors of influence today are:

- Flexible forms of teaching, like teaching the entire class, group work, teams of two and one-on-one work, should be possible in one room.
- Model *Ganztagschule* (all day schools) with expanded spatial allocation for students and teachers
- The so-called *Bewegte Schule* (or Dynamic School, see the text below), for instance according to the guidelines of the *Bundesarbeitsgemeinschaft für Haltungs- and Bewegungsförderung e.V.* (Group for the Promotion of Posture and Movement),
- Integration of electronic media

Because of this development process the classroom and its surroundings is transforming into a learning landscape. To begin with, the classroom must be able to be rearranged according to the relevant form of teaching without a great investment of time (Fig. 7).

School desks with freeform desk tops are especially useful for circular seating of the students (Fig. 8). Retreat areas for students and teachers are ideal candidates for the all day school and can also be used for group work (Fig. 9 and 10). The media centre can also be upgraded with a lounge (Fig. 11).

Because of the increasing use of electronic media, too many young children are spending too much time sitting. The concept of the *dynamic school* is an initiative of the Group for the Promotion of Posture and Movement e.V., supported by the *Bundesministerium für Familie, Senioren, Frauen und Jugend* (Federal Ministry for Family, Seniors, Women and Youth), in order to counteract certain skewed developments. According to Dieter Breithecker, the purely static seating position, which is promoted in the norms for school and office work places, must be superseded, because no human being can maintain a static position for more than a few minutes. Instead the schools need additional different seating and movement possibilities. (Fig. 12–14).

However the concept of the *dynamic school* is not limited to the maintenance or reestablishment of physical health on the basis of the general lack of movement. The insights of Maria Montessori show that movement is a necessary precondition for physical and mental development: "If one observes children, one can clearly see that their mental development depends on physical movement." She pursues this idea in more detail in her last publication:[4] "When mental development is under discussion, there are many who say: ›How does movement come into it? We are talking about the mind.‹ And when we think of intellectual activity, we always imagine people sitting still, motionless. But mental development must be connected with movement and be dependent on it. It is vital that education theory and practice should be informed by that idea."

Oliver Ludwig and Dieter Breithecker[5] have also proven that dynamic sitting activates blood circulation and improves the supply of oxygen to the brain. That means that the overall capacity for concentration increases in comparison with static sitting (Fig. 16).

4 Montessori, Maria: *The Absorbent Mind*, Adyar 1949.
5 Compare Ludwig, Oliver/Breithecker, Dieter: *Untersuchung zur Änderung der Oberkörperdurchblutung während des Sitzens auf Stühlen mit beweglicher Sitzfläche*, 2008.

Fig. 15

In contrast, the classical work ergonomic specifications currently on file in the DIN norm and the European CEN Norm is oriented more to the static sitting posture. However the norm does have important tips for size adaptation and selection of school furniture, when these items are not flexible or adjustable (Fig. 17). In principle the current growth of the students must be checked every year and where necessary the classroom furniture must be exchanged. In fact this happened seldom or not at all. If chairs which are height adjustable and support dynamic sitting are used only one chair each is needed for the primary and secondary schools. Swivel chairs can be fitted with a 3D-tilt mechanism, which continuously simulates dynamic sitting, leading to more concentration and attentiveness in class. (Fig. 16).

Fig. 9–11
After classes are through students and teachers can relax in a retreat area or media library with lounge.

Fig. 12–14
Additional opportunities to sit or move around, including some outside conventional classrooms, increase the concentration and performance of the children.

Fig. 15
The DIN EN 1729 norm is oriented to the static seating posture, for which chair and desk height are determined according to physical size.

Fig. 16
A chair equipped with a 3D tilt mechanism is a prerequisite for dynamic sitting.

Fig. 17
Unless school furniture is adjustable, the students' height will have to be checked every year and the furniture changed accordingly. Height adjustable desks and swivel chairs are available.

Fig. 16

Fig. 17

Fig. 18
Height adjustable teachers' desks (in the middle and on the right) and an adjustable stool (left) are the basis for flexible teaching situations.

Fig. 19
Electrified locker modules are for safekeeping computers, printers & etc.

Fig. 20
The Interactive Whiteboard (IAW) replaces the traditional school blackboard for the presentation of material prepared beforehand.

Fig. 21
Plan for the integration of digital technology: a wireless connection and the necessary blackboard software are the basis of digital teaching.

Fig. 18

The entire range of height through the 12th or 13th class can be covered with an adjustable desk. An inclinable desk top makes reading and writing easier especially in the primary school. Additional active possibilities for movement as a supplement to the classical school chair are stools which allow for pendulum movement (Fig. 18).

Adjustable sitting and standing positions are also helpful for teachers. In contrast to the classical teacher's desk a desk with gas lift supported sitting and standing positions can be used while teaching (Fig. 18). In the future didactic methods will undergo momentous change through the use of electronic media. While these media are only being slowly introduced in Germany, in international comparison many other countries are already better equipped in a trend that seems unstoppable.

For now the use of personal computers is limited to a room specially set up for this purpose in order to learn how to work with standard software. With the use of laptops this kind of instruction can also be conducted in the classroom. The key item here is a completely electrified laptop-cabinet module for the operation of 18 laptops with the mains adapter, mouse and cable as well as a shelf for the printer (Fig. 19). Independent of this set-up an interactive whiteboard, or IAW is in use in some schools (Fig. 20). The advantages of the interactive whiteboard can be summarized as follows:

- Images stored on the whiteboard and work that has been prepared can be recalled and processed at any time.
- Multimedia contents like graphics or images can be easily uploaded and changed and then printed out or mailed.
- The whole digital world is accessible to the classroom work.

Learning is receiving another boost from the use of tablets, which are also eBook compatible. In comparison to the printed textbook the eBook is always up to date and costs less than printed books which always must be replaced. In addition, tablets are lighter than laptops and have batteries with more capacity.

And finally, there are new possibilities for applications in the teacher- student exchange through the integrated use of the IAW. Some school districts in the USA have started to completely equip schools with tablets. According to manufacturer's statistics more than three million tablets were sold to educational facilities in 2012, with the Asian countries in the lead. South Korea's goal is to replace all school books with tablets by 2015. Although questions may be raised about this goal, the trend is clear and is increasingly evident in the European trade fairs for education and teaching materials where electronic media are playing an increasingly dominant role. Although the average age of teachers in Germany is dropping slightly, the insecurity in working with the digital world in schools is on the rise. This is in part due to the fact that almost all the manufacturers or their trading partners in the schools deliver only part of the suggested solutions. That means that the administrative effort for the school to integrate the individual components is enormous. And that means coordinating the work of a student on his tablet with the tasks assigned by the teacher and the work on the IAW. Such an integration of the digital technology can already be installed today. The following software components are employed to do that:

- The software for the classroom management (like Smart Sync) allows for the wireless control of the students' tablets by the teacher and thereby the control of the teaching contents. Conversely in order to solve a given task the students can communicate with the notebook of the teacher.
- With the notebook or whiteboard software (like the Smart Notebook) the teachers can communicate with the notebook and interactive whiteboard and present suggested solutions to the students on the electronic whiteboard.
- Remote PC access (for instance, Splashtop). This software controls the PC of the electronic whiteboard (like on and off functions) or the operating system.

Fig. 19

Fig. 20

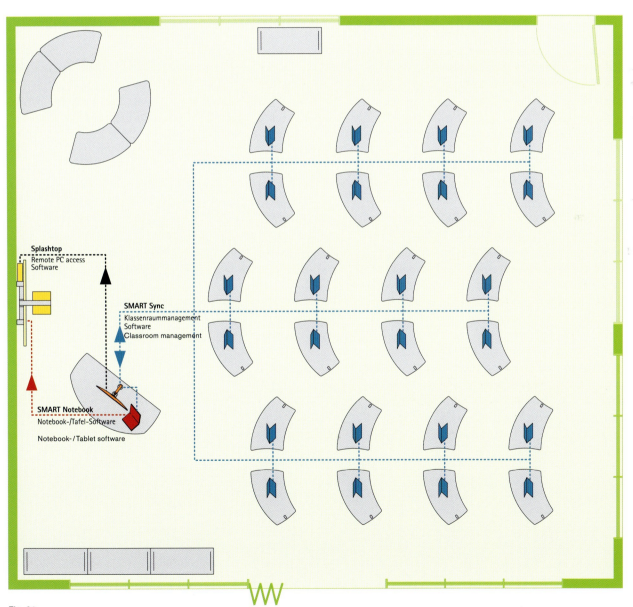

Fig. 21

From Classroom to Learning Landscape

Fig. 22
The David Stubbs concept offers new furnishing possibilities and is based on the idea of applying different forms of teaching.

Fig. 23
Computer rooms, which only have one purpose, namely computer science instruction, are more the exception today. More priority is placed on using the new media in the classroom.

Fig. 24
Adjustable stools are not just for use in conventional classroom settings. They can be taken along everywhere, for instance in the assembly hall, on the playground or in the museum.

Fig. 22

The last question to be answered is, who will pay for the student tablets? *Bring Your Own Device* (BYOD) is an organizational guideline intended to regulate how teachers and students may use their own electronic devices. This pertains especially to the access to network services and the processing and storage of internal data. In the area of education BYOD offers economical and ecological potentials: Instead of confronting the school with the procurement of the devices and the costs associated with that, the private devices should be increasingly used for school related purposes. However BYOD poses a security risk because the organization data is processed on external devices which are only partially able to be controlled and which cannot rule out break-downs and misuse of data. In addition BYOD stands in the way of a strategy for unifying an IT infrastructure. Administrative problems and data protection and liability problems can also be expected. A *Virtual Desktop Infrastructure* (VDI) could offer a possible solution. The VDI would virtualize the entire PC desktop in the computer centre.

In light of the manifold demands on the school of the future, David Stubbs, the architect and planning director of the Clarke County (USA) school district, has developed a classroom concept called *Cultural Shift*, which provides new possibilities for furnishings to take into account the most varied pedagogical forms of instruction. (Fig. 22). Five of the eight *Cultural Shift* goals are presented here as orientation:

Respond to Multiple Learning and Teaching Styles:

- Everyone learns differently so why do we offer only one seat and one desk?
- A variety of desk and seating elements in one classroom (not required but possible to fully explore ones potential).
- Various learning styles are discussed but the tools are limited to one or two options as they have not until now been designed holistically.
- Teachers and students are all different, they do not all fit in the square, creatives, intellectuals, communicative, extroverts, introverts, all benefit from different opportunities to work, to relax, to communicate, to perch, sit, stand.
- Let the teacher teach how they know, help them develop to suit what they teach.

In recent years several classes were tested in the USA according to this concept. Which means, the *From Classroom to Learning Landscape* discussion will continue in the future.

Fig. 23

Fig. 24

Learning from School Buildings
Typologies and Space Allocation Models[1]

Jochem Schneider

The considerable discussion about school building, depending on the professional point of view, ranges from an apparent need for standardisation and the demand for local, individual solutions. The fact that there are generally recognized types of schools (primary, secondary school, middle school, preparatory high school, integrated comprehensive schools etc.) indicated that schools displayed common usage requirements. The next step is an "optimized building model", which best answers all the questions concerning model space allocation and school building guidelines as well as eligibility criteria and financing stipulations that have been posed in Germany for decades. There are many detailed quantitative design requirements for the rooms planned in terms of size, shape, room height, numbers of windows and many others dealing with safety and quality. Determinations are purely quantitative – from standard surface values, like two square metres per student, which was established for classrooms.

Individualization and differentiation, cooperation and self-management, all-day schooling and inclusion, pedagogical profiling and openings to the surroundings are some of the key phrases in the current discussion about education which indicate the manifold needs leading to a diversification of the pedagogical concepts in German schools. Each school must find its own way. The school landscape is changing: non-denominational or regional schools appear alongside middle schools and preparatory high schools, while in many places the secondary school is being basically questioned, and integrated comprehensive schools are being transformed into city district schools.

If one assumes in a first approximation that the spatial structure and organization of a building is derived from the needs of the users and if one takes the idea of space as a "third teacher" seriously, then certain consequences for planning and building must be drawn from the pedagogical displacements described in every day school life: building typologies and spatial organization models undergo change. In light of ever broader tasks today it cannot only be the case to use new standards and guidelines as a basis for a quantitatively increased demand for space. Quality based criteria and changed organization models must also be discussed which respond to the increasing demands. In a good mixture of the tried and true and the new, the transferable and the specific, depending on the situation and planning, spatial needs can be defined.

The various German sets of rules to date display great differences and most often follow the logic of a spatially precise establishment of surfaces. "If one considers the prevailing guidelines for school building, one will see that they more often describe limits than characteristics of quality: especially in school funding they are generally interpreted as allowable maximum rather than minimum standards."[2] With architects and administrative officials as well as with teachers and parents this leads to permanent injustice and harsh criticism: the rules are completely antiquated and leave no leeway for adaptations. Important spaces are missing and the photo lab which no one needs anymore must be "creatively" rededicated. Often there are two planning records – one for the funding and one for the building process. Sweeping change is needed. There are many expectations regarding new guidelines, with most determined to a great degree by the self-interest of those affected. Guidelines should be general and resilient, but also to a great degree adaptable and flexible.[3] Newer guidelines and directives thereby depart from spatially specific determinations and define surface parameters for different areas of use, which can then be variously interpreted according to the local situation and pedagogical goal.[4]

1. This essay is an expanded and reworked version of *Typologien and räumliche Organisations-Modelle (Typologies and Space Organization Models)* which the author produced for and in collaboration with the Montag Stiftung Urbane Räume in 2012 in the framework of the project *Leitlinien für leistungsfähige Schulbauten* (Guidelines for Efficient School Buildings).
2. Montag Stiftung (Ed.)/Lederer, Arno/Pampe, Barbara/Seydel, Otto: *Vergleich ausgewählter Richtlinien zum Schulbau*. Abridged version, Bonn 2011.
3. See: Montag Stiftung Jugend and Gesellschaft/Montag Stiftung Urbane Räume (Ed.)/Kühn, Christian/Temel, Robert/Sammer, Florian: *Regionale Werkstattgespräche zu Schulbaurichtlinien in Deutschland*. Abridged version. Issue 2 of the series *Rahmen and Richtlinien für einen leistungsfähigen Schulbau in Deutschland*, Bonn 2011.

Flexibility, adaptability, variety, multi-usability, exchangeability – the permanent pressure of change as a consequence of countless school reforms culminates architecturally in the longing for the much quoted "one size fits all" – a school building that can be adapted to everything.

The following essay will try to approximate a "good school building" in the 21st century, with the presentation of spatial typologies and organization models which establish the foundations, but which access certain open spaces and selection possibilities. The condition for that is that before the start of construction the needs and goals of users are clearly defined and evaluated from the standpoint of their significance for the architectural concept. The building and the pedagogy must precisely fit together, like hardware and software.

In view of these interdependencies three subject areas will be treated: learning sites, team areas and common areas. Similar statements may be formulated in addition for other areas of use, like the specialist classrooms and free spaces. The contents of this essay are based on the research results of many projects from the past years which were conducted with the Montag Stiftung in Bonn.

The approaches were then practically developed and fine-tuned in an initial phase in many consultation processes with local schools and school boards.[5] The following proviso is crucial for the consideration of the subject: the challenges facing school building today cannot be met simply with the demand for more space. Changes in use and organization models are involved, which guarantee flexibility and multiple use and which must break free from the mental schema of *one room = one function*.

Learning sites must offer space for different forms of learning. The teacher-up-front style, which has until now determined the size and lay-out of the classrooms, will only be one form of teaching among many in the future. But how can individual or group work be done in the existing rooms or the rooms that are being built now? Schools are increasingly designing an ongoing daily rhythm for the school. Teaching and all-day spaces are being correspondingly conceptualized as a unit. The requirement of inclusion broadens the heterogeneity in the student body. The flexibility frequently called for requires precise activity analyses and needs assessment; use procedures must be investigated and design criteria specified according to activity. Instead of a mono-functionality, this involves intelligent combinations, spatial connections and multiple use that makes sense. In reference to learning sites these key terms in the school construction debate can be represented in three development model prototypes: Classroom Plus, Learning Cluster and Learning Landscape.

---

4   See: Musterflächenprogramm Hamburg (2012); Montag Stiftung Jugend and Gesellschaft/Montag Stiftung Urbane Räume (Ed.): *Leitlinien für leistungsfähige Schulbauten in Deutschland,* Berlin 2013; Schulbauleitlinien Darmstadt-Dieburg (2013); Ministerium für Kultus, Jugend and Sport Baden-Württemberg/ Schneider, Jochem/Seydel, Otto: *Empfehlungen für einen zeitgemäßen Schulbau in Baden-Württemberg,* Stuttgart/Überlingen 2013.

5   See: www.schulen-planen-und-bauen.de/konzept/phase-null.html; Montag Stiftung Jugend and Gesellschaft/Montag Stiftung Urbane Räume (Ed.)/ Hubel, Ernst/Passlick, Ulrich/Reich, Kersten/Schneider, Jochem/Seydel, Otto: *Schulen planen and bauen. Grundlagen and Prozesse,* Berlin 2012. Montag Stiftungen (Ed.)/Schneider, Jochem/Backes, Michael: *Schulumbau – Strategien zur Anpassung von Bestandsgebäuden,* Köln/Bonn 2012.

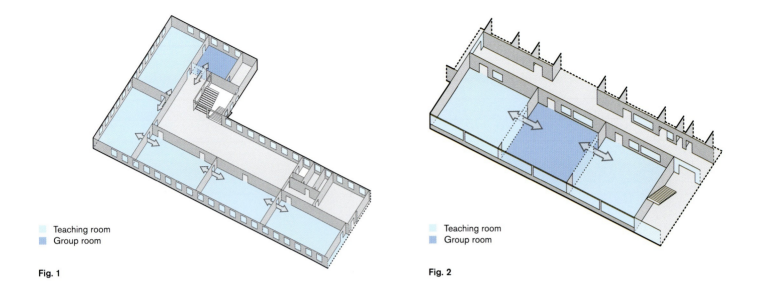

■ Teaching room
■ Group room

Fig. 1

■ Teaching room
■ Group room

Fig. 2

The work day of the teachers changes along with the school. Good team work in interdisciplinary teams is the key to successful work in education. Effective team structures and a cooperative climate among teachers, pedagogical staff and special teachers form the basis for a continued development of the school as location of learning and living. That makes possible an exchange of experience among colleagues and the implementation of contemporary learning concepts constitutes a significant health care building block. The relevant central criterion for success is: "No school development without team development". However as a consequence of the change in form of the team work new spatial needs arise and organizational structures emerge: the central staff room, where the functions of conference, communication, discussions, individual work and filing are jammed into far too little space was conceptualized for the break periods of the half-day school and has no future. Whether it is a central or decentralized organizational model, team areas require a disentangling of competing functions and usage requirements. That in turn means defining the pedagogical and spatial interfaces in relationship to the students and teachers. The spectrum ranges from common work areas to zones which are completely separate.

Common rooms as locations for exchange and communication are indispensable building blocks of a contemporary school, and are rightfully called the "heart of the school". Convertibility and openness also play a central role with canteens, auditoriums, libraries and gyms. These areas of use must be interconnected with access zones. In many schools foyer areas are being enhanced with concrete use functions so that a stage and a café can then be located in a spatial continuum along with reading and work areas without leading to an ominous cacophony. Access, encounter and lingering a while proceed in parallel. Can the stage area be set up in such a way that it can be decoupled from the day-to-day operation for rehearsals, set-up and striking the set? What can be learned from using an auditorium as a library? In a pinch can a stage interposed between a canteen and a sports area operate as a spectator room?

These are only a few examples. They show what is possible, which draws in different degrees on what is known while venturing something new at the same time. Generalized organization models and central criteria for decisions can be derived for the contemporary school building. Models and projects do not represent *the* solution or *copy-and-paste* patterns. They show much more a catalogue of solutions and are in that sense more indebted to a *copy-and-learn* idea.

Fig. 1
The large classrooms with approximately 80 square metres in the Milchbuck School converted by B.E.R.G. Architekten in Zurich feature high flexibility and can be used with different learning formats in each room. The doors of the classrooms can be opened with connecting doors to create an "enfilade".

Fig. 2
The classrooms of the Landsberger Straße primary school in Herford designed by SITTIG + VOGES are furnished in twos with an intermediate assembly area. The walls are transparent, allowing a direct view inside. According to need, a group room can be used by both classes, either individually or together.

Fig. 3
Four classes are located in the Wartburg School House of Learning in Münster, designed by Helmut Rentrop. The structuring in pairs creates clear lines.

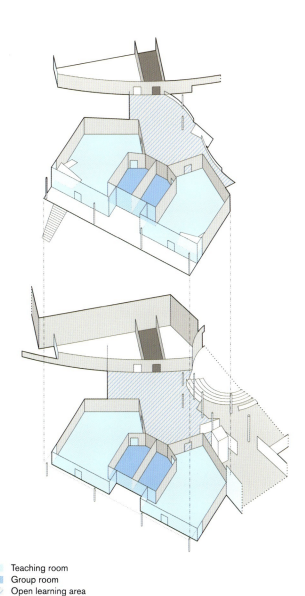

Teaching room
Group room
Open learning area
Access
Ancillary spaces

Fig. 3

Learning Areas

Classroom Plus

More classroom space means that the need for multi-optional use space for different forms of learning will be increasingly addressed by larger, especially more networked teaching rooms. One-on-one and group work with three to eight students, sitting in a circle or teaching the entire class then becomes possible in close proximity.

- Beginning with 70 square metres, with an allocation of 25 students significant improvements occur in the flexibility of classroom use.
- The backpack principle enables the classroom to be used in conjunction with another class by adding an adjacent space. Two classrooms with a group room between them then become a tandem class. Partitions are equipped with doors and/or are glazed. In spite of the acoustic separation there is a spatial continuum. Different activities and forms of learning can take place in parallel in the teaching and group rooms, without losing eye contact. A pedagogical concept that is tailored to that arrangement and a direct accord between the two classes is essential for the use model. The rooms most often have several accesses, with a hallway either directly into the classroom or to the group room.
- With a two storey learning facility two classrooms with central group rooms are positioned together on one level. Each tandem has a common entryway, connected side rooms and a direct access to a space outside. The levels are displaced by a half storey towards the main access.

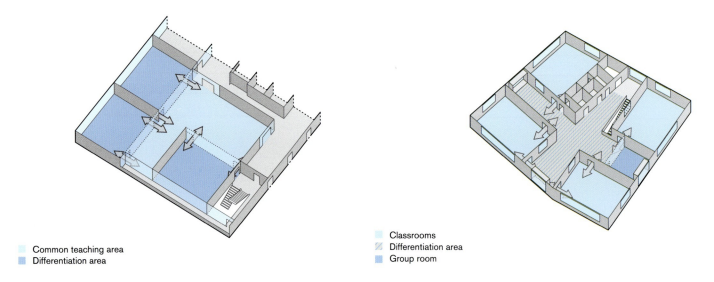

Common teaching area
Differentiation area

Fig. 4

Classrooms
Differentiation area
Group room

Fig. 5

Learning Cluster

In the cluster model two to six classes or learning groups are joined either by or across age groups. The relevant classrooms together with the differentiation spaces, rest and relaxation areas for all-day and inclusion are combined in an identifiable unit. Work places for teachers (team bases) and the storage and toilet and washroom facilities can be integrated in the cluster. As an alternative to age group teams, a cluster can also be set up according to joint specialist rooms (mathematics, English, languages, social sciences etc.).

Through the combination of adjacent spaces the cluster model creates relations that make sense with far-reaching flexibility.

- The cluster makes it possible in the immediate teaching environment to offer a multitude of spatial situations, from confines to expansiveness, introversion and openness, individuality and community.
- Because of spatial variation network structures are adaptable to changes in demand. The palette of combinations is extensive.
- The spatial network supports day-to-day communication and exchange. Communication niches are formed in the informal transition areas between the rooms. As indeterminate interstices they are an important spatial resource. They require the relevant fire protection solution.
- Open group rooms, flexible relaxation areas and access spaces, window niches, balconies and etc. expand the spatial possibilities especially for phases of one-on-one or small group work.
- By means of the network and the inclusion of access spaces a significant increase in usable space in the teaching area can be achieved. Current space allocation programs for this kind of teaching area calculate up to five square metres per student.
- The clear association of spatial blocks with pedagogical teams creates identification and responsibility.

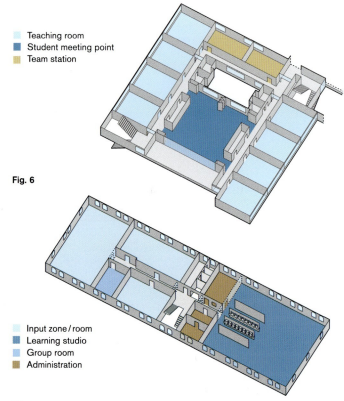

Teaching room
Student meeting point
Team station

Fig. 6

Input zone/room
Learning studio
Group room
Administration

Fig. 7

Fig. 4
Three classes of the *Im Birch* school in Zurich by Peter Märkli and Gody Kühnis share a common forum, with transparent partitions. The spatial organization enables a level of flexibility ranging all the way to a return to the original utilization distribution: the forum becomes a learning site with individual work places with the outer walls as differentiation.

Fig. 5
Four classrooms of the primary school by Klaus Hellweger in Welsberg Italy, are located on one floor. They share a common access area which as an open learning workshop can be used for free group work. Each class has two doors, the group room being separated only by a glass wall.

Fig. 6
According to the plans by Zaeske and Partner for the converted Alexej von Jawlensky Integrated Comprehensive School (*Integrierte Gesamtschule* or IGS) in Wiesbaden two age group teams for every four classes are located in a common block. Team areas, storage space, open areas and sanitary areas are integrated. A jointly used student meeting point which can be subdivided is located in the middle of the school.

Fig. 7
Half of each floor of the education supplier *SBW Haus des Lernens* in Romanshorn, Switzerland, converted according to plans by J. Ineichen, consists of a learning studio and different, specifically furnished input rooms which can be arranged according to need. A large, open space for multiple as well as individual learning formats is augmented by fixed, closed rooms.

Fig. 8
In the Ringstabekk Skole Baerum, Norway, planned by Div. A arkitekter, two learning sites each for 60 students are arranged around an auditorium with space for 60. They contain a large joint learning area, group rooms and little *think tanks* for up to five persons. Team rooms for the teachers are integrated.

Fig. 9
Four classrooms are located on each floor of the half-storey offset Corlaer College planned by Broekbakema In Nijkerk, Holland. Transparent teaching rooms and open learning areas alternate within an age group.

<u>Learning Landscape</u>

The furthest step away from the classroom as building block of a school is the so-called *learning landscape*, in which the students can pick and choose between individual or group work depending on the situation. Instead of fixed classrooms there are open learning areas and group and instruction rooms. Access and intermediate areas are integrated as communication zones in the learning landscape.

The concept is spatially shaped directly by the idea of individualization and self-reliance in learning, so that every student can choose between different learning areas and atmospheres. It is especially useful in the higher forms and requires a greater degree of self-sufficiency. Open learning areas are always augmented by instruction rooms with special equipment. With a clearly defined function they offer a precise framework for a teaching format which may include technical equipment and fixed furniture. They are occupied with prior consultation on an alternating basis. If they are free, they are used for group work.

Among the spatial organization model learning landscapes which are prevalent in Scandinavia in the secondary schools are the base concepts. A base consisting of a large group of 60 to 120 students is brought together in a room. Depending on need the group is then subdivided in learning groups of 30, 20 or 15 students. The schools have open spatial zones for free use. Team work is possible in adjacent group spaces which can be sequestered. A centrally located lecture hall for 60 augments the spatial array and provides a counterpole to the smallest room in a base, the *Think Tanks*, which can be used for up to five persons for a joint discussion. The interchange between open, multiple use areas for free allocation and functionally defined spaces with clearly defined use profiles is also apparent here.

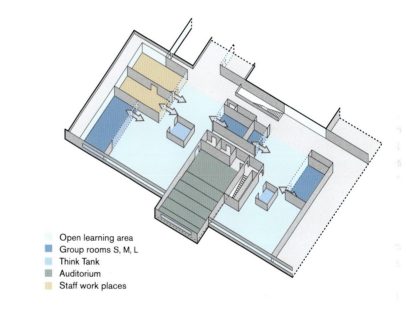

- Open learning area
- Group rooms S, M, L
- Think Tank
- Auditorium
- Staff work places

Fig. 8

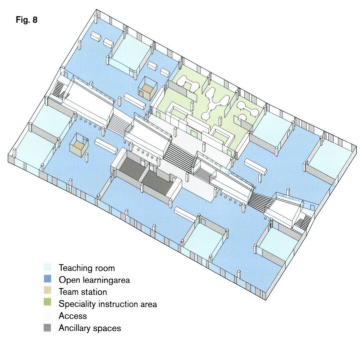

- Teaching room
- Open learningarea
- Team station
- Speciality instruction area
- Access
- Ancillary spaces

Fig. 9

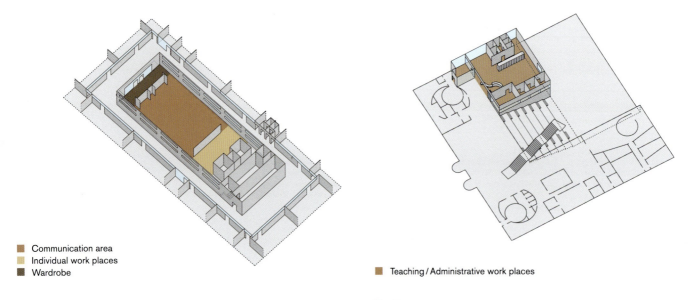

■ Communication area
■ Individual work places
■ Wardrobe

Fig. 10

■ Teaching / Administrative work places

Fig. 11

Team Areas

Since the introduction of the all-day concept the established requirements for contemporary work places also pertain to teachers. The appropriate spatial conditions had to be created for the teams made up of teachers, pedagogical employees and in the context of inclusion, the special education staff. The classical staff room can no longer fulfil those needs. In these "break rooms" with an average of 1.5 to two square metres of space per person, the teaching staff has completely inadequate conditions to work. In a normal office setting the allocation is eight to twelve square metres per person. In addition, since faculty rooms until now have been set up for individual work, filing, discussions, communication and conferences, they are completely overloaded from a functional standpoint. These needs must be disentangled so areas which are separate from each other are made available for individual preparatory work and filing, for discussions and for informal exchange. This arrangement is independent of whether space is available in a centralized or decentralized location.

The central solution is the one most often selected in schools which have at their disposal a manageable enough size, that all the teachers in the team can still meet in one room. Nevertheless, in this arrangement there must also be clear differentiation among the various use areas: communication, discussions and individual work and filing. The acoustic decoupling of the individual areas becomes especially important here in order to avoid competitive use and mutual hindrances. At the same time it is necessary from the standpoint of a collective space for encounter to maintain transparency and clear orientation:

- The entryway should be viewed as a communicative interface and access channel, which has a central meaning for the teacher-student relationship.
- The communication area should feature an informal, cafeteria-like ambiance. Opportunities to be informed (electronic notice board or blackboard) are appropriate.
- Some schools pick the flexible model with mobile writing desks for individual work places, others prefer fixed work places, even when these are extremely cramped. Enough storage space is available in any case.
- Possibilities for meetings in groups of four to six persons are envisioned.
- The orientation of the size of the team area to the conference area is no longer relevant. A multi-function room that can otherwise be used for teaching should be used for faculty meetings.
- In addition to these active function areas places of retreat or rest areas are envisioned. They provide needed downtime in an all-day school schedule that can be gruelling.
- In some schools team and administrative areas can be combined in a targeted way as a spatial unity.

Decentralized organization models for the spatial arrangement of team areas as an alternative to centralized solutions are finding increasing acceptance. They are mostly used in connection with pedagogical concepts of age groups or specialist teams. The decentralized arrangement allows for work together in small, easy to manage units. It enhances the team structures and creates possibilities for identification between places and people.

Fig. 10
The École Secondaire Nyon-Marens in Switzerland built according to plans by CCHE Architecture features a centrally located joint staff room with clearly defined individual work places, a communication area and an entryway.

Fig. 11
Some teacher's work places in the 3XN Architekten designed Ørestad College in Copenhagen were arranged in a central location in the administrative tract. At the same time every teacher and student has the opportunity to pick out a temporary work location anywhere in the building.

Fig. 12
Team stations are integrated in the bases, the open group areas for the students, in the Ringstabekk Skole designed by the office of Div. A arkitekter. Meeting and work areas are connected with a sliding door. In the administrative area another team room provides space for retreat and communication.

Fig. 13
Work and meeting rooms for the teams are located in the decentralized "homeland areas" in the Hellerup Skole in Copenhagen, planned by Arkitema Architects. 75 students can be taught in each of them. There is an additional team room at a central location.

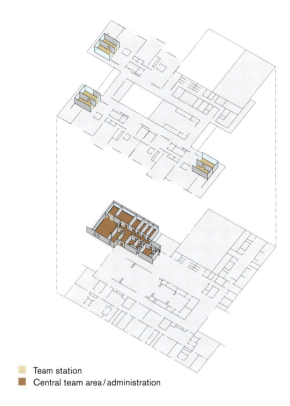

▓ Team station
▓ Central team area / administration

Fig. 12

This goes for the teachers as well as the students. Reservations concerning a possibly too great density can be alleviated with architectural buffers and clear rules for communication. The role of the teachers as consultants and learning companions is explicitly underscored with this spatial model:

- In decentralized team bases – on the basis of age groups or department – more workplaces for teachers will be set up. Room units with space for up to eight workplaces have proven to be effective.
- Meeting areas are joined to or integrated in the team bases. These must be acoustically insulated so that confidential discussions with colleagues, students and parents can be conducted.
- Some schools combine decentralized work and meeting rooms with communication zones at a central point – often attached to the administration –, so that the team can socialize outside the classroom.
- Conferences are held in multi-purpose rooms.

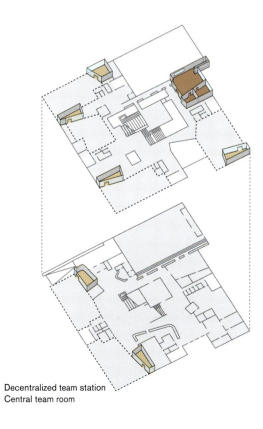

▓ Decentralized team station
▓ Central team room

Fig. 13

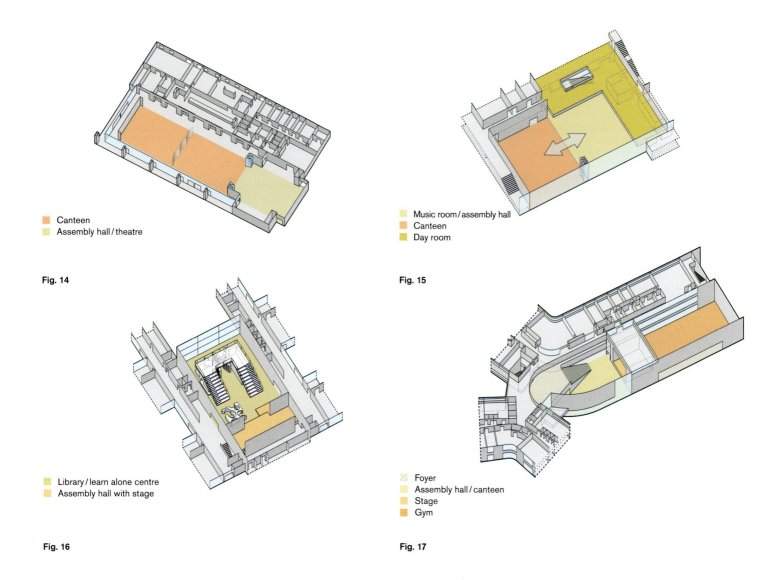

■ Canteen
■ Assembly hall / theatre

Fig. 14

■ Music room / assembly hall
■ Canteen
■ Day room

Fig. 15

■ Library / learn alone centre
■ Assembly hall with stage

Fig. 16

▨ Foyer
■ Assembly hall / canteen
■ Stage
■ Gym

Fig. 17

Common Areas

The watchword for the common areas, the auditorium, canteen, all-day areas, sport halls, libraries, forums etc., is multiple use. Very often these areas have a double use, like the combination of canteen and auditorium, if these two functions can be separated by a flexible, but acoustically effective partition. If an event is being held, both spaces can be combined and used together. A double use as auditorium and library can also make sense for smaller schools.

In many schools, by converting the access areas and using the foyers as meeting and movement rooms, new, open room typologies are created. They are marked by a broad palette of usage possibilities which emerge from overlapping, so that day-to-day and holiday situations become merged. The clear boundaries which prevailed as functional areas – work and recreation areas, canteen, auditorium, music room, and library, become blurred. The rooms open up to the access areas, making possible a reciprocal activation. Transitional areas emerge –

spatially and functionally: the foyer becomes a ballroom, a library, stairway, stage, workroom, cafe … The location of the stage has a special meaning. It should by all means be acoustically decoupled and separately accessed. That allows the organization of set-up and dismantling to be done independently. The stage can also operate as the transition to the gym, which in turn can become the auditorium. In many schools the canteen is multi-use, opening up possibilities for significantly more activities than a place to dispense meals. In an expanded constellation it can become a meeting point and communicative hub in the life of the school. The basic canteen program is often augmented by additional building blocks, like reading lounges, internet cafes, recreation and rest areas and consultation rooms. The space can also function as a docking station for youth welfare programs and interfaces for extracurricular education. The canteen should also feature an open area for public, non-school related events, with an appropriate independent access. The more that functions overlap, the more important it becomes to use definitions and agreements concerning mutual consideration.

Fig. 14
The canteen and assembly hall of the Alexej von Jawlensky Integrated Comprehensive School in Wiesbaden, designed by Zaeske and Partner are accessible via a flexible sub-dividable and optionally combinable partition. Meals and theatre production are an important part of the day-to-day pedagogical life of the school.

Fig. 15
The assembly hall of the Zurich school *Im Birch*, designed by Peter Märkli and Gody Kühnis, can be combined with the adjacent canteen into a large event hall. A gallery for free time and rest is located above the food service area.

Fig. 16
This room becomes additionally usable by the installation of seating in the assembly hall of the Munkegaard Skole Gentofte, Denmark, designed by Arne Jacobsen and reconstructed 60 years later by Dorte Mandrup, without relinquishing the character of its original use: the bleachers are formed by the "roof" of a small library.

Fig. 17
Even more seldom than the canteen and assembly hall combination is the canteen, assembly hall and gym combination that one may find in the Kirkkojarvi Comprehensive School Espoo, Finland, designed according to plans by VERSTAS Architects. The stage area is an insertion that is separately usable and open on both sides.

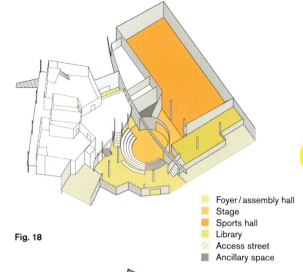

▨ Foyer / assembly hall
▨ Stage
▨ Sports hall
▨ Library
▨ Access street
▨ Ancillary space

Fig. 18

Fig. 18
With its semi-circular auditorium and a stage the multiple use entryway of the Wartburg Primary School in the city district of Gievenbeck west of downtown Münster is the centre of the school built according to plans by Helmut Rentrop. The library and gym are directly connected.

Fig. 19
The central hall of the A. P. Møller School in Schleswig, planned by C.F. Møller, is both a location for movement and relaxation: the library is just as much a part of the whole as the work places for students and teachers. The assembly hall is also directly connected.

Fig. 20
More leeway is needed to create transition and day rooms. By overlapping the functions of stairway, meeting point, stage and Café in the school De Titaan in Hoorn, Holland (Architectuurstudio Herman Hertzberger) a central location with multiple use possibilities emerges.

Fig. 21
Entryway, bleachers and gym on the ground floor are separate in Ørestad College in Copenhagen, but still usable together. The open spatial design, planned by 3XN, extends into all floors of the gym.

▨ Foyer
▨ Assembly hall
▨ Library / learn alone centre

Fig. 19

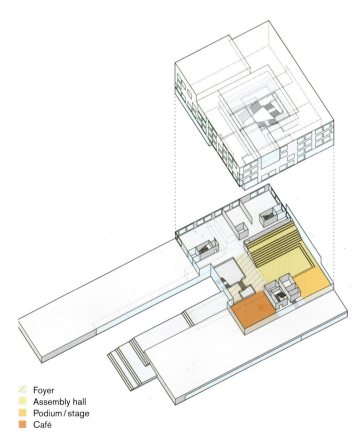

▨ Foyer
▨ Assembly hall
▨ Podium / stage
▨ Café

Fig. 20

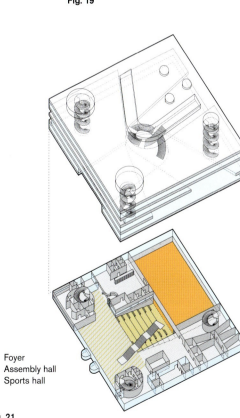

▨ Foyer
▨ Assembly hall
▨ Sports hall

Fig. 21

Learning from School Buildings 55

Publications

Ford, Alan: *Designing the Sustainable School,* Melbourne 2007.

Wirz, Heinz (Ed.): *Cartesian Caves,* Luzern 2012.

Selected Books

Ainscow, Mel/Booth, Tony/Dyson, Alan: *Improving Schools. Developing Inclusion,* London 2006.

Bamford, Anne: *The Wow Factor. Global research compendium on the impact of the arts in education,* Münster/New York et al. 2006.

Billimore, Brian/Department for Education and Skills (UK): *The Outdoor Classroom,* London 1999.

Brubaker, Charles William: *Planning and Designing Schools,* New York 1998.

Ceppi, Giulio/Zini, Michele (Ed.): *Children, Spaces, Relations. Metaproject for an Environment for Young Children,* Milan 1998.

Crosbie, Michael J.: *Class Architecture,* Melbourne 2001.

Curtis, Eleanor: *School Builders,* Chichester 2003.

Daniels, Klaus: *Advanced Building Systems. A Technical Guide for Architects and Engineers,* Basel/Boston/Berlin 2003.

DeMause, Lloyd (Ed.): *The History of Childhood,* New Jersey 1974.

Dewey, John: *Democracy and Education,* New York 1916.

Dudek, Mark: *Architecture of Schools. The New Learning Environments,* Oxford/Boston 2000.

Dudek, Mark: *Building for Young Children,* London 2001.

Dudek, Mark: *Children's Spaces,* Oxford 2005.

Dudek, Mark: *Schools and Kindergartens. A Design Manual,* Basel 2008.

Ehmann, Sven/Borges, Sofia/Klanten, Robert: *Learn for Life. New Architecture for New Learning,* Berlin 2012.

Encyclopædia Britannica: *History of Education,* London 2007.

Ford, Alan: *Designing the Sustainable School,* Melbourne 2007.

Gardener, Howard: *Extraordinary Minds. Portraits of Exeptional Individuals and an Examination of our Extraordinariness,* New York 1997.

Gardener, Howard: *Frames of Mind. The Theory of Multiple Intelligences,* New York 1993.

Gardener, Howard: *The Unschooled Mind. How Children Think and how Schools Should Teach,* New York 1991.

Graves, Ben E./Pearson, Clifford A.: *School Ways. The Planning and Design of America's schools,* New York 1993.

Grosvenor, Ian/Lawn, Martin/Rousmaniere, Kate: *Silences and Images. The Social History of the Classroom,* New York 1999.

Haar, Sharon (Ed.): *Schools for Cities. Urban Strategies,* New York 2002.

Hendricks, Barbara E.: *Designing for Play,* Burlington 2001.

Knapp, Eberhard/Noschis, Kaj/Pasalar, Çelen (Ed.): *School Building Design and Learning Performance. With a Focus on Schools in Developing Countries,* Lausanne 2007.

Kurz, Daniel/Wakefield, Alan: *School Buildings. The State of Affairs,* Basel 2004.

Lackney, Jeffery A.: *Thirty-three Educational Design Principles for Schools and Community Learning Centers,* Mississippi State University 2000.

Lackney, Jeffery A.: *Educational Facilities. The Impact and Role of the Physical Environment of the School on Teaching,* University of Wisconsin, Milwaukee 2002.

Lippman, Peter C.: *Evidence-Based Design of Elementary and Secondary Schools. A Responsive Approach to Creating Learning Environments,* New York 2010.

LPA Architects (Ed.): *Green School Primer. Lessons in Sustainability,* Melbourne 2009.

Meuser, Philipp (Ed.): *Construction and Design Manual. Accessible Architecture,* Berlin 2012.

Meuser, Philipp/Pogade, Daniela: *Construction and Design Manual. Wayfinding and Signage,* Berlin 2010.

Montessori, Maria: *The Absorbent Mind,* Adyar (India) 1949.

Müller, Thomas/Schneider, Romana: *Montessori. Educational Material for Early Childhood and School,* München 2002.

Müller, Thomas/Schneider, Romana: *The Classroom. From the Late 19th Century until the Present Day,* Tübingen 2010.

Nair, Prakash/Fielding, Randall: *The Language of School Design. Design Patterns for the 21st Century Schools,* Minneapolis 2009.

Müller, Thomas/Schneider, Romana: *The Classroom,* Tübingen 2010.

Meuser, Philipp (Ed.): *Accessible Architecture,* Berlin 2012.

Meuser, Philipp/Pogade, Daniela: *Wayfinding and Signage,* Berlin 2010.

OECD (Ed.): *Designs for Learning. 55 Exemplary Educational Facilities,* Paris 2001.
Olds, Anita Rui: *Child Care Design Guide,* New York 2001.
Omrod, Jeanne Ellis: *Human Learning,* Columbus, Ohio 2004.
Omrod, Jeanne Ellis: *Educational Psychology. Developing Learners,* Upper Saddle River, New Jersey 2006.
OWP/P Architects/VS Furniture et al.: *The Third Teacher,* New York 2010.
Perkins, Bradford/Kliment, Stephen: *Building Type Basics – Elementary and Secondary Schools,* New York 2001.
Pollock, Linda A.: *Forgotten Children – Parent – Child Relations from 1500 to 1900,* Cambridge 1983.
Robson, Edward R.: *School Architecture (with an introducing from Malcolm Seaborne),* Leicester 1972.
Rocheleau, Paul: *The One-Room Schoolhouse. A Tribute to a Beloved National Icon,* New York 2003.
Schools Buildings and Design Unit, Department for Education and Stills (UK): *Acoustic Design of Schools – A Design Guide,* London 2003.
Sennett, Richard: *The Fall of Public Man,* Cambridge 1974.
Sorell, John and Frances: *Joined up Design for Schools,* London/New York 2006.
Tanner, C. Kenneth/Lackney, Jeffery A.: *Educational Facilities Planning,* Boston 2006.

Von Wiley, Bradford: *Building Type Basics for Elementary and Secondary Schools,* New York 2001.
Walden, Rotraut (Ed.): *Schools for the Future. Design proposals from Architectural Psychology,* Göttingen 2009.
Weinstein, Carol S./David, Thomas G.: *Spaces for Children. The Built Environment and Child Development,* New York 1987.
Wilson, Brent G. (Ed.): *Constructivist Learning Environments. Case Studies in Instructional Design,* New Jersey 1996.
Wirz, Heinz (Ed.): *Kartesanische Höhlen/Cartesian Caves. Schulhaus/ School Building Eichmatt, Cham/Hünenberg,* Luzern 2012.
Yee, Roger: *Educational Environments. No. 1–5,* New York 2002–2012.

Selected Articles

Blatchford, Peter/Baines, Ed/Kutnick, Peter/Martin, Clare: *Classroom Contexts. Connections Between Class Size and Within Class Grouping,* in: British Journal of Educational Psychology 71/2001, p. 282–302.
Earthman, Glen I.: *The Quality of School Buildings. Student Achievement and Student Behavior,* in: Bildung und Erziehung 52/1999, p. 353–372.
Edwards, Carolyn Pope: *"Fine Designs" from Italy: Montessori Education and the Reggio Emilia Approach,* in: Montessori Life 1/2003, p. 34–39.

Herrington, Susan: *Garden Pedagogy. Romanticism to Reform,* in: Landscape Journal 1/2001, p. 30–47.
Evans, Gary W.: *The Built Environment and Mental Health,* in: Journal of Urban Health 80/2003, p. 536–555.
Müller, Rikard/Lindsten, Carin: *Health and Behavior of Children in Classrooms With and Without windows,* in: Journal of Environmental Psychology 12/1992, p. 305–317.
Lackney, Jeffery A.: *Forming Small Learning Communities. Implementing Neighborhoods in an Existing High School,* in: CEFPI Journal, 3/2002, p. 5–10.
Places of Learning, in: Canadian Architect 10/2006, p. 26–42, 53.
Read, Marilyn A./Sugawara, Alan I./Brandt, Jeanette A.: *Impact of space and color in the physical environment on preschool childrens cooperative behavior,* in: Environment and Behavior 31/1999, p. 413–428.
Schauss, Alexander G.: *Tranquilizing Effect of Colour Reduces Aggressive Behaviour and Potential Violence,* in: Journal of Orthomogical Psychology 4/1979, p. 218–221.
Spodek, Bernhard/Saracho, Olivia N.: *On the Shoulders of Giants,* in: Early Childhood Education Journal 1/2003, p. 3–10.
Wells, Nancy M.: *At Home with Nature. Effects on "Greenness" on Children's Cognitive Functioning,* in: Environment and Behavior 32/2000, p. 775–795.
Wien, Carol Anne: *Scene for a Reflection. Neruda School, Reggio Emilia,* in: Canadian Children 1/2004, p. 44–45.

Primary Schools

Hardenberg · Holland	60
London · United Kingdom	68
Schulzendorf · Germany	76
Rudrapur · Bangladesh	84
Cressy · Switzerland	92
Rolle · Switzerland	100
Hamburg · Germany	108
Leusden · Holland	116
Chemnitz · Germany	126
Siegertsbrunn · Germany	136
Berlin · Germany	144
Grono · Switzerland	150

De Matrix Community School
Hardenberg

Architect: Marlies Rohmer
Staff: Simone van the Brink, Floris Hund, Gieneke Pieterse, Charles Hueber, Boris Briels, Klaas Nienhuis, Irene Zandhuis, Rijkan Scholten, Quirijin Oudegeest
Structural design: ABC Management Groep, Schreuders Baouwtechniek
Planning and construction phase: 2004–2007

School type: Community School – primary school with childcare, family counselling and family education
Number of students: 500 + 80 (day care centre)
Grades: 1–5
Age of students: 0–12 years
Average class size: 25 pupils
Number of classes: 13 classes (protestant primary school), 7 classes (public primary school)

Plot size: 6,000 square metres
Gross floor space: 6,465 square metres
Type of energy supply: district heating
Construction costs: 5.6 million euros

Awards: School Architectural Prize (Scholenbouwprijs) 2008, Building Business Golden Green Award 2009

In the middle of a district of former farmland belonging to the community of Hardenberg in Holland, this school is not just an educational facility. The dominance of the complex consisting of five cubes is derived from the position of the *Brede School*, which in its role as a non-denominational school next to the primary school, combines a network of childcare and counselling for parents and children from birth to twelve years of age. The school is the visible expression of the concern for education in the centre of the town. As a community centre the building is simultaneously a meeting point for the whole region. This character can already be seen at a good distance in the architecture of the central cube looming above the other buildings as the prize of the property, flanked on its corners by four other cubes. The rationale of the shape is a give-away of the life inside it. The one and two storey neighbouring buildings house the public and the Protestant primary school, while the facilities for health and social affairs, a childcare centre with group room and sleeping quarters, a crafts room and rooms for after school care and administration are located in the other cubes. While each cube is connected with another part of the building, it stands on its own as a unity. With its community and conference room the middle section is the marketplace of the non-denominational school, a site where different facilities which all belong together are located next to the childcare centre with its own kitchen, storage space and quarters for the caretaker. The common rooms are intended to offer a high degree of flexibility and freedom, and can be used for a library, PC room and many other purposes, or for larger events, celebrations and church services. If all the space is still not enough, the whole complex can be extended at any time by additional floors. The sports field is located on the roof of the middle section. The grounds can be used as a vegetable or school garden, or playground. Based on the idea of Frank Lloyd Wright to combine the functions of art, nature and areas of human living, a building has been created which strives to give a contemporary response to the needs of young people.

With the grid-like façade made of glass fibre reinforced plastic slabs (GRP) a school building was created which looks both robust and decorative. Because of the multiple usage together with the offer of free space, it is not surprising that in addition to the students who use the 9,000 square metre roof terrace during their breaks, people from the surrounding region also use the terrace to relax.

In addition to the teaching offered in the De Matrix Community School in the most varied subjects for the students, there are also health and social facilities, a child care centre and an after school care facility in the school. The core is the central section which is used as a library, media centre, waiting room, games room, among others. As needed, the adjacent classes can also be combined, creating one large hall.

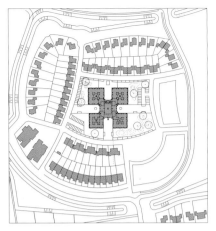
Site plan

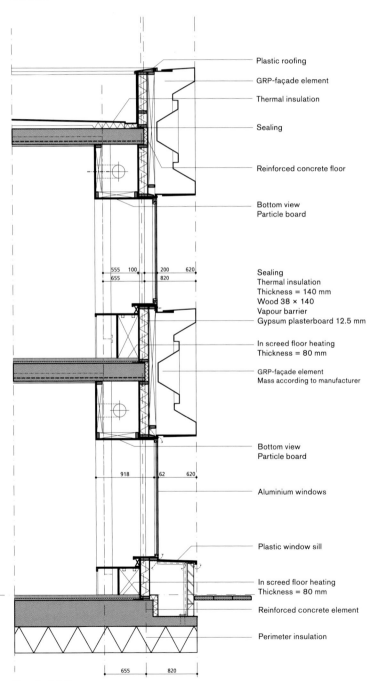
Façade detail

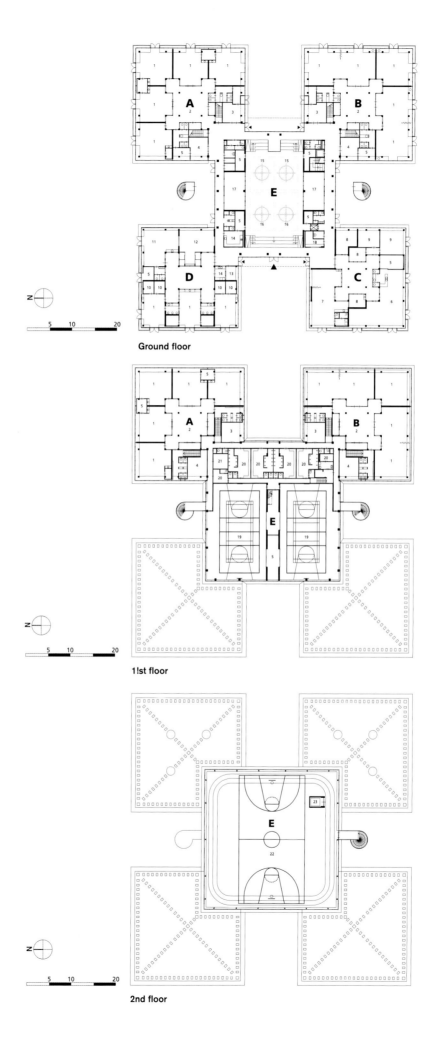

Ground floor

1!st floor

2nd floor

PRIMARY SCHOOLS

Hampden Gurney School
London

Architect: Building Design Partnership (BDP)
Staff: Tony McGuirk, John Toovey
Structural design: BDP
BSE Planning: BDP

Planning time/Construction time: 1995–1998 / 2000–2002

School type: primary school and kindergarten
Number of students: 223
Grades: 1–4
Age of students: 3.5–11 years
Average class size: 30 pupils
Number of classes: 8 classes

Plot size: 886 square metres
Built-up area: 660 square metres
Gross floor space: 4,400 square metres
Type of energy supply: gas and electricity
Construction costs: 7.2 million euros

Awards: RIBA Award for Architecture 2002 (short-listed for the Stirling Prize), Civic Trust Award 2004, Structural Steel Design Award 2003 (commendation)

The full name of this primary school located in the exclusive Westminster district of London is the *Hampden Gurney Church School of England*. The name already says a great deal about the orientation and goals of the institution. For lack of its own financing the school previously had to make do with two successor buildings built in the 1950s on a former plot of rubble from World War II. This arrangement in no way reflected 21st century demands, never mind the quality called up by the reputation of the academic level of the proud Church of England School. For this reason and that of the financial deficit a collaboration was initiated between the foundation board as land owner and building sponsor on the one hand, and the town planning office and the architects on the other hand which resulted in a solution that was both architecturally elegant and financially clever. On the corner of a new block of flats, with multiple storey playground terraces on each floor, a school was built whose refined transparency articulates with a distinctive verve the level of education appropriate for an urban jewel on the bustling Edgware Road. Financed with the profit from the construction of 52 flats, the new school is also now on a sound economical footing. The glass skin of the building ensures optimal solar irradiation and an assertive transparency as a social institution in the prime location in the cityscape. The combined kindergarten and school facility is arranged as a vertical "Kinder-tower". A play garden discernible from outside dominates the appearance of the ground floor which is flanked to the right and left by a lobby. The school children may access the classrooms, the library and the multi-media room directly on three levels from there. The roof is equipped with a group teaching room. In addition the students may move freely outside, protected on all levels from the elements by the roof. During warm weather the verandas may also be used for classes. When the children meet in high-spirited occasion beneath the broad tent roof, places of community and creative activity like the auditorium, chapel, music and theatre room are located in the basement.

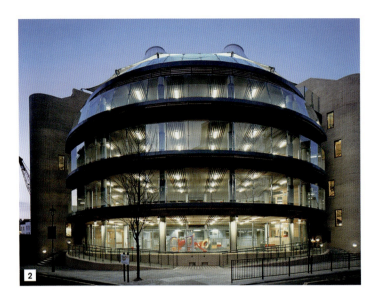

2

3

4

Seen in an urban context with its open free spaces the school creates the association of a car park. The cramped space in an urban fabric was optimally used here. In good weather one can enjoy a break on the tent-protected terrace.

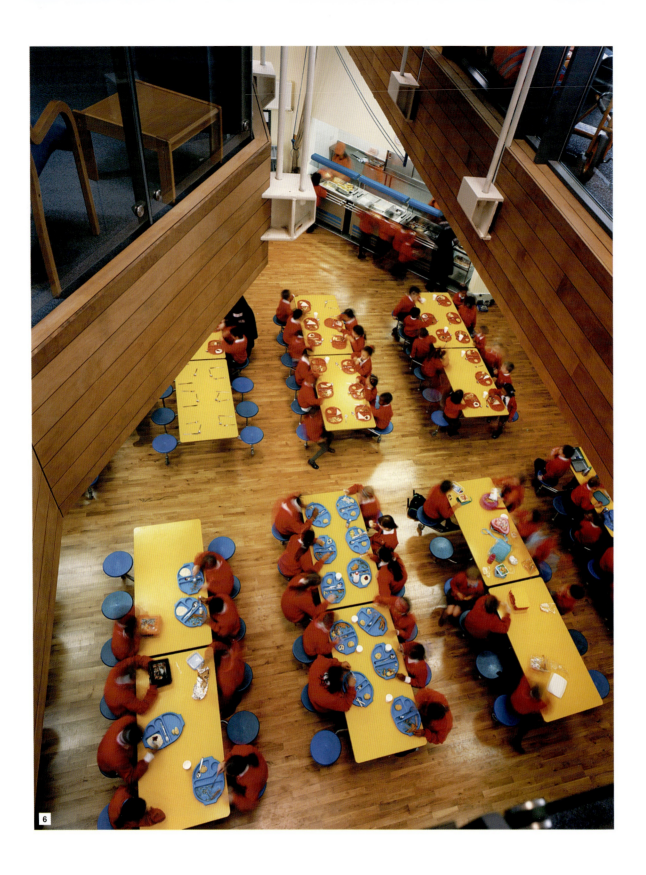

The auditorium, chapel, music and theatre room are located in the basement. While the children can romp on the south-oriented terraces of the upper floors, quiet is the rule in the northern part of the building. In addition to the classrooms, the library on the second floor is located here.

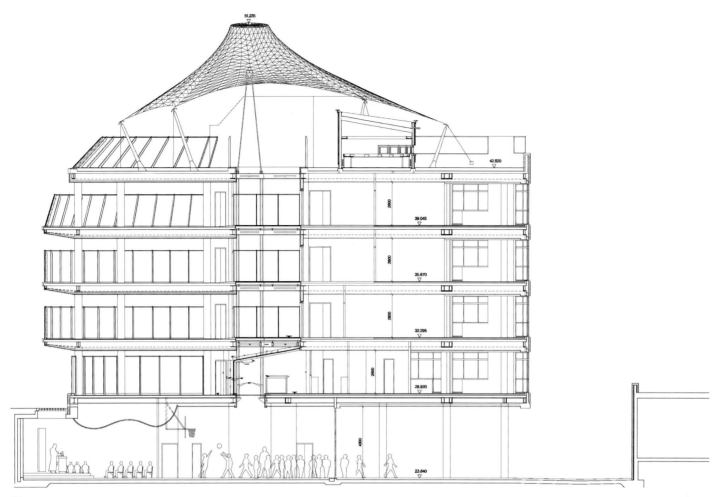

View

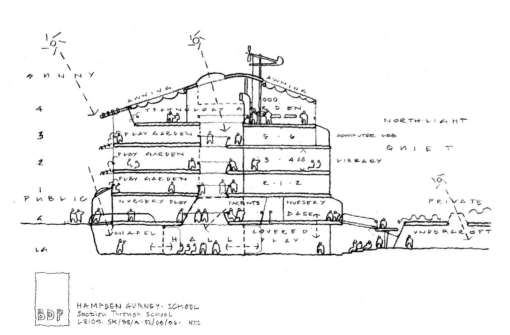

Drawing

Ground floor

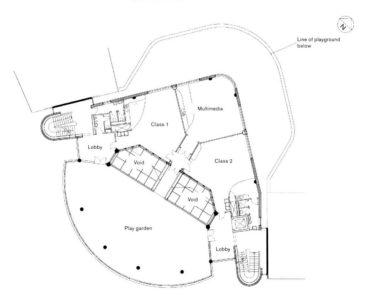

1st floor

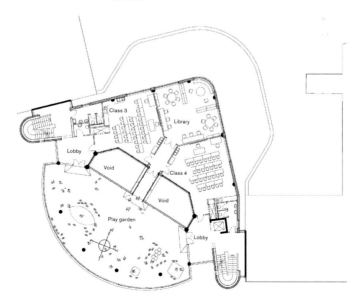

2nd floor

Music Oriented Primary School
Schulzendorf

371

Architect: zanderroth architekten with Guido Neubeck
Staff: Sascha Zander, Christian Roth, Guido Nebeck, Hanael Sfez
Structural design: Ingenieurbüro für Bauwesen Volker Krienitz
BSE Planning: Ingenieurbüro Jürgen Reimann,
Ingenieurbüro Gerhard Frenzel

Planning and construction phase : 2004–2006

School type: primary school (expansion)
Number of students: 371
Grades: 1–6
Age of students: 5–13 years
Average class size: 23 pupils
Number of classes: 16 classes

Plot size: 33,316 square metres
Built-up area: 2,815 square metres
Gross floor space: 3,079 square metres
Gross volume: 12,468 cubic metres
Useful area: 2,429 square metres
Type of energy supply: on-site cogeneration unit
Construction costs: 3.6 million euros

Awards: Hans Schäfer Prize 2007, BDA (Association of German Architects) Prize 2008, Brandenburg Architecture Prize 2007

Communities which have the good fortune to expand in population need new schools. One of those is in Schulzendorf south of Berlin. The primary school in Schulzendorf is surrounded by one-family houses in the middle of a newly developed area. To be precise it is an expansion within a conglomerate of school buildings which was built in the 1930s. In order to at least visually tie together what belonged together the *Magdeburg* type school building built in 1965 was expanded on both sides of the floor plan by an "H" and consolidated in a block. The two interior courtyards form a figure eight. The glazed atriums are flanked by the accesses between the old and new classrooms. Two lateral incisions in the cube provide interstices, one of which functions as an entryway and roof covered extension of the school courtyard and the other as an entryway for the canteen. The building with its dark façade on the basement level is surrounded on both of the upper stories by a suspended rear ventilated façade made of locally braided willow, merging the old and new building into one. Because of this special optical effect and also because of its size, the building serves as a bridge to the detail work of the school grounds. In that sense it is a place of tranquillity while at the same time providing a link with the environs. The architectural message of the austerely symmetrical form is: the mid-point, not only of the educational facility, but of a whole colony of individuals, which otherwise live insulated from each other, lies in the expanded and converted *Magdeburg* type school building from 1965. This character of the school building is also functionally justified in that with canteen, community library and the public auditorium, the school is a meeting point for the educational and local communities. The auditorium as market place is accessed at the ground level and opens upwards to all floors above. Surrounding galleries connect the rooms with each other. The fact that school is everyone's business and not just the student's is underscored by the colour concept of the interior design, which connects each floor but retains a unique identity at the same time. And the teachers may decide which colour their classroom should have.

A seamless envelope around the existing stock and the two extensions makes a single building from the old and new. The unifying element is the suspended back-ventilated façade made of locally caned willow. The basement level is plastered for fire and climbing protection.

5

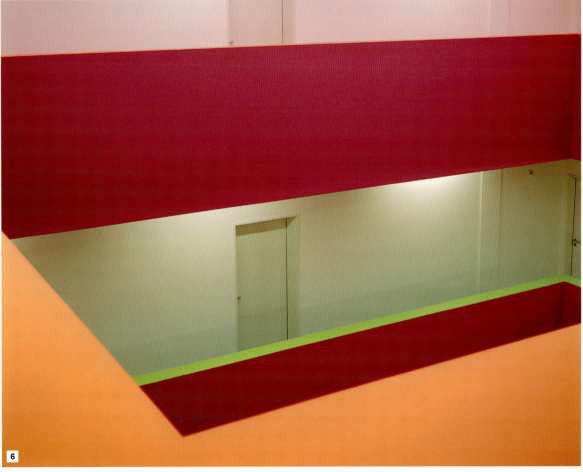

6

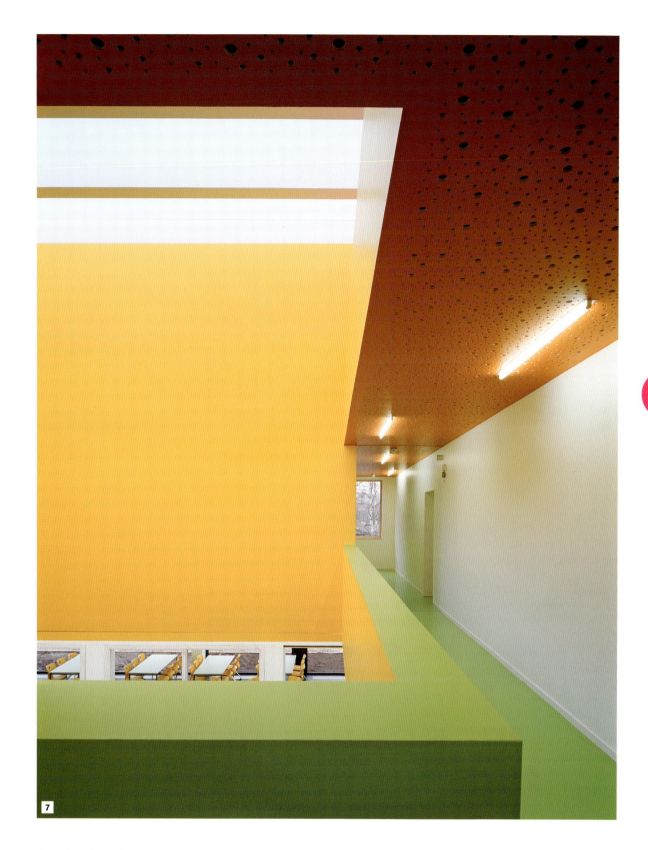

7

A complex colour scheme winds through the building according to a clever architectural concept. Every floor and each atrium has its own colour. The walls, the floor, and the ceiling are monochrome, generating a special room atmosphere. The teachers may decide the colour scheme of their classrooms.

Site plan

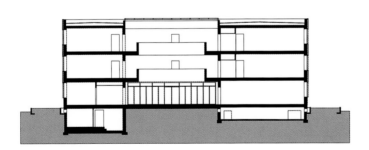

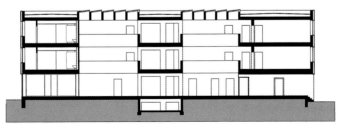

Sections

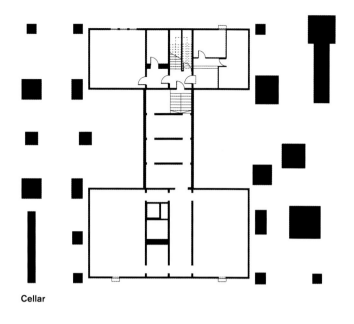
Cellar

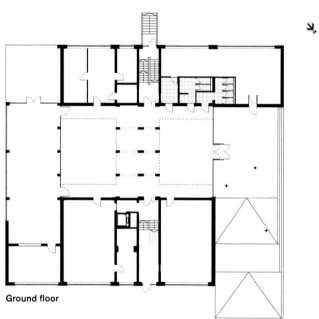
Ground floor

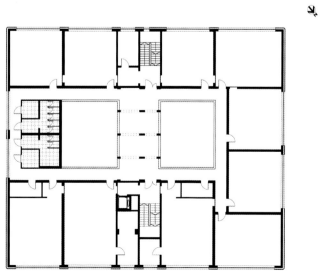
1st and 2nd floor

METI School
Rudrapur

Architect: Anna Heringer, Elke Roswag
Staff: Emmanuel Heringer, Stefanie Heringer, Khondaker Hasibul Kabir, Abdun Nime
Structural design: Dr. Christof Ziegert, Uwe Seiler, Rudolf Sackmauer
BSE Planning: Oskar Pankratz (energy concept)

Planning and construction phase: 2004–2006

School type: village school
Number of students: 130
Grades: 1–6
Age of students: 5–12 years
Average class size: 10–35 pupils
Number of classes: 5–6 classes

Built-up area: 275 square metres
Useful area: 325 square metres
Type of energy supply: natural ventilation and illumination
Construction costs: 23,000 euros

Awards: Architectural Association (AA) and Environments, Ecology and Sustainability Research Cluster (EES), Environmental Technotics Competition London 2006 (Honourable Mention), Aga Khan Award for Architecture Tenth Award Circle 2007, Emerging Architecture Award, Architectural Review London 2006, International Bamboo Building Design Competition 2007, Kenneth F. Brown Asia Pacific Culture and Architecture Design Award 2007, Nomination for the DAM (German Architectural Museum) Architecture Prize 2007/2008, Global Award for Sustainable Architecture 2010

Whoever wants to experience the fascination of the school, must find a place where education is viewed as a gift and not just taken for granted. For instance Bangladesh. Near to the district capital of Mymensingh, in the town of Rudrapur, there is a school built with clay and bamboo, looking as if it were part of the surroundings. The architecture of this school is as impressively natural as the means of teaching. The basement level made of massive clay walls with its coloured doors and sari cloth contrasts with the ease of the open upper floor made of bamboo, which optically dissipates in the play of shadow in the cracks between the bamboo and the view over the trees and the village pond. While on the ground floor the classrooms together with a cave made of clay provide a retreat for concentrated individual and team work, the upper floor, in addition to a bold view culminating in a row of trees rising up to a patio, also offers the necessary freedom of movement. This bold view over the compact clay houses was not even needed to make clear to the people there the importance of education because all the local residents were involved in the construction of the school building. The students and their teachers manufactured the bundled straw for the door and lintels. The door panels which bear the Bengali names of the children, evolve in an annually developing school chronicle. Along with and on behalf of the *Modern Education and Training Institute* (METI) together with the partnership of *Shanti Bangladesch e.V. Deutschland* and the *Päpstliche Missionswerk der Kinder* (PMK) a school was built which from the beginning was a training centre for the local residents. The school is also an institutional focal point of the town. Since its inception the residents have have found out what the school building has to offer, with its natural materials and the array of different rooms and multiple usages. These aspects all contribute to fostering the capabilities and interests of the individual and a variable work pace of the students and apprentices in a free form for learning as an alternative to the face-the-front and beware-the-cane type of instruction common throughout the country. The basic METI issue of experience and design has been broadcast beyond Rudrapur, because the realization of this school has shown how with local resources and manpower economical, high-quality buildings can be built using the creative potential in the traditional method of building.

On the ground floor, with its massive clay walls, three classrooms are located, each of which is connected by two round loopholes with a dynamically formed relaxation room. The spacious bamboo open upper floor has plenty of space for movement. From here one can look out over the trees and the village pond. The bamboo gaps create fine plays of shadow, which together with the sari material generate a fascinating pattern on the clay floor and ceiling. The clay and bamboo techniques used were recreated and further developed from traditional building methods and taught to the people from the surrounding area. They collaborated with the architect and her staff to build the school in Rudrapur.

PRIMARY SCHOOLS

89

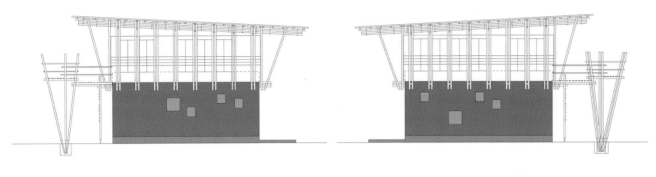
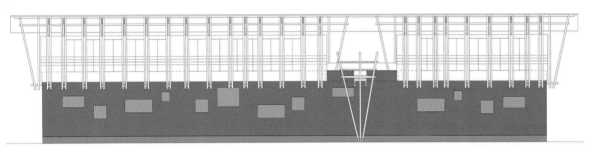
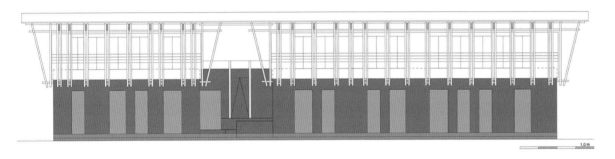

Views

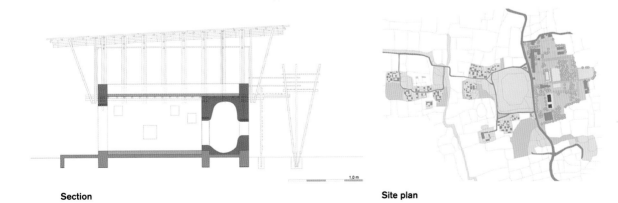

Section

Site plan

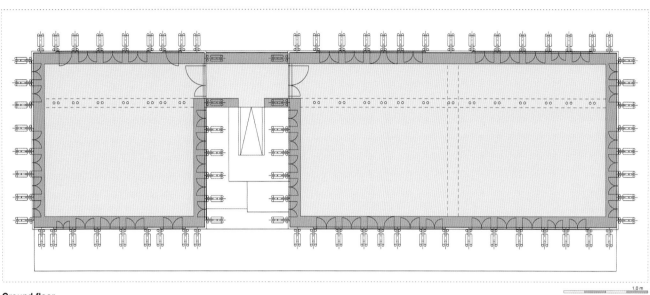
Ground floor

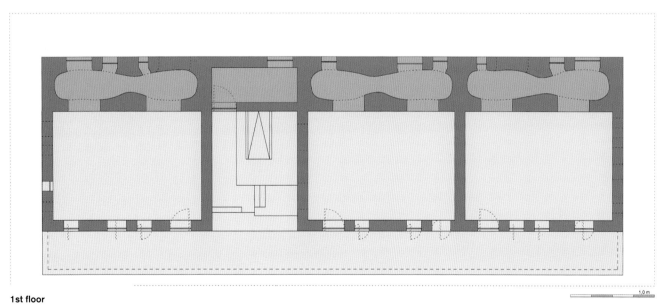
1st floor

School Centre Lucciole
Cressy

Architect: Devanthéry & Lamunière Architectes
Staff: Frédéric Crausaz, Frédéric Dayer, Franziska Gygax
Structural design: B + S, A. Sumi – G. Babel
BSE Planning: Sorane, Dumont – Schneider, Ryser Eco, Mike Humbert

Planning and construction phase: 2002–2006

School type: primary school
Number of students: 336
Grades: 1–5
Age of students: 5–11 years
Number of classes: 13 classes

Plot size: 12,000 square metres
Built-up area: 6,175 square metres
Gross floor space: 6,042 square metres
Gross volume: 27,545 cubic metres
Type of energy supply: district heating from waste recovery
Construction costs: 19.1 million euros

Awards: Compendium of Exemplary Education Facilities 2011 (OECD – Centre for Effective Learning Environments)

When a new residential district was created in Cressy, a suburb of Geneva, a school was built that consisted of three structures: a large square structure for teaching, a small, also square one for the auditorium, canteen and a youth and club rooms, and a rectangular gymnasium recessed in the ground. The new school in the midst of a settlement built with traditional masonry work is both an educational facility and community centre. The functionally separate buildings are accessible independently of each other. Reflecting its role as a focal point of the community, the premises may be used during as well as after school hours. Group and multi-purpose rooms arranged classrooms are distributed on three floors throughout the school building. The custodian's apartment and a room for non-school activities and a language lab are located in the cellar, which receives half its illumination from daylight. The harmonious design of the class and group rooms allows for additional multi-facetted use. Music and utility rooms are located in the cellar of the auditorium, while to the west the gymnasium houses wardrobes and storage rooms. What seems to be architecturally separate is connected by subterranean passageways. A generously laid out forecourt underscores the role of the three buildings as a local meeting point whose status is also emphasized by a fascinating and cleverly assembled façade design which displays the structures like pearls on a necklace. All three buildings are completely glazed and are flooded with daylight. The classrooms, movement and play rooms are equipped with large-scale glass encased modules which may be opened and closed, and which are furnished with variously coloured draperies. When the sun shines on them, they act like a light filter and provide agreeable lighting throughout the building, so that during the day the building needs only a modicum of artificial light. As soon as it becomes dark outside, the glass spaces are transformed into colourful lamps, which is why the school and community centre in Cressy is also called *Lucciole*, in English, firefly. The architects worked with Swiss light artist Daniel Schläpfer on the realization of the unique lighting concept. At night the school house in the Swiss canton of Geneva is perceived as a town jewel.

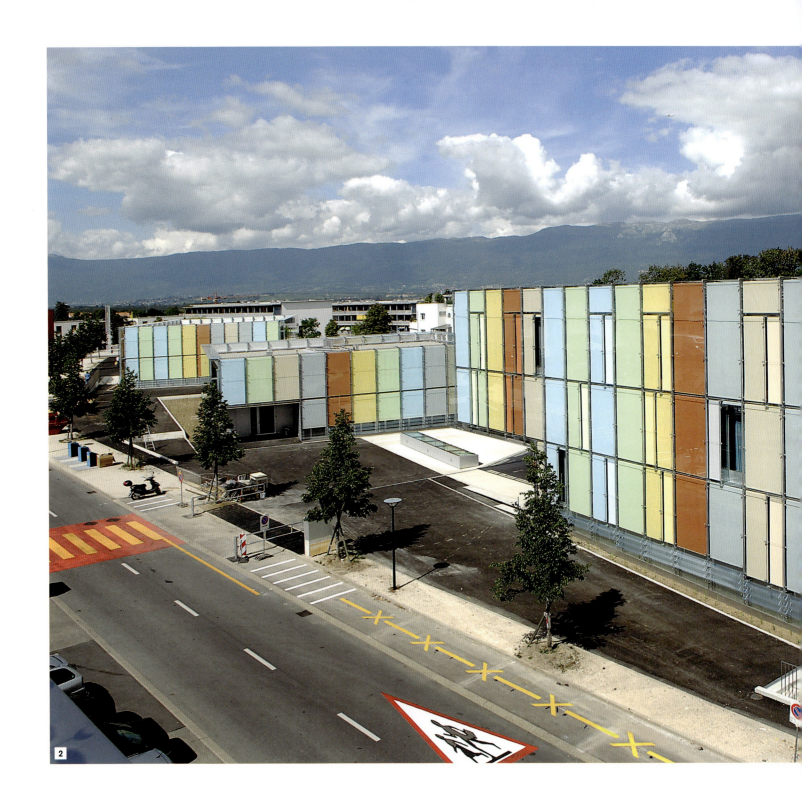

The façade details, the exterior design and the selection of materials contribute to the perception of the three buildings as one. The volumes are compact, the incisions clear, and the geometry is rational. In addition to adapting to the weather conditions (sunny, cloudy, rainy) the illumination is also adjusted to the time of year. For instance, on a sunny day, the façades reflect intensive shades of yellow and orange. In contrast, on a rainy day the façades turn a matt blue.

An optimized support structure (supporting walls in the middle and supports in the façade area) allows for flexible organization and room division. The classrooms of the teaching building are distributed on three levels around the stairwell with circumferential galleries. All buildings are provided with natural air circulation from the double façade. The high insulation value of the outer shell and the sun protection integrated in the façade contribute to an agreeable building climate.

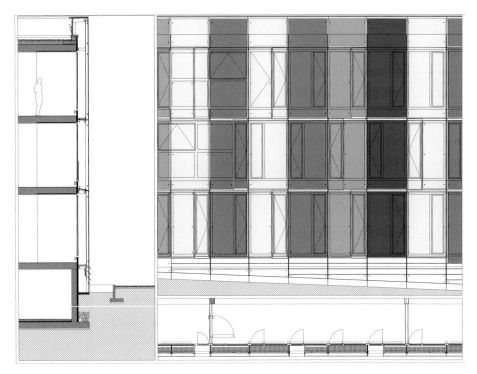

Façade detail

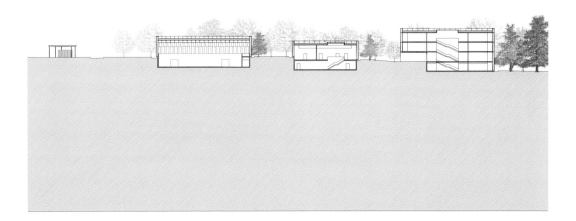

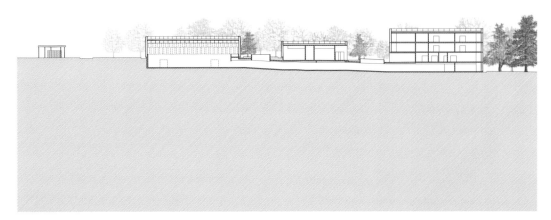

Sections

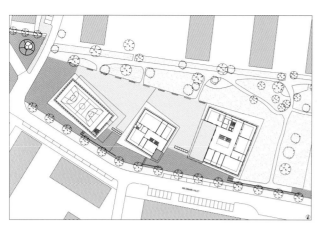
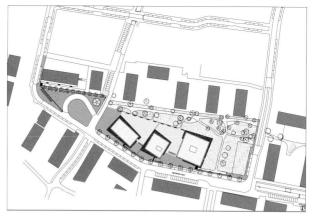

Site plan

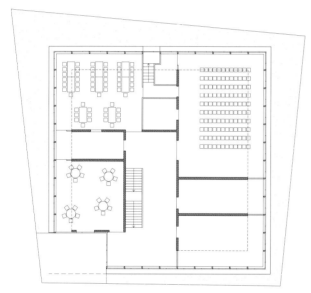

Ground floor auditorium building

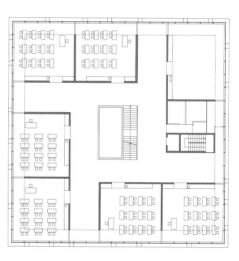

1st floor teaching building

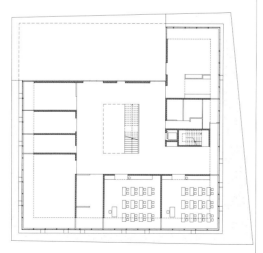

Ground floor teaching building

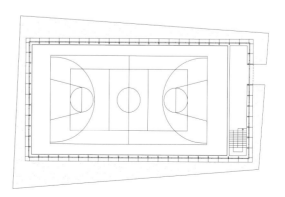

Gym

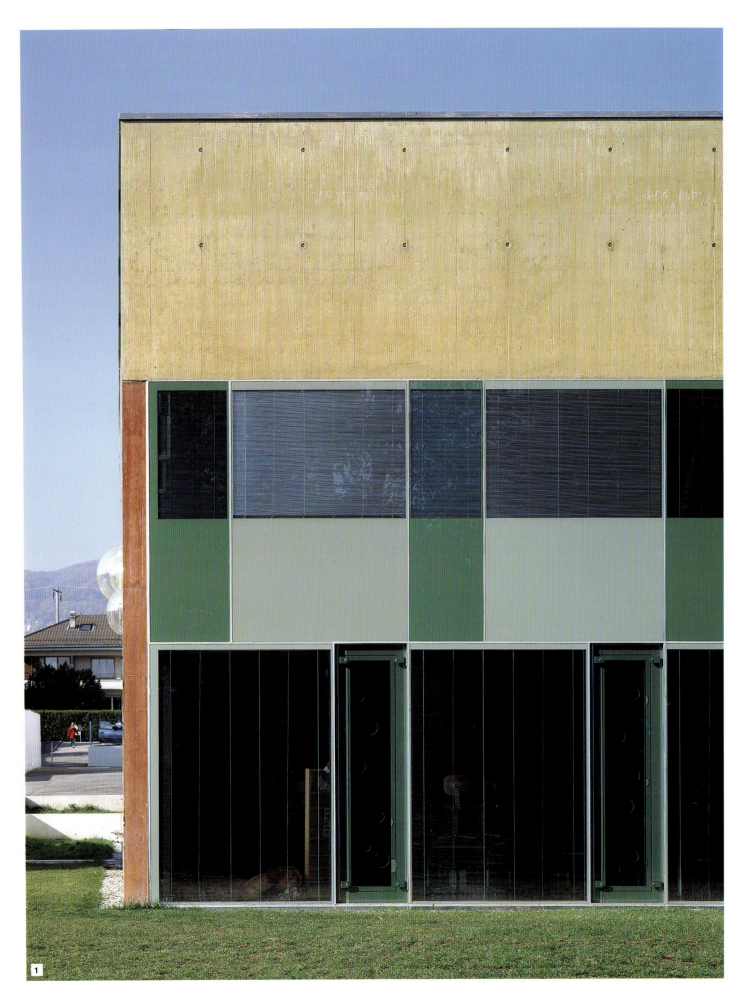

Rolle Primary School
Rolle

Architect: *Devanthéry & Lamunière Architectes*
Staff: *Alexandre Clerc (project assistant)*
Structural design: *Frauncis Liard*
BSE Planning: *Marc de Wurstemberger, Saniplan, Pierre Chuard*

Planning and construction phase: *1999–2003*

School type: *primary school*
Number of students: *150*
Grades: *1–5*
Age of students: *5–11 years*
Number of classes: *5 classes*

Built-up area: *1,541 square metres*
Gross floor space: *2,717 square metres*
Gross volume: *11,120 cubic metres*
Type of energy supply: *district heating from the existing plant*
Construction costs: *5.2 million euros*

The extension of the College des Buttes on the north-west bank of Lake Geneva houses a total of eight classrooms, a school kitchen and canteen, a music room and several computer and multifunctional rooms. With its expansive flat roof stretching along the promenade from the building complex, floating over a forecourt, it surprisingly overturns preconceptions about building modern structures in culturally significant, delicately natural surroundings. Across from the old main building a new structure fitted in with the topography has been built which is integrated like a modern sculpture in the landscape, providing a flowing transition from the historical architecture to the landscape. The new building opens up points of vantage to the sloped garden and exposes the children in the classrooms facing the park and in the open areas to the benevolent rays of the sun. The stimulating landscape view from the rectangular two storey new building also has a decidedly positive effect on the learning climate. The architectural reference point is the old school house. The bold ease with which the flat roof of the extension building juts outwards gives the new building its own impressive forecourt, finishing off with the upper edge of the class window from the ground floor of the old main building. This design also provides the students in the old building with a view and natural sunlight in the classrooms. The façades of the new buildings with their earthy matt colours reflect the light and throw shadows. The blue-green, shimmering glass surfaces augment the effect. Seen from the classrooms, the landscape seems to appear at uniform intervals. At the same time the windows are mirrors of their environment. A new building has been created with the expansion of the school, which draws on the qualities of the surroundings including the existing stock, taking its place in the historical context while at the same time maintaining its own unmistakable identity.

The architects played with concrete in the design of the façade: brightly coloured exposed concrete elements are woven together like a patchwork. In between are light coloured, greenish glass surfaces which provide a view onto the surrounding landscape. The circular openings on the first floor which resemble soap bubbles, billiard balls or balloons, continue the playfulness of the design.

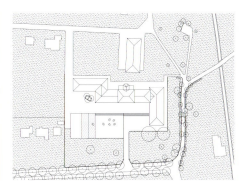

The classrooms open up to the adjacent garden. Because of the reflection in the glass surfaces, the connection between inside and out is especially evident. Side rooms and computer rooms are located on the street side. A wardrobe for the children is located in front of each classroom.

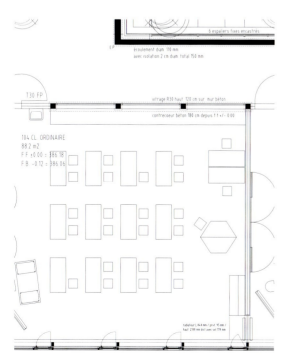

PRIMARY SCHOOLS

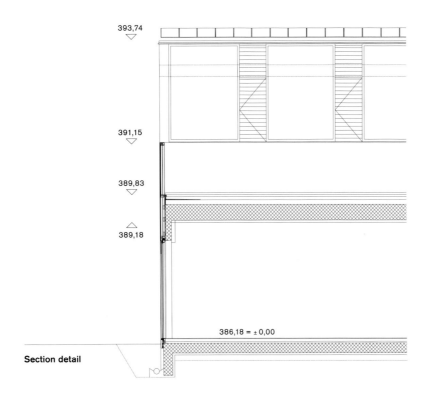

Section detail

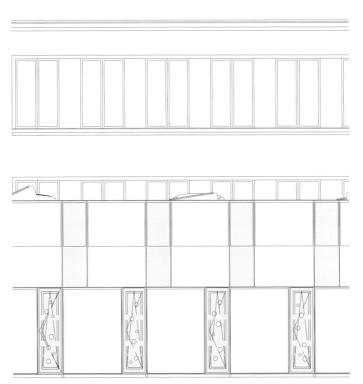

View detail

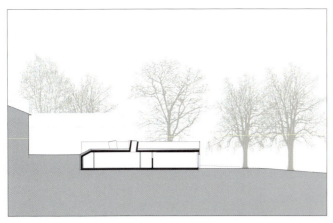
Cross section

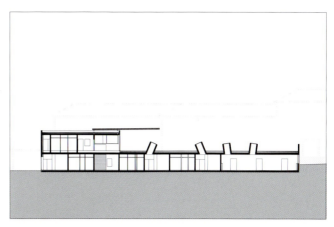
Longitudinal section

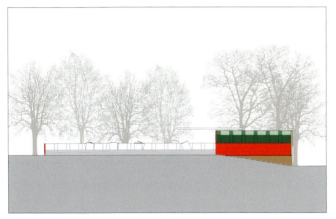
View west

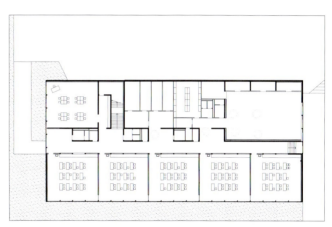
Ground floor

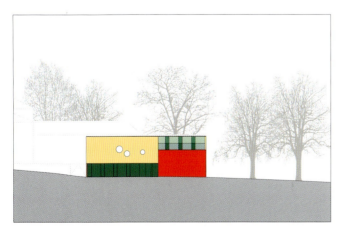
View south

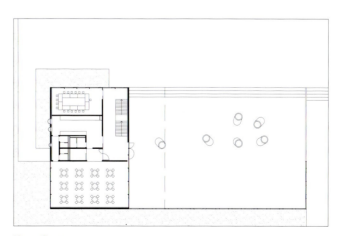
Upper floor

PRIMARY SCHOOLS

107

Katharinen School Hafencity
Hamburg

Architect: Spengler · Wiescholek Architekten and Stadtplaner
Staff: Jens Tepel, Johannes Gaußmann, Michal Zirau, Birgit Ascher, Gesine Seyffert, Sven Dunker
Structural design: Otto Wulff Bauunternehmung, Hamburg
BSE planning: IB Sommer (plumbing), Ingenieurbüro Scholz (ventilation), Frank Eggers (ventilation and electrical equipment)

Planning and construction phase: 2006–2009

School type: primary school with day-care and 30 apartments
Number of students: 340
Grades: 1–4
Age of students: 6–10 years
Average class size: 28 pupils
Number of classes: 12 classes

Plot size: 3,072 square metres
Built-up area: 2,450 square metres
Gross floor space: 10,924 square metres
Gross volume: 23,400 cubic metres (school), 2,800 cubic metres (day-care), 9,200 cubic metres (apartments)
Useful area: 4,600 square metres (school), 670 square metres (day-care), 2,200 square metres (apartments)
Type of energy supply: district heating
Construction costs: 6.6 million euros

Awards: Hafencity Environmental Gold Medal Prize 2010, German Urban Development Prize 2010

The Katharinen School Hafencity-Hamburg is located there, where the great passenger ships awake a longing for far-away lands. It is not just the central location in the Hamburg-Mitte district within sight of its sacred namesake that lends the school its identity. The outward appearance of the unmistakable architecture is what is special about the first public building to be erected in the new city district Hafencity in 2009. The light beige and grey toned Danish clinkers and the slanted embrasures, lending the massive structure a wave-like movement and thereby the necessary ease, follow the rules of this densely built city. The secret is in the quadrilateral. The interior of the building creates an urban diversity with the day care and primary school, along with a public gymnasium, cafeteria, library and, rather unusual for a school building, 30 apartments. The building is a school and townhouse in one connected via a one storey central block with the neighbouring seven storey apartment building. The spatial program features a central, open atrium. In addition to natural ventilation and light in all the rooms the atrium also provides views into the multi-purpose recreation hall and auditorium on the ground floor as well as into the classrooms and teaching rooms located on the upper floors. This rational ordering principle guarantees short paths and perfect orientation. The schoolyard on the ground floor is augmented by another schoolyard on the roof. Virginia creeper and a sun shield in the form of a canvas covered pergola make the romping on the rooftop every day an unforgettable experience, as the coloured capital letters on a just as coloured background show, with a view over the city and the harbour. In addition to the well thought out spatial program the other ordering principle is colour, which penetrates all levels of the house, from the floor covering to the wall design and the door surfaces to the hand railings on the roof. The compact and efficient building ensemble is especially sustainable, with its extraordinary life cycle assessment (KfW-60-Standard) not only because of the building materials used, but also through the use of grey water, waterless urinals and the implementation of regenerative energies in the form of solar heating. The innovative school building truly earned the Hafencity Environmental Gold Medal Prize in 2010.

From a bird's eye perspective the educational building on the Dalman Quay in the newly built Hafencity district in Hamburg is conspicuous for its brightly coloured roof garden. The roof together with the space on the ground floor provides 2,000 square metres of covered open space for the children of the Katharinen School to romp and play. A multi-purpose recess hall on the ground floor and 1st floor are sufficiently lit by the open atrium, surrounded by rooms for special purposes.

5

6

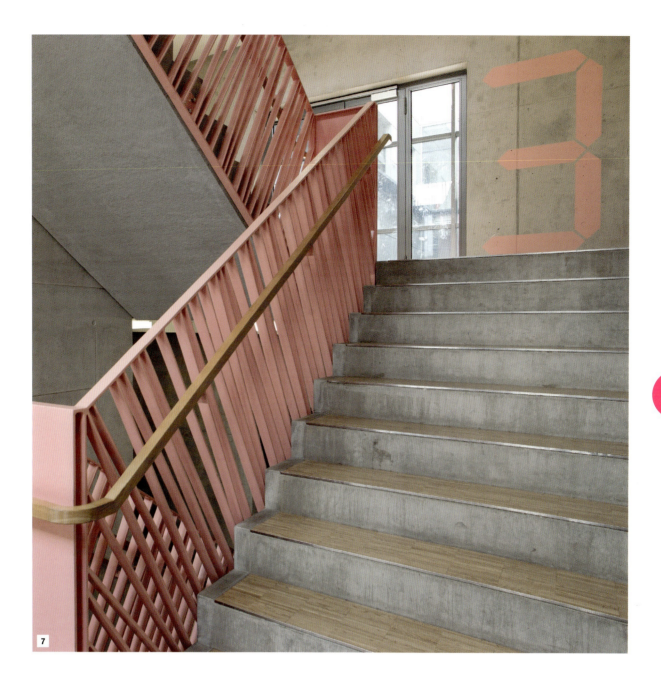

7

The design of the hallways and classrooms refrained from the use of strong colours. In contrast, the public areas like the stairways, canteen, auditorium and the schoolyard on the roof display conscious colour accents, like pink coloured bannisters. Exposed concrete was used for the walls, supports and beams, which the individual colours not only emphasize, but which also serve as a leitmotiv of the otherwise white wall and doors. Even the gymnasium receives a special atmosphere from the skylight in combination with the raw concrete and the coloured padded impact protections.

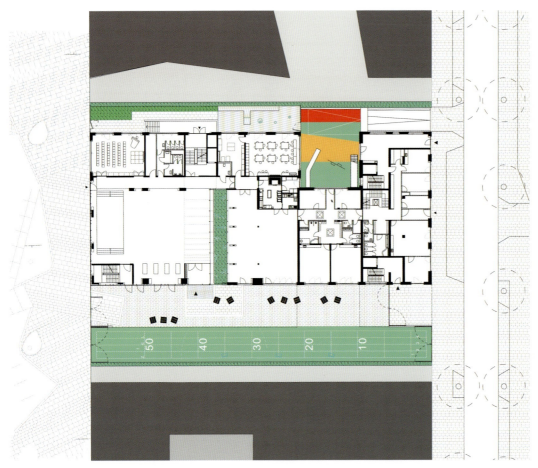

Ground floor

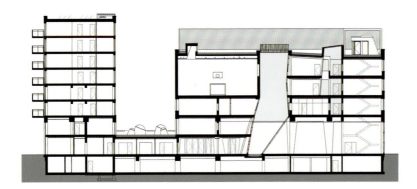

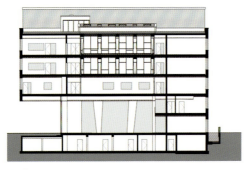

Sections

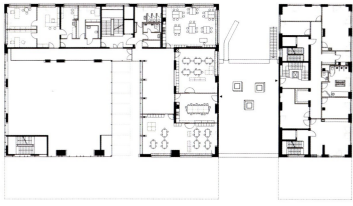

1st floor

2nd floor

Attic

3rd Upper floor

4th Upper floor

PRIMARY SCHOOLS

115

Brede School Antares
Leusden

Architect: RAU Architects
Staff: Ernst-Peter Everraardt, Peter Hasink, Peter Hol
Structural design: Alferink – Van Schieveen
BSE Planning: De Groot Projecttechniek

Planning and construction phase: 2005–2011

School type: 2 primary schools
Number of students: 320
Grades: 1–8
Age of students: 4–12 years
Average class size: 20 pupils
Number of classes: 16 classes

Gross floor space: 8,400 square metres

The school is part of the new community centre *MFC Antares* in Leusden, Holland, built in a former tobacco cultivation area from the 17th and 18th century. The different roof forms of the *Brede School* (English: non-denominational school) style recall the tobacco sheds and the vertical and horizontal red and white frame-like structured glass fronts. The spatial structure is oriented to the so-called *Hallenboerderijen* farmhouses of the former tobacco producers arranged around a community square and several terraces. The school was designed to maintain the identity of several different users in one building. The community centre built in 2011, along with two primary schools, a day-care, public library and gymnasium for the district and several rooms for different purposes, are based on the principle of inner flexibility. The classrooms are arranged in such a way that they can be quickly combined in a community hall. They also allow for the teaching of a larger number of students, group work, one-on-one or work in teams of two. Traditional teacher-centred frontal instruction is also possible. In addition to the main entrance which is clearly marked by a yellow gable, the school, kindergarten and the other social facilities have a separate access which may be used after the school opening hours. The variety of this pedagogical city district is reflected in the sedum vegetation roof, which in this case is the essence of a roof landscape, harmonizing in gentle waves with the roofs of the surrounding houses. Both large green inner courtyards let in an abundance of light and fresh air into the building. Playgrounds for the small children, the large schoolyard and terraces, also usable after school hours, offer a richly diverse view of the neighbouring buildings on the grounds. Along with the *MFC Antares m*ulti-purpose centre the Tabaksteeg district of Leusden has attained a significant social and spatial focus.

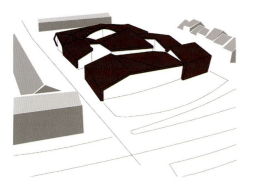

Grounds model

From the outside the school building resembles the old halls where tobacco was stored. Up until the 18th century the majority of the citizens of Leusden depended on the proceeds from the tobacco economy. In order to maintain the identity of the area in spite of the new building, 18 months before the opening of the building in 2011, a diversified program in the school rooms was started in order to familiarize the residents by degrees with their new centre.

View

A variety of colours were used in the interior of the building complex in keeping with its multi-functionality. The ramp accessible gymnasium shows this clearly. Yellow seating niches mark the bleachers area and separate it from the aisle with grey floor covering. In combination with the banisters, that provides not only exciting contrasts, but also smooth transitions.

Some important components of the RAU Architects design concept are openness, cooperation and flexibility. These three aspects are especially reflected in the multi-functional use which is also intended for after-school hours and the extension of the classrooms. For instance, the library together with the adjacent multi-purpose room continues to hum with activity on the weekends.

Longitudinal section

Cross section

Ground floor access

1 Main entrance
2 Day-care entrance 1
3 Day-care entrance 2
4 Entrance play rooms
5 Entrance classrooms
6 Entrance multi-purpose rooms
7 Schoolyard (open area)
8 Entrance gymnasium
9 Schoolyard (open area)
10 Classrooms
11 Library
12 Entrance community centre

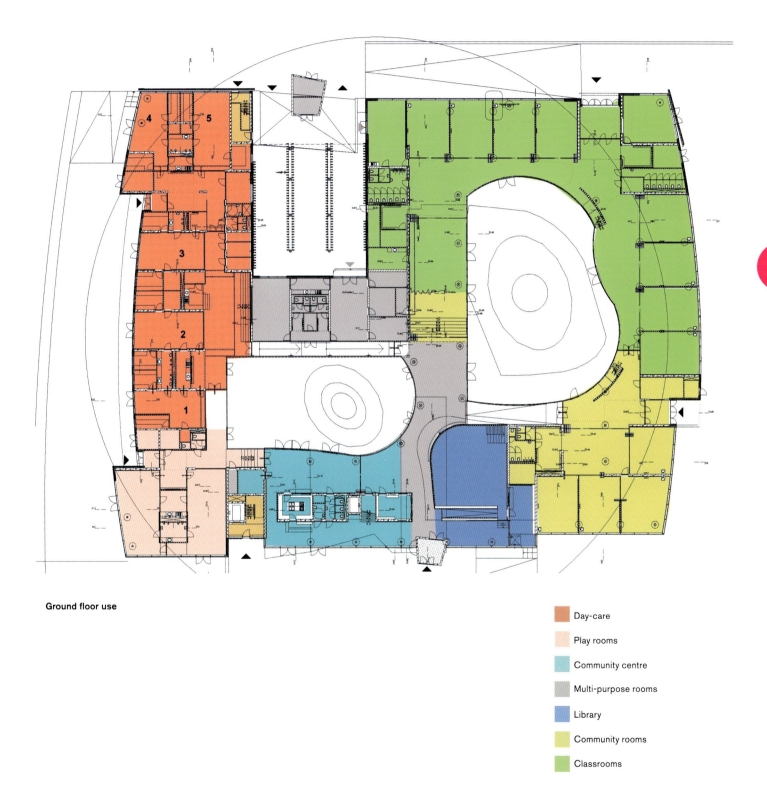

Ground floor use

- Day-care
- Play rooms
- Community centre
- Multi-purpose rooms
- Library
- Community rooms
- Classrooms

Rudolf School
Chemnitz

`213`

Architect: bhss Architekten
Staff: Georg Blüthner, Robert Laser
Structural design: IB F & M (Ingenieurbüro Fankhänel & Müller)
BSE Planning: Ingenieurbüro Prof. Dr. Scheibe

Planning and construction phase: 2007–2009 (1st phase), 2009–2010 (2nd phase)

School type: primary school
Number of students: 213
Grades: 1–4
Age of students: 6–10 years
Average class size: 23 pupils
Number of classes: 9 classes

Plot size: 7,100 square metres
Built-up area: 844 square metres (1st phase), 325 square metres (2nd)
Gross floor space: 844 square metres (1st phase) 3,490 square metres (2nd)
Gross volume: 2,955 cubic metres (1st phase), 17,799 cubic metres (2nd)
Useful area: 567 square metres (1st phase), 1,937 square metres (2nd phase)
Type of energy supply: central gas heating
Construction costs: 3.3 million euros (2nd phase)

The Rudolf School in the Chemnitz Lutherviertel city district was built in 1889 (or 1901 – there are two completion dates) as a symmetrical facility with one entrance for the boys and one for the girls. During the war the main building to the north was completely destroyed, so that at the time of the building application there were three buildings and an annex on the property. In spite of a few damp spots where the chimneys penetrated the roof and the dilapidation of the annex in the rear, the builder and the architectural firm decided to preserve the ensemble. One of the reasons was the increased need for space which argued for the inclusion of the existing building. The listed main building was completely renovated in 2009 and 2010. Significant renovations involved the outer building shell, including the vertical sealing of the cellar, the cleaning and renovation of the façade including the replacement of the windows and a new roof. The classrooms along with the group rooms, a computer workshop and the staff area are located in the main building. A staircase which was built for fire protection reasons is housed in an annex in front of one of the gables. This new building incorporates the symmetry of the school building, storey by storey forming different sized loggias dedicated to the students. Annex 1 has three sections: to the south on the grounds the gym is accessed by a connecting building, which in turns provides an entrance to the third section which was completely renovated from 2007 to 2009. It now is home to a workshop area and a multi-purpose room. The dining room and school library are located in Annex 2, whose façade also incorporates the reddish colour of the clinker walls of the existing building.

In the framework of pre-planning, an extension of individual areas of the roof and cellar was examined for use for the recreation rooms. For reasons pertaining to fire protection, statics, and functional and financial aspects, the idea was rejected. In its place a second stairway built in accordance with the building code was attached to the existing main building, providing an additional covered open area for the children. The new stairwell tower is distinct from the existing building. In contrast to the other existing buildings the annex to the west also has a façade made of reddish-brown cement slabs, whose colour still harmonizes with the clinker walls.

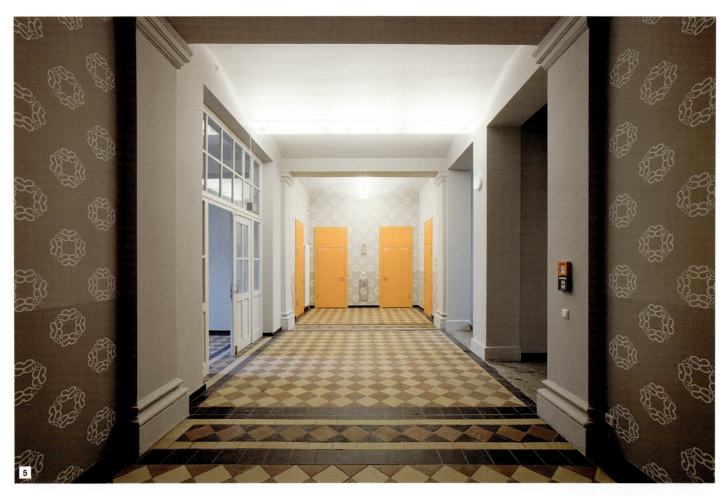

The walls in the hallways of the main building decorated with wallpaper of different patterns. Each floor had its own flair. Following a suggestion by the architects the patterns were developed by the primary schoolers in the art class. The task posed was to create an axially symmetric pattern by turning and reflecting letters and numbers in obverse. The children's drawings were further abstracted by the architects and digitalized. The self-designed wall paper enhanced the identification of the children with their school. In front of the stairwells on each floor seating arrangements have been built which are hung on the wall like a wardrobe, referring to the relevant floor.

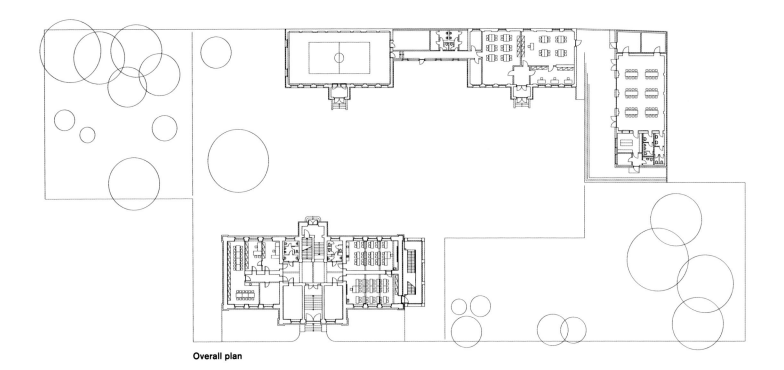
Overall plan

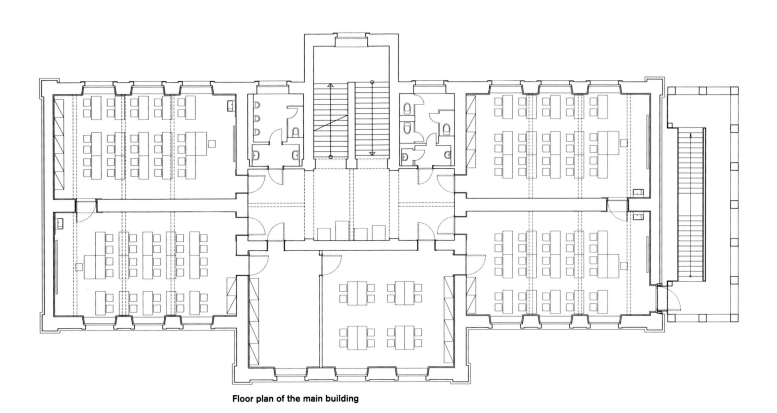
Floor plan of the main building

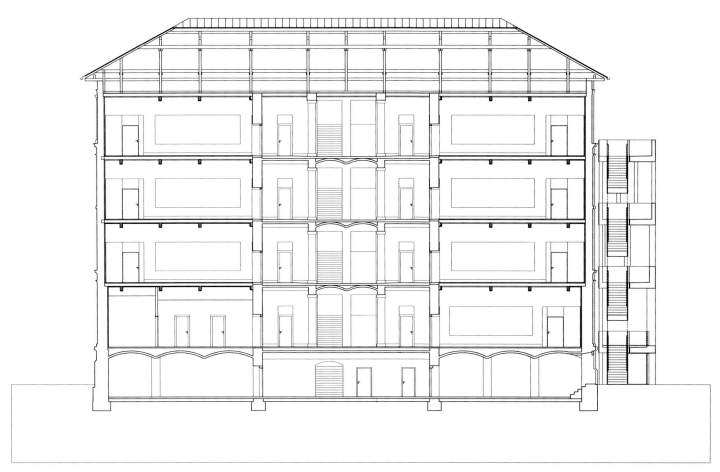

Section of the main building

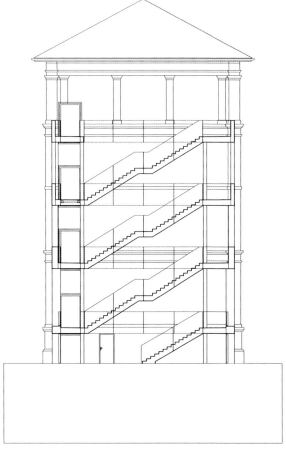

Section of the stairway

Façade design annex 2

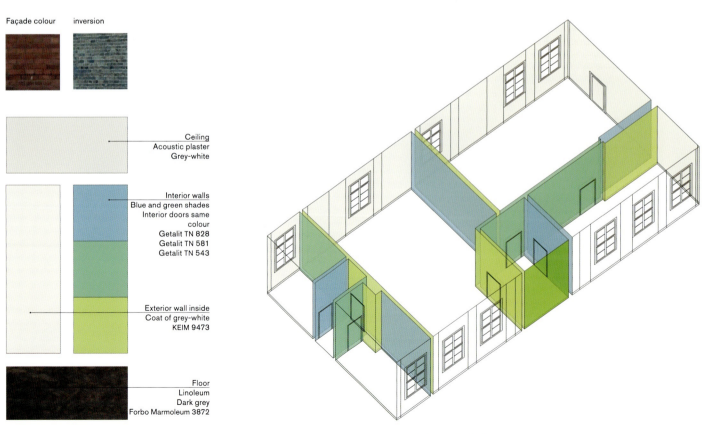

Colour concept Annex 1

View of main building with entryway

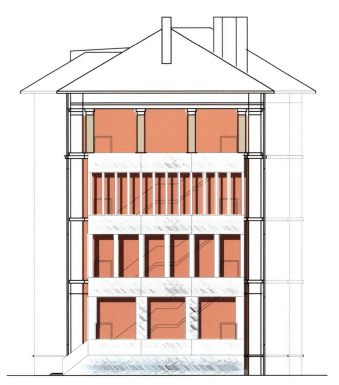

View of main building with stairway tower

Erich Kästner School
Höhenkirchen-Siegertsbrunn

Architect: Fischer Architekten
Staff: Sibylle Staltmayr (project director), Heinz R. Hugler, Michel Flaßkamp, Stefanie Wagner
Local builder: Heinz R. Hugler
Landscape architecture: LUZ landscape architects
Structural design: Ingenieurbüro Max Wagmann
BSE Planning: Bloos, Däumling, Huber – Consulting Engineer for Supply engineering, Ingenieurbüro Groben

Planning and construction phase: 2009–2012

School type: primary and middle school, all-day school
Number of students: 185
Grades: 1–10
Age of students: 6–16 years
Average class size: 26 pupils
Number of classes: 4 classes (extension)

Plot size: 15,910 square metres
Built-up area: 680 square metres
Gross floor space: 1,690 square metres
Gross volume: 5,416 cubic metres
Useful area: 945 square metres
Type of energy supply: centrally supplied from existing plant
Construction costs: 2.9 million euros

The school complex of the Erich Kästner Primary and Secondary School in Höhenkirchen-Siegertsbrunn, about 20 kilometres from Munich, had to be expanded for the afternoon care by adding a building with four classrooms and side rooms, canteen, music, a homework and reading room, and a teacher's kitchen. The nucleus of the facility is the school house built in the 1930s which was expanded in the 1950s and 70s. A temporary *Isartaler Holzhaus* pavilion was the last addition in 1980. This pavilion with the newly coloured, open building provides a counterpoint to the austere, monochromatic main building with its perforated façade. The main design element of the expansion is the façade with its strong profile. The load-bearing mullions are located outside, with the resulting gap filled at irregular intervals with coloured panels. The new building's elongated figure interrupted by two breaks is parallel to the dominant classroom structure from the 1950s standing perpendicular to the street. By lowering the basement levels the new work yard was created between the two buildings. The former cellar of the existing building was thereby upgraded to a full floor. The school house is located at the edge of the town in the transition between the urban area and nature. Its precise urban developmental and internal organization define the transition into the open landscape. The one storey block, where the classrooms face the Brunnthal Forest in the west, seems to float. A few stairs anchor the building with the lawn. The new structure is joined with the existing building via a connecting bridge. Two expansive hallways, with space for play and learning, lead from the central hall to the class and group rooms, with one stairway leading to the courtyard. A hallway illuminated with daylight from a light shaft provides access. All rooms in the courtyard are oriented to the work yard in the east. Vertical structural elements are reduced to a minimum through the use of ribbed ceilings. Slender steel stanchions in the canteen are the only support of the ceiling construction. In order to economize the overall volume, all installations are integrated here. The nether side of the ribs were left exposed and give the ceiling its look. The work yard is the new creative centre of the outdoor facilities. A generous bleacher and stair unit for relaxation, spectating and play leads from the schoolyard in this protected open area. A broad green strip in the slope in the courtyard, planted with choke berry bushes and cranesbill shrubs maintains the distance to the work yard and the classrooms of the existing building.

The pronounced profile of the extension façade green and red colour panels provides a stark contrast to the perforated façade grid of the existing stock. Two creases in the longitudinal façades create a wave-like form which lends the building a certain lightness. A footbridge running over the playground and work yard connects the new building and the old.

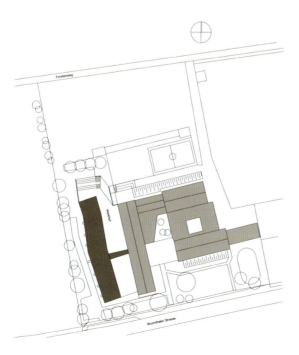

Site plan

While the classrooms on the ground floor of the extension are oriented to the neighbouring Brunnthal Wood in the west, the rooms in the courtyard underneath, with teaching kitchen and canteen, homework, reading and music room provide a good view of the work yard, which can also be used for specific experiments.

Slender steel stanchions in the canteen are the only support of the ceiling construction. Aside from them, the vertical construction elements are kept to a minimum. In addition to serving as mounting for the plumbing, ribbed panels are also an important design element. To the extent that the nether side is left visible, a ceiling view emerges which provides a contrasting horizontal organization to the vertical structure of the façade.

7

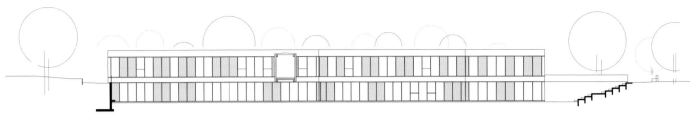
Sectional view east

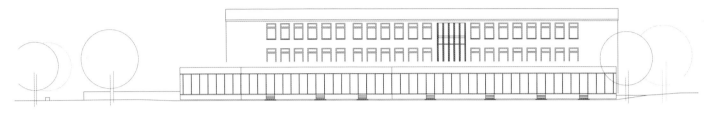
View west

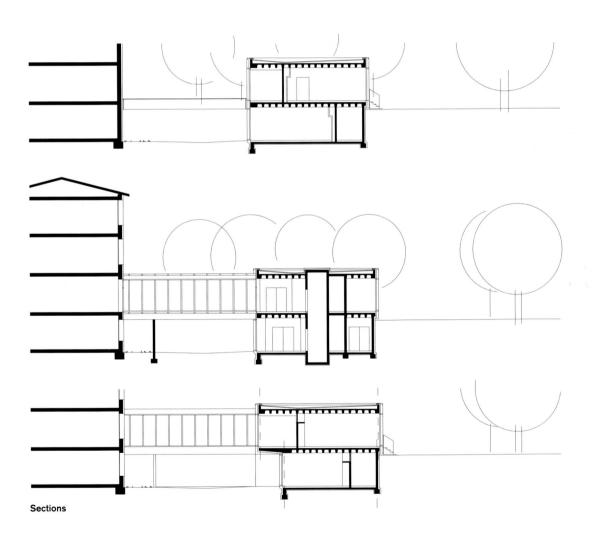
Sections

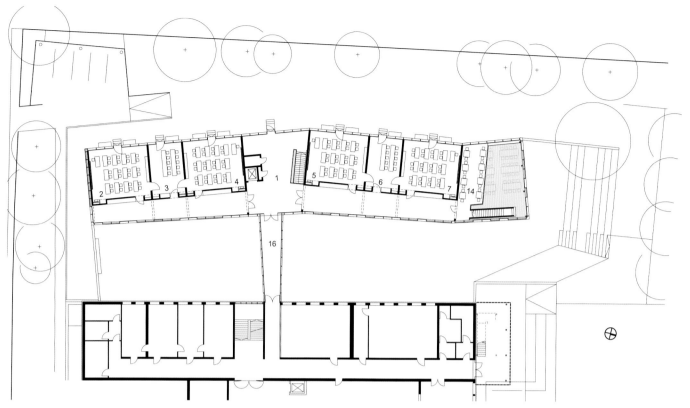

Floor plan ground floor

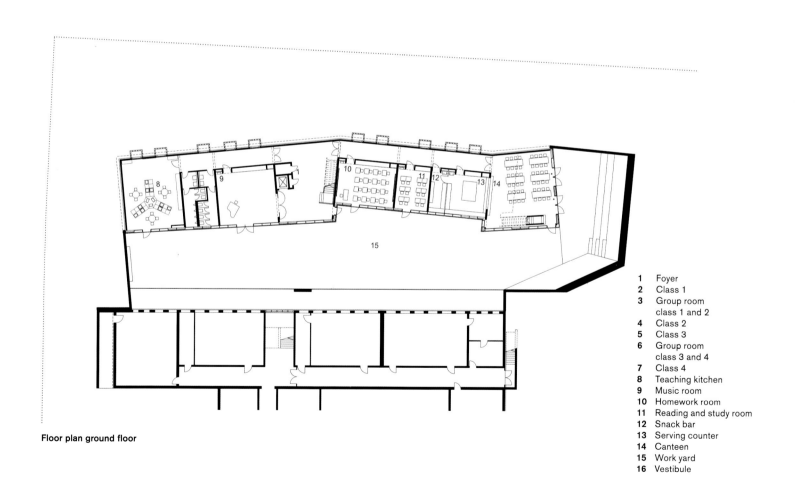

Floor plan ground floor

1 Foyer
2 Class 1
3 Group room class 1 and 2
4 Class 2
5 Class 3
6 Group room class 3 and 4
7 Class 4
8 Teaching kitchen
9 Music room
10 Homework room
11 Reading and study room
12 Snack bar
13 Serving counter
14 Canteen
15 Work yard
16 Vestibule

Wilhelm von Humboldt School
Berlin

Architect: Numrich Albrecht Klumpp
Staff: Daniel Gleißenberg (project director)
Structural design: Laschinski Ingenieure
BSE Planning: Riethmüller Plan

Planning and construction phase: 2009–2012

School type: non-denominational school
Number of students: 411
Grades: 1–7
Age of students: 5–13 years
Average class size: 20 pupils
Number of classes: 20 learning groups with combined age groups

Plot size: 6,850 square metres
Built-up area: 1,129 square metres
Gross floor space: 9,181 square metres
Gross volume: 6,890 cubic metres
Useful area: 4,010 square metres
Type of energy supply: district heating
Construction costs: approx. 2.2 million euros

The listed building ensemble of what is now the Wilhelm von Humboldt School in Berlin-Pankow was built from 1913 to 1916 as a neoclassical inner courtyard school typical for Berlin according to plans of the municipal planner and builder, Ludwig Hoffmann. A director's house and a classroom section on the courtyard are part of the building complex today. The school building in the Gudvanger Straße from the late 1950s is also listed and in spite of all the reminders of classical traditional architectural forms is clearly oriented to a sleek design language. In 2008 the non-denominational Wilhelm von Humboldt School was started up in the framework of the Berlin pilot project with same name. In the project children learn multi-disciplinarily in mixed age groups, from the first day at school to graduation. However the historically important building had to first be completely renovated and rebuilt. The spatial adaptation of the building to contemporary pedagogical demands and modern safety and technical standards, maintaining handicap access, energy efficiency and the building's protected status, are in the foreground. The space for the canteen which is now operated on an all-day basis was created in the former heating and coal cellar on the courtyard side in the cellar of the building from the 1950s. The new dining room expansion is now located partly unter the school house and partly under the courtyard. A skylight shed for additional illumination creates a bright and open spatial character. The raw substance of the existing brick walls is in stark contrast to the new exposed concrete walls and a filigree wood slat ceiling. The glazed façade front with large doors opens up to the new atrium. A flight of stairs leads from here to the schoolyard. The conversion is actually an extension because this connection between schoolyard and canteen creates a new focal point in the school life. The relevant spatial situation can also be used after the mealtime, with the broad stairs to the atrium as seating. And in addition to providing another meeting point, it can also be used for classes in open spaces, events and theatre productions.

The former furnace and coal cellar in the cellar from the 1950s is the canteen for the students today. The broad steps which lead to the school kitchen and dining area are an occasion to relax during the breaks. Outdoor instruction as well as school events can be held here.

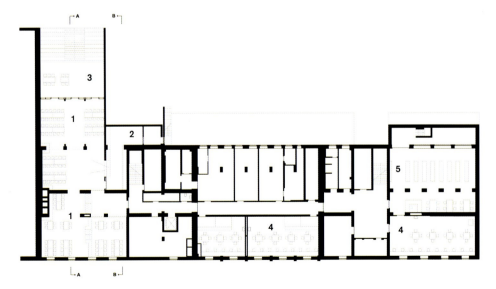

1 Canteen
2 Kitchen
3 Terrace
4 Workshop
5 Library

Floor plan cellar

4

5

PRIMARY SCHOOLS

The warm and at the same time vibrant raw wood lumber was used for the visible ceiling structure. A fleece based insulation layer improved the acoustical properties. That is especially important because during the breaks the open spaces are used as communications zones.

School House and Kindergarten
Grono

144

Architect: Raphael Zuber
Staff: David Gianinazzi, Kosuke Yutani,
Thomas Melliger (project director)
Builders: Devis Bruni, Giulio Cereghetti
Structural design: Patrick Gartmann, Conzett Bronzini Gartmann
Landscape architecture: Maurus Schifferli,
4d Landschaftsarchitekten AG

Planning and construction phase: 2007–2011

School type: primary school and Kindergarten
Number of students: 144
Grades: 1–5
Age of students: 4–12 years
Average class size: 24 pupils
Number of classes: 4 classes (primary school) + 2 (Kindergarten)

Plot size: 3,046 square metres
Built-up area: 615 square metres
Gross floor space: 2,105 square metres
Gross volume: 7,803 cubic metres
Type of energy supply: heat pump (geothermal)
Construction costs: approximately 4.8 million euros
Awards: Architecture and Engineering prize for Earthquake-proof Building 2012, ›Gutes Bauen‹ Graubünden Award 2013

At less than 1,000 inhabitants and with a usable surface of five percent, with the rest consisting of forest and unproductive ground, the small town of Grono, as well as the surrounding Valle Mesolcina in the canton of Graubunden is not exactly one of the more economically robust regions in Switzerland. The primary school building built in 2011 with an integrated kindergarten is located in the middle of the village, at the interface between the village and the periphery, in a garden on a public square. The garden is the playground for the kindergarten, and the square is the recess area for the primary school. With its design language, the square floor plan and slightly skewed placement on the plot with the building not quite parallel to the street, the Chur architects Raphael Zuber designed a school house which hearkens back to the small palazzi of the regional architecture of the Graubündner southtal from the 15th and 16th century. The school forms an axis with the community centre across the street, which holds together the frayed environs of the old village centre, with its one family houses which have sprung up over the past years. The kindergarten as well as the school each has its own entrance and main façade. The kindergarten is located on the ground floor and is accessible on the east side of the property on the ground floor, while the classrooms are situated on the upper floor. Common rooms are located on the main floor. The exterior appearance of the building is mainly an expression of the distribution of forces. The almost closed façade openings, each with the identical geometry of a quarter ellipse form bent curves at right angles, which transmit the load through the middle of the façade into the ground. Both entryway façades stabilize the building in one direction, while a round wall section in the middle of the building does the same in the other direction. The entire support structure is made of light brown coloured reinforced concrete. All non-load bearing parts are inserted additively. The fragmentary perception of the support structure in the building interior creates a direct connection from each room to a unity and its centre.

A centrally located stairwell is the connecting element between the three floors, where in addition to the classrooms, staff rooms and community rooms a kindergarten is also located. With its untreated concrete which owes its light brown colour to the admixture of yellow and black iron oxide pigments, the stairway resembles a sculpture hewn from a cliff or a cave. The stairway walls and the elevator shaft provide support for the vertical loads and a stiffening of the building in the y-direction, while the 40 centimetre thick outer walls deflect horizontal stress like wind and earthquakes.

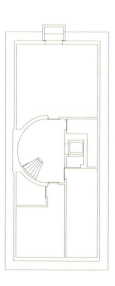

Floorplan cellar

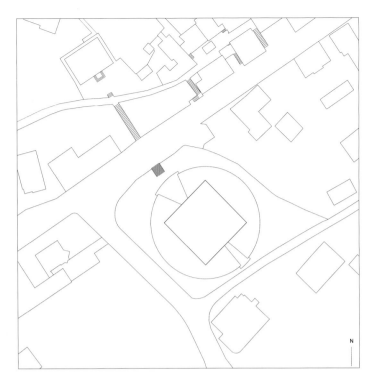

Site plan

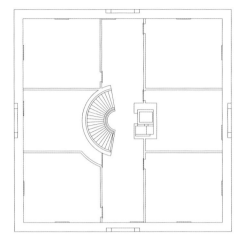

2nd floor with primary school

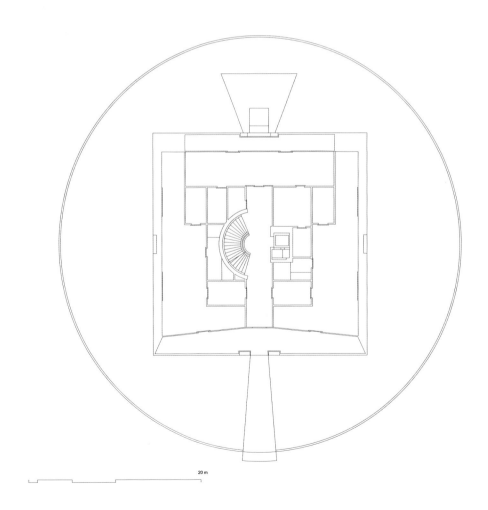

Ground floor with kindergarten

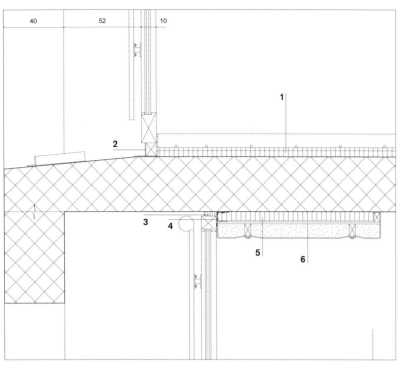

1 Floor construction:
  Industrial screed with
  under-floor heating
  PE film separation layer
  Footstep sound insulation
  Thermal insulation,
  laminated aluminium
  Reinforced concrete ceiling panel
2 Sealing, liquid plastic
3 Compriband
4 Wind barrier
5 Thermal insulation
6 Acoustic element:
  non-flammable carrier plate
  Foam plastic
  Cotton fleece
  Artificial leather cover

Section detail

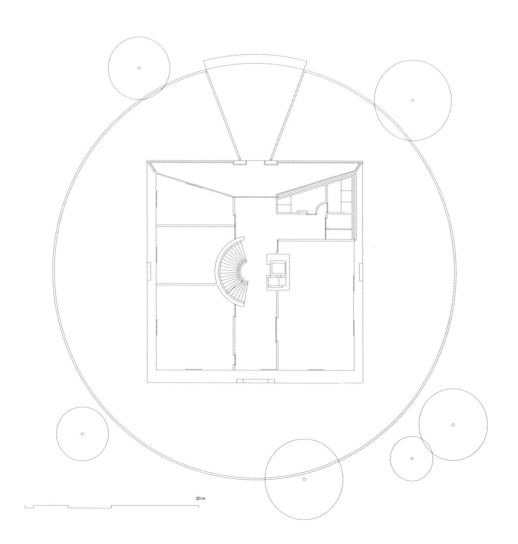

1st floor

Secondary Schools

Copenhagen • Denmark 162
Slough • United Kingdom 172
Nijkerk • Holland 182
Zutphen • Holland 190
Cape Town • South Africa 198
Melbourne • Australia 206
Schleswig • Germany 214
Vienna • Austria 224
Gjerdrum • Norway 232
La Orotava • Spain 238
Deutsch-Wagram • Austria 246
Mosfellsbær • Island 256
Eidsvoll • Norway 266
Dinkelsbühl • Germany 274
Berlin • Germany 284

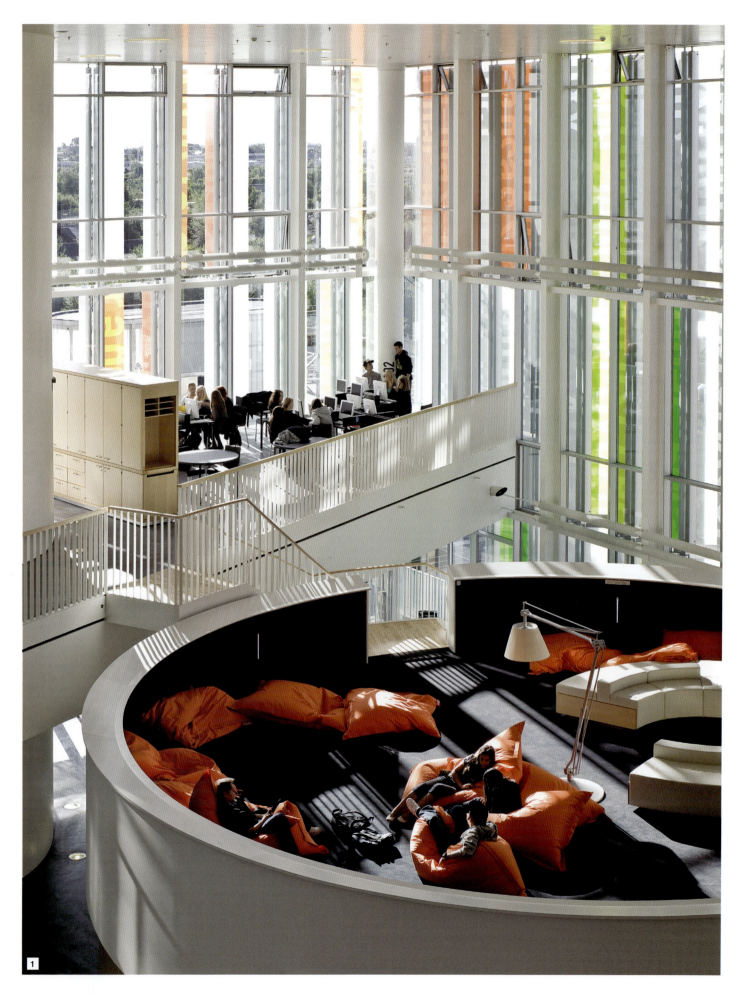

Ørestad College
Copenhagen

Architects: 3XN (Kim Herforth Nielsen, Bo Boje Larsen, Jan Ammundsen, Kasper Guldager Jørgensen)
Structural design: Søren Jensen
BSE Planning: Søren Jensen

Planning and construction phase: 2003–2007

School type: preparatory high school
Number of students: 1,200
Grades: 11–13
Age of students: 16–19 years
Average class size: 28–30 pupils
Number of classes: none

Gross floor space: 12,000 square metres
Type of energy supply: district heating
Construction costs: 27 million euros

Awards: Forum AID – Best Scandinavian Building 2008, Mies van der Rohe Award (Nomination) 2009

The Ørestad preparatory high school is the first of its kind in Denmark. It is based on a new conception, in which content, subject matter, organization and the form of instruction are part of an education reform passed in Denmark in 2005 for the high schools for 16 to 19 year olds. The accelerated scientific courses, mutual exchange, team work and interdisciplinary learning are intended to strengthen the abilities of the students, in order to ease the transition to study in a university. These goals of the Danish educational reform were the starting point for the design of the high school in Copenhagen's newest district of Ørestad. The five storey building in the south of the city is located on the boulevard with the same name, on one of the many canals in the capital. The exterior of the white cube is striking, with its glazed portico, whose gallery on the fourth floor opens up the almost regular alternation of massive white floor-wide bands and ribbon windows. The building changes its face at night. The white bands disappear between the darkness and the illuminated glass surfaces. The building does entirely without classrooms and staff rooms, with a multitude of passages, niches and open, flexibly designed spaces instead. With its organic fixtures and the boomerang-like twisted surfaces supported by three cylinders, the interior concept of the school has nothing to do with the exterior orderliness. A gigantic wooden stairway winding through the hall, a work of art and an occasion to linger connects all levels of the school. The support cylinders house the toilettes, building technology and emergency stairways. Only a few areas are separated from the other open spaces. Among them are the administration tract and some technical classrooms. The latter can be used in different configurations with the aid of sliding doors. The circular islands strewn with orange and green bean bag cushions on the roofs of the cylinders are the places to relax. Everything is designed to support education, which in a mutually interdisciplinary exchange occurs among colleagues according to the motto *teachers teach pupils who teach other pupils*. The goal of a maximally life-like learning environment has found an architectural form in the Ørestad-preparatory high school.

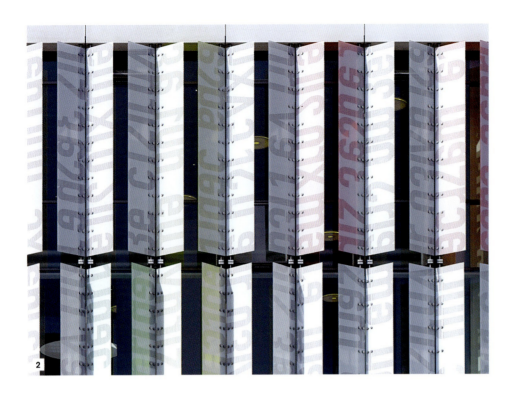

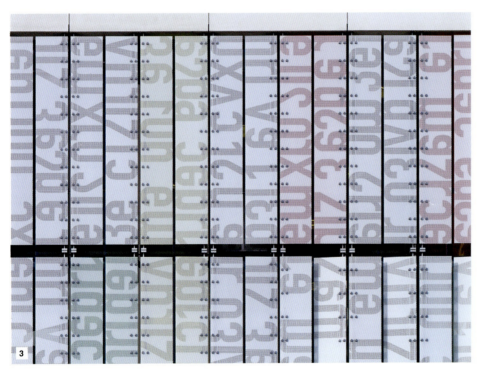

The four floors of the horizontally structured building at the Ørestad Canal in Copenhagen are mounted on a glass pedestal which formally draws the students into the building. The massive white floor-wide bands and the ceilings above them fit flush with windows on each floor. The regularity of the structure is interrupted by the vertical, half-transparent, movable glass sun protection louvers. Their dabs of colour and letters lend the façade a special character.

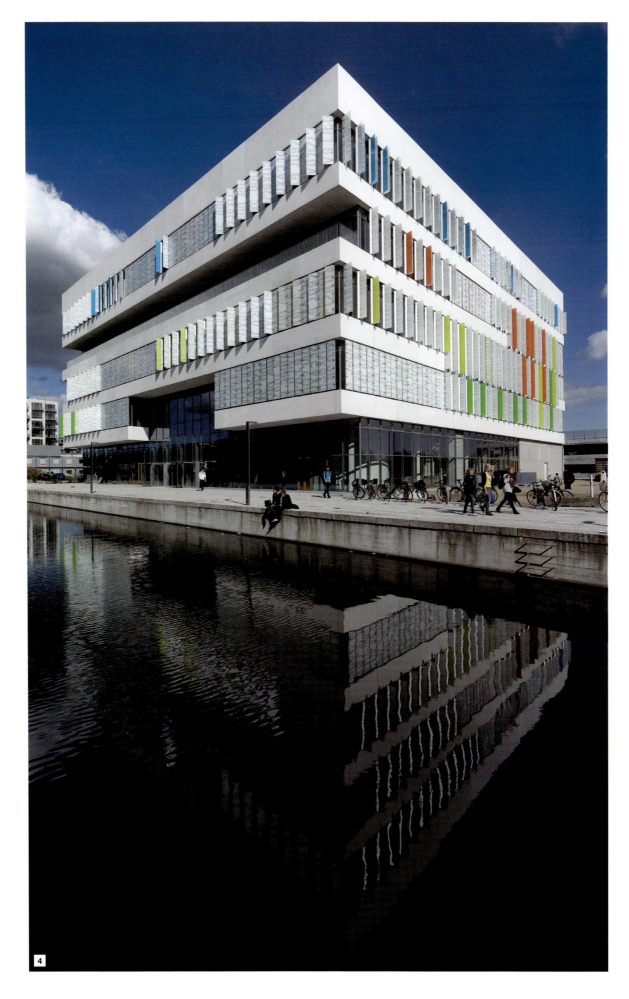

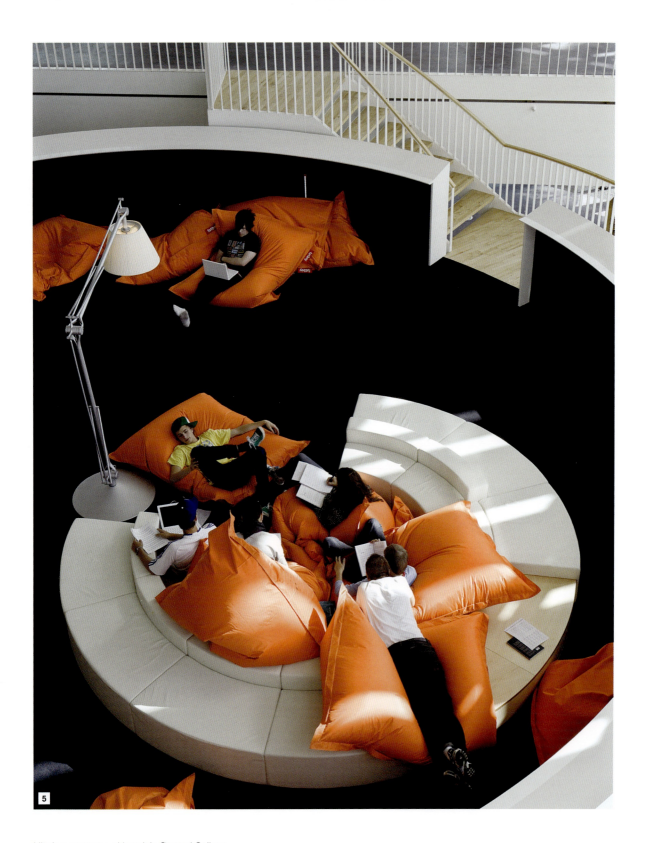

Like in a commune, although in Ørestad College not even the classes have their own rooms, the teaching is loft-style, so to speak. Except for a few rooms for special purposes the teaching and learning areas are only separated by a few fixtures and flexibly adjustable book shelves and cabinets. The open space concept with the sculptural stairs in the middle is intended to simulate as much as possible a life-like learning environment and to support the communication among the students.

Those who teach and learn at Ørestad College can enjoy the special atmosphere of the open space concept, with the ample light, air and sun of the 3XN design. The space coordinating element on the four upper floors is an atrium which ensures that daylight penetrates into the rear areas on each floor.

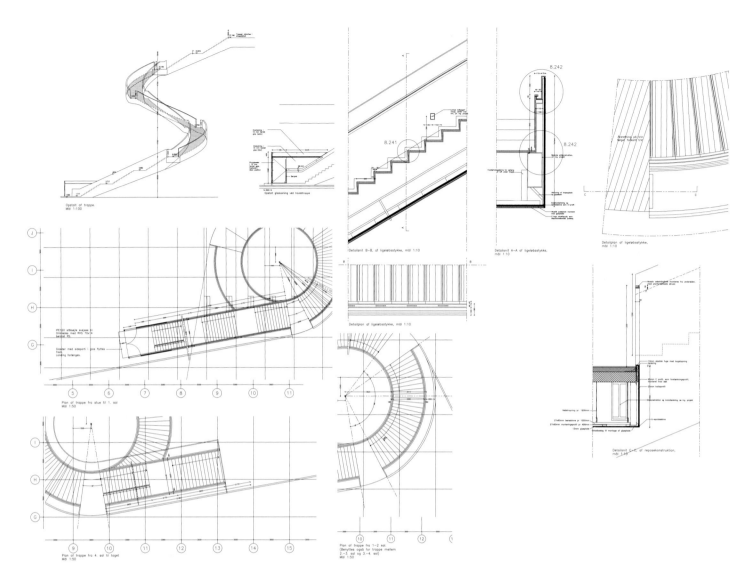

Stair construction

Sections

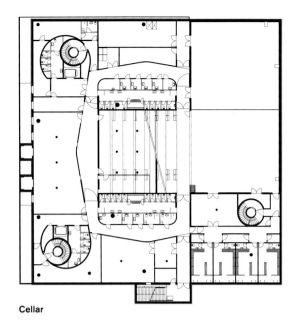
Cellar

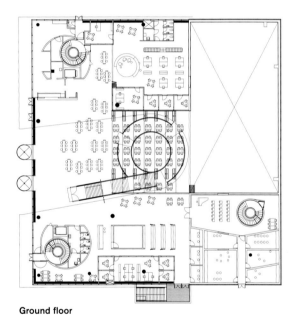
Ground floor

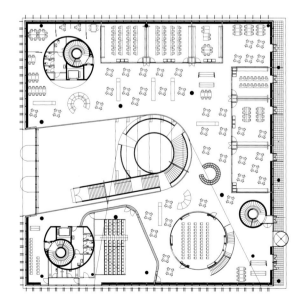
1st floor

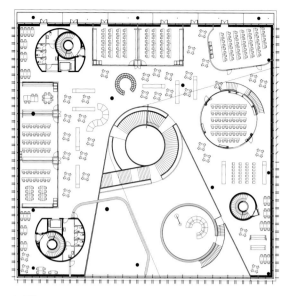
2nd floor

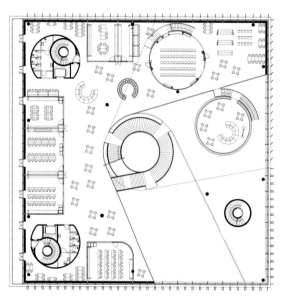
3rd floor

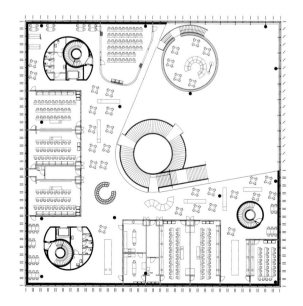
4th floor

SECONDARY SCHOOLS

Langley Academy
Slough

1.150

Architect: Foster + Partners
Staff: Norman Foster, Nigel Dancey, Iwan Jones,
Dominik Hauser, Racel MacIntyre, Adran Nicholas, Declan Sharkey,
Stefan Unnewehr, Pietje Witt, Levin Lo
Structural design: Büro Happold
BSE Planning: Büro Happold

Planning and construction phase: 2004–2008

School type: academy
Number of students: 1,150
Grades: 7–11
Age of students: 11–18 years
Average class size: 30 pupils

Plot size: 65,270 square metres
Built-up area: 3,700 square metres
Gross floor space: 10,000 square metres
Type of energy supply: biomass, geothermal and photovoltaic
Construction costs: confidential

Awards: Royal Institute of Chartered Surveyors (RICS)
Building of the Year, RICS Sustainability Prize

The Langley Academy is located in Slough, a few kilometres west of London. The instruction is distinguished by more specialised scientific subjects like forensics. But practical museum pedagogical subjects are also taught here to show children suitable presentation technologies. Since the best way to do that is with an on-site exhibition, it was deemed necessary in the planning of the building to include possible exhibition spaces in the space allocation. Another focus is sports, especially cricket and rowing. The form of the floor plan is unusual for a school built in 2008 in the middle of a residential district. It consists of three ovals which represent a cricket playing field and two longitudinal figures spreading apart from each other, as a stylized representation of the direction of movement of the cricket players. Movement is the leitmotiv of the design. Everything is in flow: 657 wooden slats were installed on top of the building glazing, through which the illumination of the classrooms, laboratories and work areas and depending on their position, the face of the house changes. The fact that the academy operates almost energy independently with its own solar unit and a utilization and treatment plant for rain and service water makes the two to three storey building the model for the subject of *sustainable technology*. The management of the academy is governed by the science of interconnections. Economy is ecology. Which is convincing. The unusual here is matter-of-fact from the standpoint of the space organization. The main entrance is not just a place of transition. It is also shaped as an agora. Conferences, meetings and exhibitions of the students' work are held here. This atrium with its ten laboratories, classrooms and the art and IT rooms is optically connected in two sleeve-shaped wings. It incorporates the circulatory principle of incessant interdisciplinary exchange of a rather less formal method of instruction. The outward ergonomic shape of the building is also reflected inside with the adaptability of each of the classrooms to the preferred teaching method. The atrium has a direct view of the restaurant and sport fields – those places on the school grounds which stand for the interpersonal solidarity and along with that the community of those who are learning and those who teach them. In time these community rooms round off the self-conception of a learning life-partnership.

The floor plan of the structure with sweeping curves is both extravagant and refined. The red cedar façade is made from wood harvested from sustainably managed forests. Especially in the morning and evening hours the vertical wood slats on the west and east side of the of the structure serve as sun protection. Horizontal ribs and a photo-voltaic installation on the roof lend character to the south and north side. The students have the opportunity in the atrium to look through a window into the utility room, where digital displays show the actual energy gain and water consumption of the school building.

5

6

7

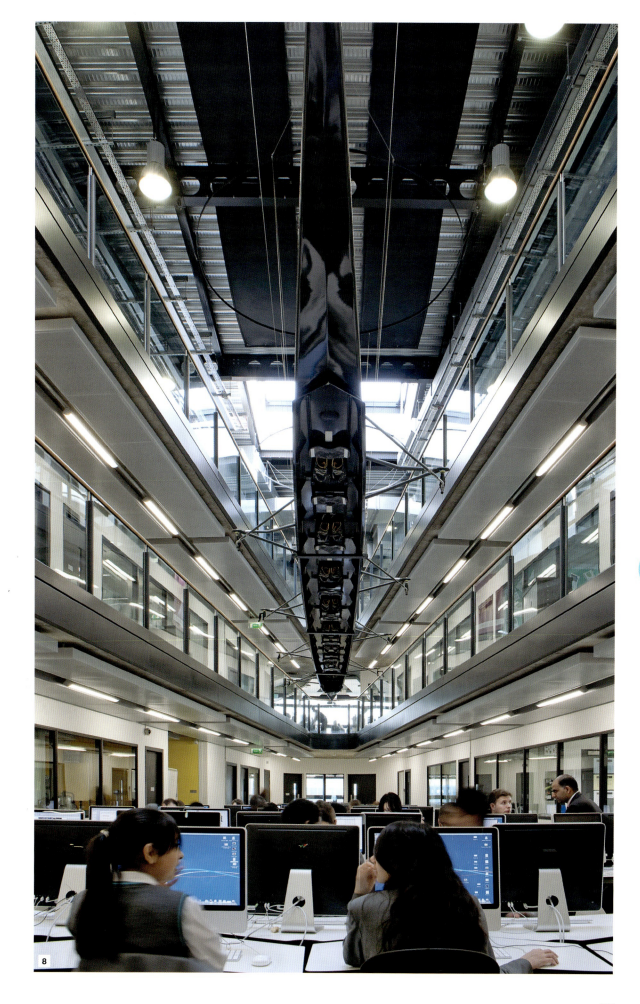

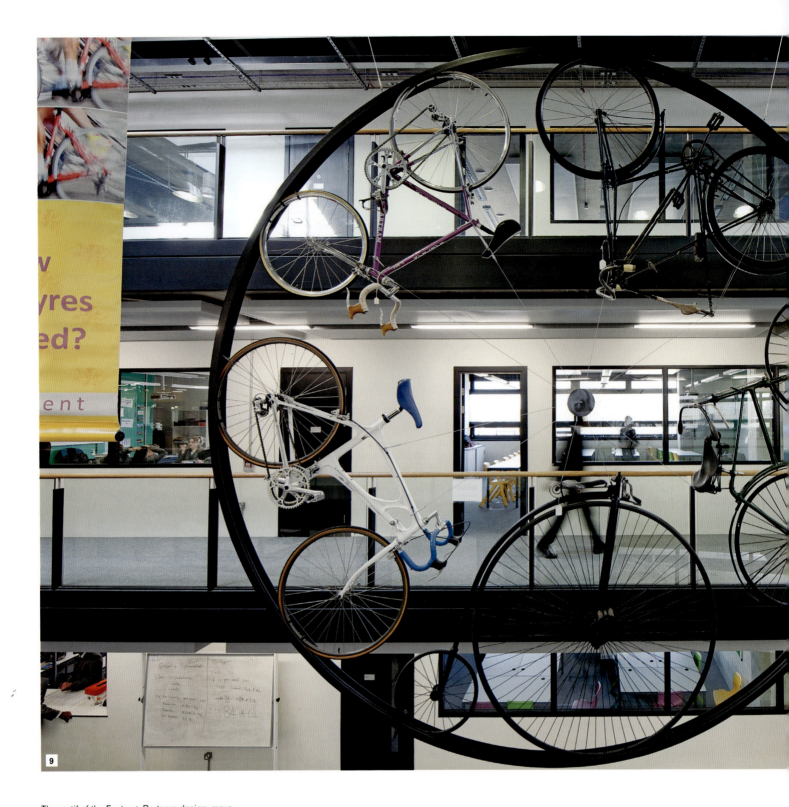

The motif of the Foster + Partners design, movement, is shown by a more than two storey high sculpture. The classrooms are painted in plain grey, so that in addition to the coloured chairs the individually painted walls come into play in order to focus the class in the traditional frontal orientation on the teacher. The gymnasium in the western section of the building complex is connected with the central atrium.

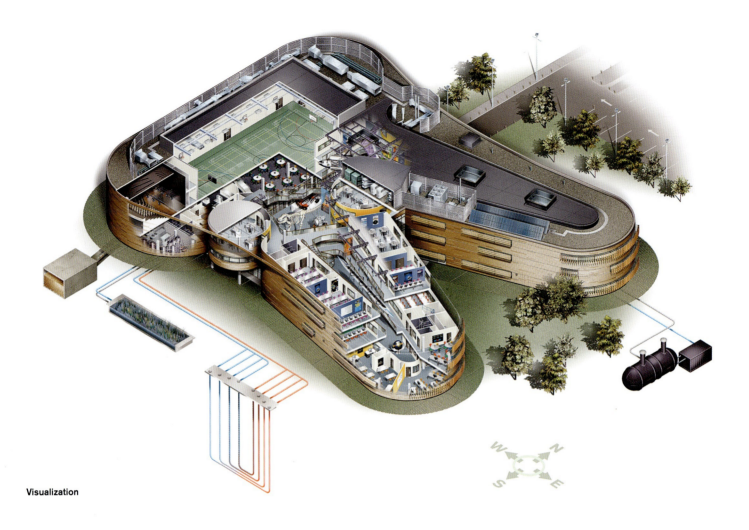
Visualization

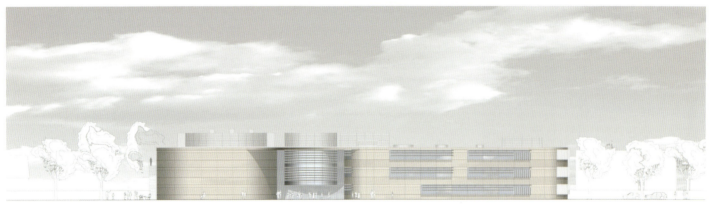
View

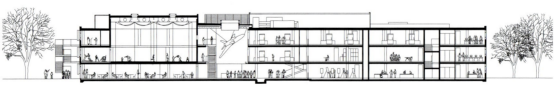
Section

180

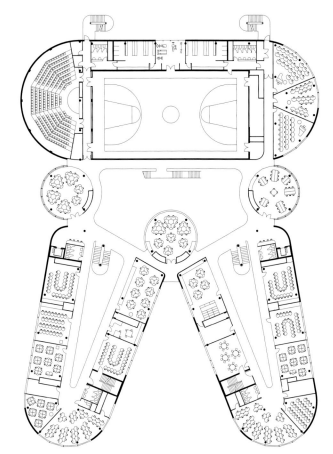
Ground floor

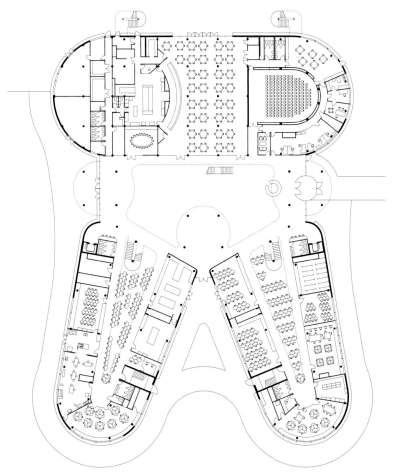
1st floor

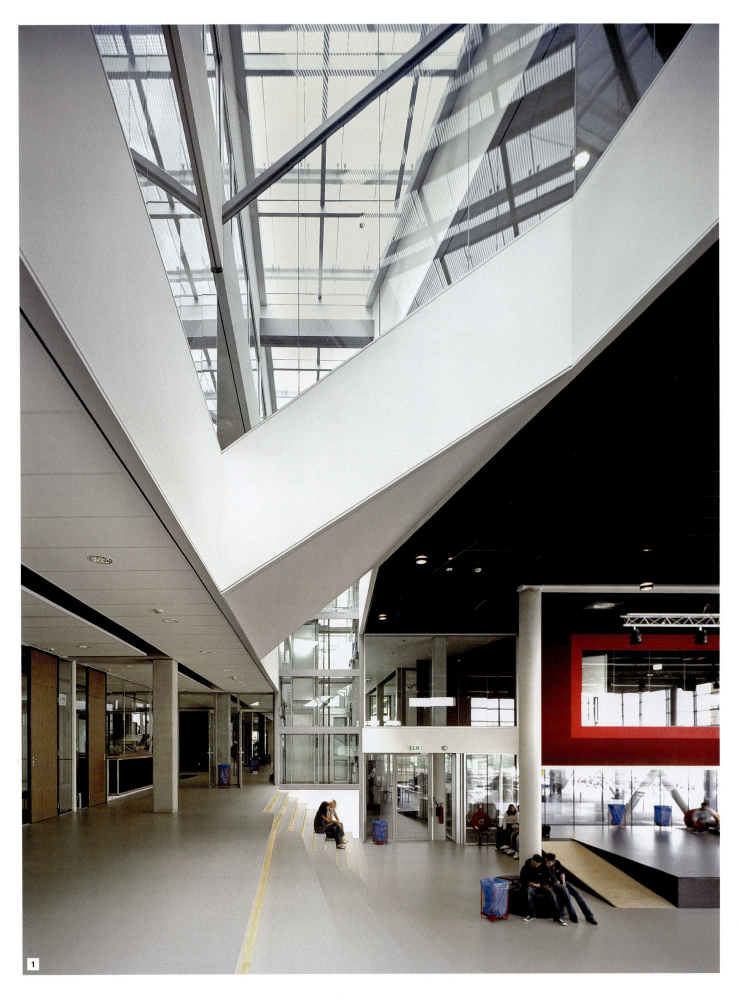

Corlaer College
Nijkerk

Architect: Broekbakema, Rotterdam
Staff: Jan van Iersel, Michaela Stegerwald, Kees van Zwol
Structural design: Raadgevend Ing. bureau Heijm-de Heer bv Velp
BSE Planning: Herman de Groot Project Techniek Leusden

Planning and construction phase: 2003–2006

School type: preparatory high school
Number of students: 800
Grades: 11–13
Age of students: 16–19 years
Number of classes: 13 classes + 5 learning landscapes

Plot size: 4,200 square metres
Built-up area: 2,340 square metres
Gross floor space: 6,000 square metres
Gross volume: 21,600 cubic metres
Useful area: 4,800 square metres
Construction costs: 4 million euros

Awards: BNA Building of the Year 2007 Region East

Fortresses were formerly built on heights surrounded by moats. The town of Nijkerk is located between Amsterdam and Apeldoorn, where these moats are an indispensable and characteristic part of the landscape. Corlaer College rises up in the form of a cross on one of those islands to the south of the old city. The extension completed in 2006 is attached in the south-west and with a different façade on each side provides a contrast to the brown clinker main building. The hilly grounds determine the topography of the structure of the building, freely straddling on supports on one side. Towards the water the building is wrapped by a circumferential corner glazing stretching out over two floors. The manifold design of the façades expresses the inner pedagogical variety of the college which prepares the students to attend a higher education institution. Clarity, safety, group work, the connection to teaching objectives and a suitable training concept are the marks of a humanist athaenum which fosters the formation of personality by conveying knowledge. The interior design bridges and a central stairway which provides a smooth connection to the split level and space allocated according to need make the teaching attitude of the school apparent. Like the structures that can be built up and torn down again in a computer, the work areas for the group work, with individual rooms and common areas with the character of relaxation islands, can be combined and disassembled according to need. An inspiring environment for learning in the building interior enabling personal style in conjunction with others has been created. The entire teaching program is based on a form of instruction which relies little on traditional classrooms, drawing instead on a series of study rooms for more or less personal instruction. The split levels are not an obstacle and actually support the desired learning method and concept with teams of alternating sizes. The entire building, from the entrance to the roof is filled with spaces for instruction, which are artistically expressed in the individual subject areas like the music room, the room for computer graphics or the rooms for biology, physics and chemistry.

Regardless of the direction from which one views the school building, it always looks different: from the north-east the view is through the two storey corner window in the auditorium, in the north-west one looks down the stairs through all the floors. The south-west side of the school is characterized by smaller horizontal window surfaces. The façade concept was derived from the school's multitude of teaching methodologies.

Split level construction supports the transmission of knowledge, by making it possible to teach as flexibly as possible. Group work in groups of different sizes is possible. Those who do not want to sit in the separate study rooms can be taught throughout the entire school. For this reason, and not just during the breaks, students and teachers often congregate on the central stairway with seating steps.

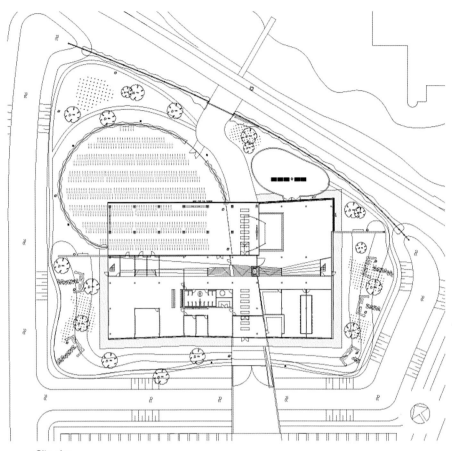
Site plan

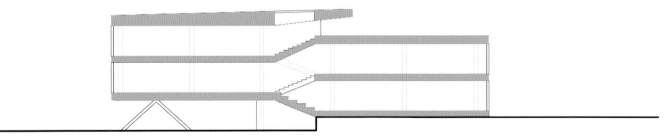
Section

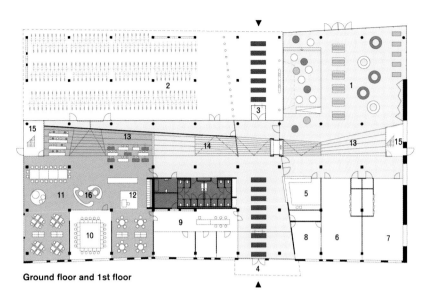

Ground floor and 1st floor

1	Auditorium
2	Bicycle parking lot
3	School entrance
4	Main entrance
5	Doorman
6	Music room
7	Drawing room
8	Work shops
9	Administration
10	Class room
11	Learning room
12	Group leader (teacher)
13	Seating steps
14	Main stairs
15	Escape route
16	Rest area
17	Lecture hall
18	Personnel area
19	Specialist room
20	Conference room

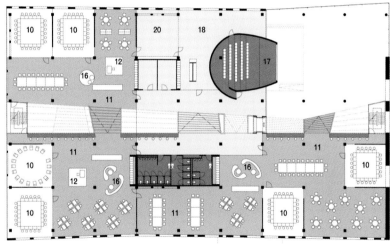

2nd floor and 3rd floor

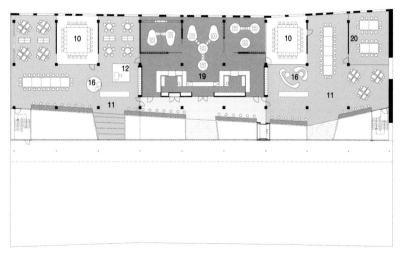

4th floor

ROC Aventus
Zutphen

Architects: RAU Architects
Staff: Thomas Rau, Martin van Kampenhout, Ernst-Peter Everraardt, Peter Horsink
Structural design: Corsmit
BSE Planning: Schreuder, Corsmit

Planning and construction phase: 2006–2010

School type: vocational school
Number of students: 800
Grades: 9–12
Age of students: 14–18 years

Plot size: 2,160 square metres
Built-up area: 1,210 square metres
Gross floor space: 4,200 square metres
Gross volume: 17,500 cubic metres
Useful area: 3,940 square metres
Construction costs: 7.0 million euros

The ROC (*Regionaal opleidingencentrum*) is a Dutch facility for professional training which offers a broad spectrum of courses annually to more than 15,000 students from Apeldroon, Deventer and Zutphen. The new ROC Aventus subsidiary in Zutphen is located at the junction between the train station and the picturesque old town. The blue, white and gold colour of the building is identifiable with the local trains and buses and refers to the train station. The building was built by NS Poort, the development arm of the Dutch rail system. The new training centre provides mobility and continuity between the train station and the old town. The street pattern repeats in abstract form in the criss-crossing narrow blue ribbon windows of the façade profile of the trapezoidal shaped building. Everything else in this building has a reference and relationship. The stone facing made of alternating light and darker grey tones on the ground floor lends an element of style to the station forecourt, while the gold-yellow coloured wood panelling on the first floor refers to the old town. The metal sheathing on the second floor refers to the activities of the school in the urban developmental area of *De Mars* north of the station, while the white plaster in the attic was inspired by the IJssel and the white houses on the quay. The building consists of four L-shaped floors turned towards each other. This creates niches on each floor, which because of the turning are located in a different angle on each level. The construction makes it seem that each floor opens its arms to another part of the city. The stacked floor plan also generates a central open area passing through all levels of the house, which together with the open spaces ensures that the school is illuminated by daylight from all sides. To the south the overhangs that are created provided the necessary shade. The open areas fulfil their pedagogical purpose as break areas and as a location for interdisciplinary exchange. These areas outside the teaching rooms connect the four teaching floors for culture and theatre, health, technology and economics. They are places for the exchange of ideas and knowledge and useful collaboration among human beings.

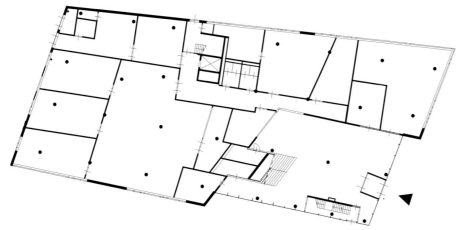

Ground floor

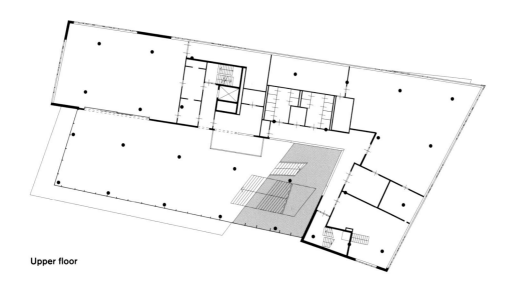

Upper floor

Four L-shaped levels reflect each other so that due to the rotation there is always enough open space for each level. Each level faces a different side of the city. Above all, the empty rooms which result from the stacking of levels fulfil a social function. They are used as platforms for spontaneous meetings, for the exchange of ideas and for collaboration between the study courses.

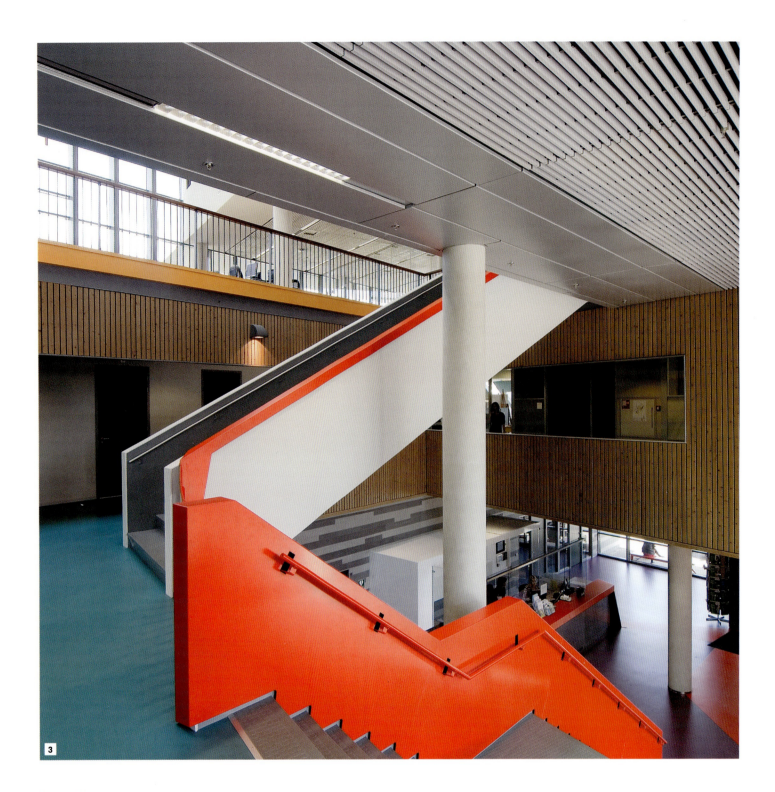

The use of sustainable materials and an energy efficient means of construction were the key to the building design. Only untreated wood was used for the wooden parts. The deployment of a geothermal heat pump, sufficient exposure to daylight and thermal activation of building structures ensure that the school can do without conventional heating and cooling. The result of this method of construction is a healthy building climate, with a substantial reduction of dust accumulation and less allergies and headaches, which means increased concentration on learning.

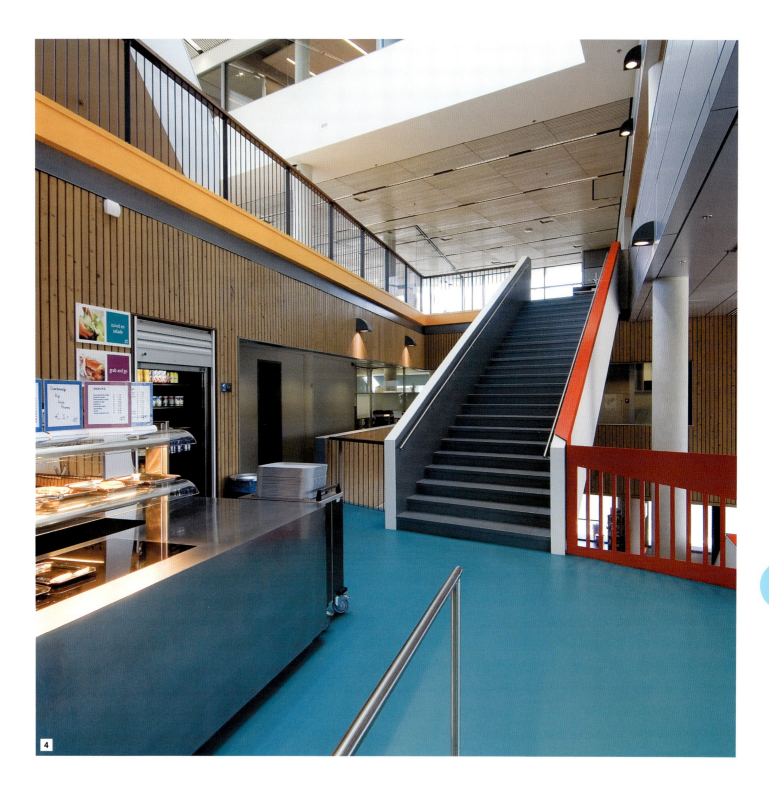

Another connecting link is a red sculpture by the designer duo of Marleen Kaptein and Stijn Roodnat (Kaptein Roodnat), which winds through the building like a red thread, from the entryway on the first floor to the ceiling of the top floor. Stijn Roodnat call their work "the organ" of the building.

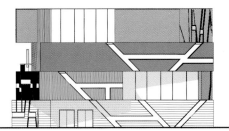

View west

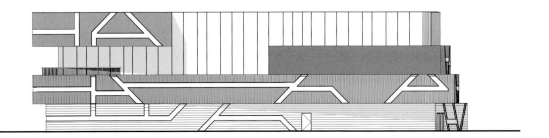

View north

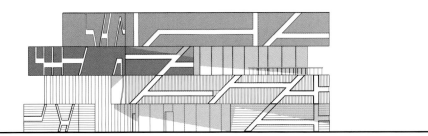

View east

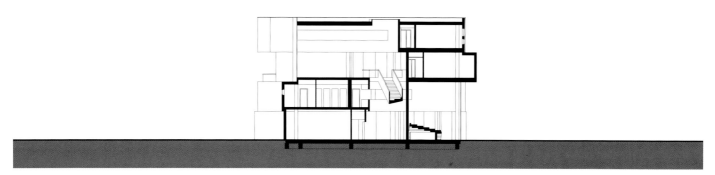
Cross section

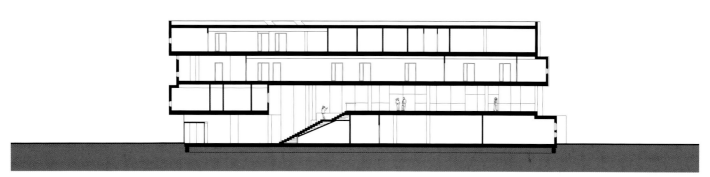
Longitudinal section

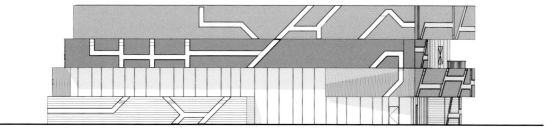
View south

Inkwenkwezi Secondary School
Cape Town

Architect: Sonja Petrus Spamer Architects, Noero Wolff Architects
Structural design: PDA Naidoo and Associates Structural Engineers
BSE Planning: SAWE Consulting Engineers

Planning and construction phase: 2004–2007

School type: secondary school
Number of students: 1,163
Grades: 8–12
Age of students: 13–20 years
Average class size: 40–50 students
Number of classes: 27 classes

Plot size: 14,000 square metres
Built-up area: 1,800 square metres
Gross floor space: 3,000 square metres
Construction costs: 1.0 million euros

Awards: Cape Institute for Architecture – Regional Award of Merit, Cityscape Architectural Award – Best Community Building in the World, BAQ Awards (3rd place), Chicago Athenaeum International Architecture Award

The township of Dunoon on the edge of Cape Town is one of those dustbins of civilisation for the unwelcome, for whom the educational facilities and the chances in life that go with them are denied. Although apartheid ended in 1994, the relicts of this period and its aftermath continue today. The school in the Township of Dunoon is an attempt to bring the effects of this period to an end. In the *mélange* of coloured houses and sad sheet metal huts which sometimes serve as stores, its topography recreates in a wave-like form an optical mid-point. In order to articulate the identity of the school with its surroundings, the occurrence of painted signs on the businesses in the township was utilized. The name of the school *Inkwenkwezi*, in English "morning star", complete with a yellow star, is emblazoned on the otherwise gleaming white building. The community areas like the entryway, library and administration are located in the middle of the main entrance. The specialist classes are accessed from there. In the adjacent, landscape oriented building wing, the upper class teaching rooms are located, with the classrooms for the lower grades on the side facing the settlement. Both wings with their circumferential galleries generate a kind of school forum with direct access to the athletics field. The stylized mother-like figure protects the children from the hot winds and criminality. The courtyard planted with trees is located on the periphery. There are different levels which offer everyone the possibility to relax. Rock climbing and various games can be enjoyed. The clear structure and the clever use of coloured elements show how modern and traditional forms of expression can be combined in an aesthetic typical for the country. The school is also designed to be used by the local residents, offering them the opportunity to earn money here. Computer rooms and the library serve as workplaces; they are closely packed together at the entrance and may be used until late in the evening. The entrance hall serves as community hall and ballroom.

The challenge of this project was to find an architectural solution which could be accepted by the inhabitants of the Township of Dunoon. There was not one public building in the entire settlement. Some of the dwellings were converted into stores whose façades now sported large lettering or images referring to the business inside. This kind of identification is also part of the school, whose white façade is decorated with a yellow morning star along with the name of the school.

The sculptural form of the building is noticeable from outside and continues into the building interior. Although the individual classrooms are repetitively arranged, the corridors widen like caves, so that there is no danger of monotony. The illumination from above increases the drama of the space. The façade in turn reflects the interior of the school to the outside.

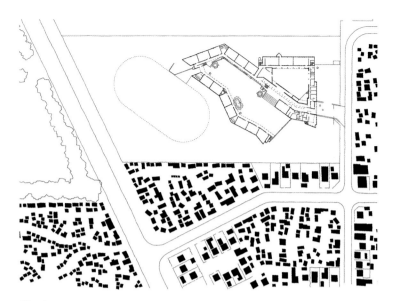

Site plan

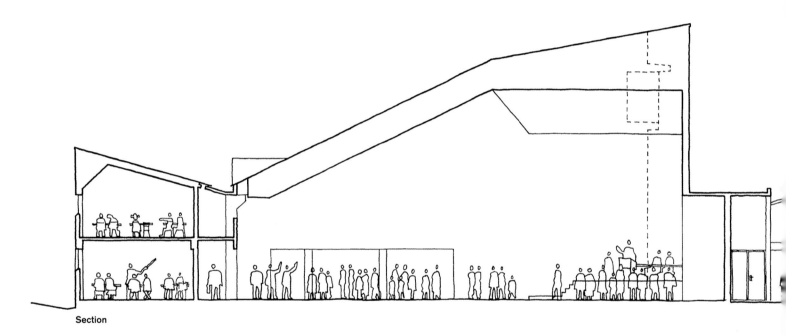

Section

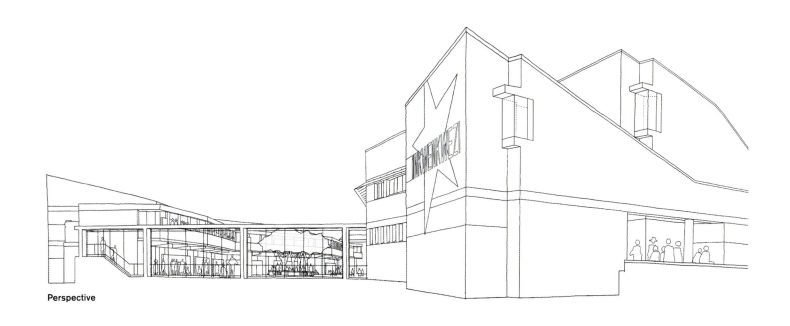
Perspective

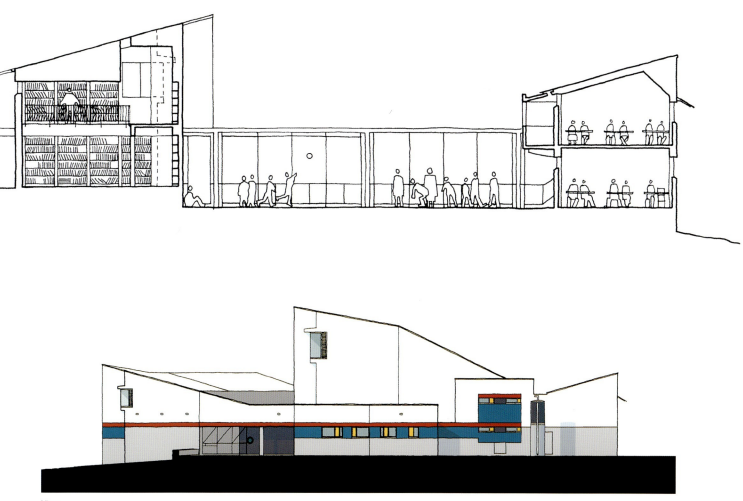

View

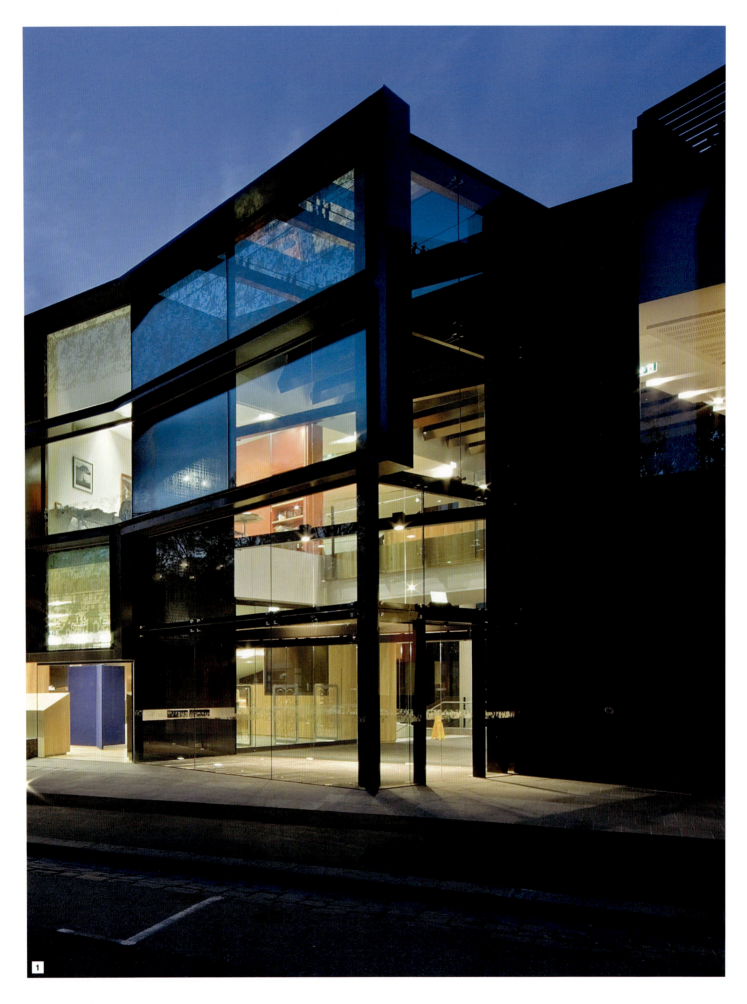

Melbourne Grammar School
Melbourne

Architect: John Wardle Architects
Staff: John Wardle, Stefan Mee, Andy Wong, Diego Bekinschstein, Barry Hayes, Kirrilly Wilson, Nick Harding, Stuart Mann, Paul Evans, Fiona Dunin
Structural design: Connell Wagner
BSE Planning: Webb Australia (Lighting technology), Umow Lai (Information technology)

Planning and construction phase: 2004–2007

School type: preparatory high school
Number of students: 800
Grades: 9–12
Age of students: 15–18 years

Gross floor space: 3,430 square metres
Construction costs: 12.5 million euros

Awards: Victorian Architecture Medal 2008, Premier's Design Mark Award – State of Design 2008, National Award of Public Architecture 2008, The Emil Soderstan Award for Interior Architecture, William Wardell Public Architecture Award 2008

Located as it is in direct proximity to the capital city government facilities of the south-eastern Australian state of Victoria, the Melbourne Grammar School, founded in 1858, also known as the *The Nigel Peck Centre for Learning & Leadership* – is the right place for a training centre for young talent. One need only view the location at the threshold of the city centre to the historically significant and charming surrounding environs of the *Royal Botanic Gardens* in order to appreciate the bold extension of the old Victorian building. With the completion of the building in 2007, a learning campus was created which shields the existing three-wing facility with the church on the main street. The new building with its prestigious stairway, pooled library facilities, an additional lecture hall and seminar rooms, is presented on the street side as a series of conjoined pavilions which cleverly simulate a direct connection with the old town with an optical reflection on the main entrance. A curtain wall shows the new growing out of the old. The route is clear, even if both architectures do not come into contact with each other. The annex represents a sophisticated nod to the past. With its sequence of pavilions with giant windows in different shapes, the building manages equability and change. The reading room windows with privacy protection in the library look like they have been fitted with gossamer frost flowers. From outside the interior appears with impressive effects, while from inside the various windows afford different views of the historical garden to the rear. As if in an oversized showcase window, the students sit on the street side in their elegant library reading room – a building which from the main street allows a glimpse inside the school life, while offering the students a learning experience with an optical connection to their surroundings. The new building also thrives on these reciprocal optical and historical visual references to the campus: where the main library surrounds a huge old elm tree, a glazed administrative section stands as a counterpart to the brick clad library, which with its book-like layered and polished bricks, lends a down-to-earth gravity to the building's openness.

Depending on where one stands in the building, the environs are perceived differently, due to the street-side glazing in different forms, inclinations and size. While the façade facing the street looks like an arrangement of several show windows, the courtyard side in the south of the facility is noticeably more closed and massive. The auditorium in the cellar emerges here on the surface as a sculptural flight of stairs, creating an intimate space between the library stack room and the campus courtyard.

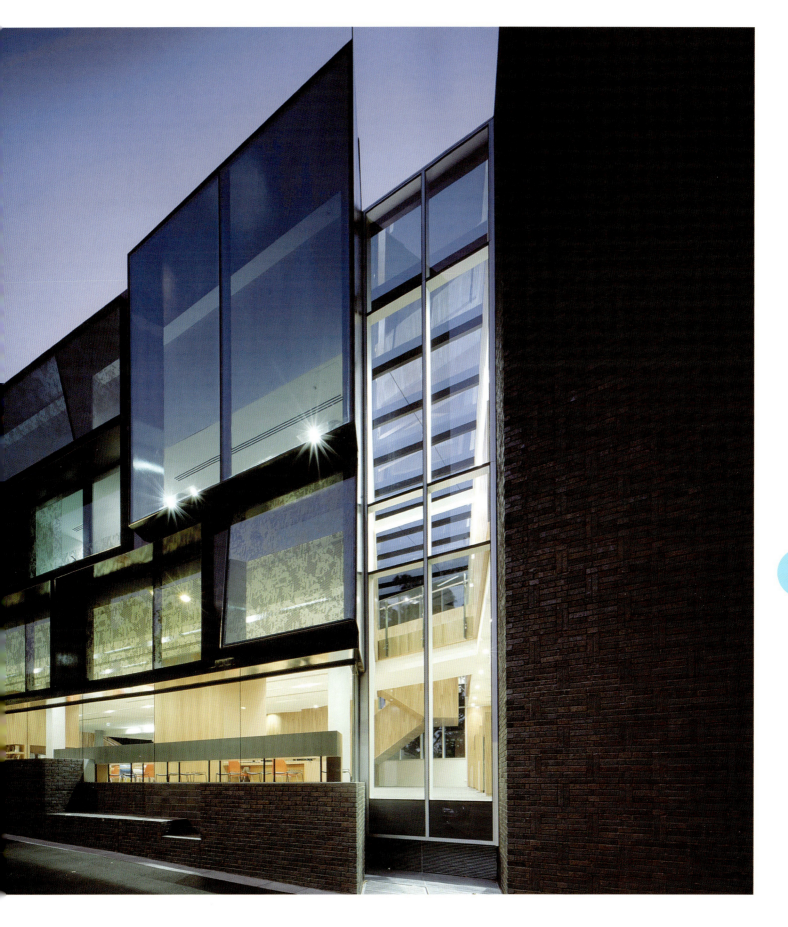

The connection to the outside plays an important role in the building. In addition to furnishing a view of the adjacent street which in turn allows pedestrians a look inside, the library building is also oriented to the green covered campus courtyard. An imposing staircase in the interior of the school harmonizes with the open spatial concept of the learning centre.

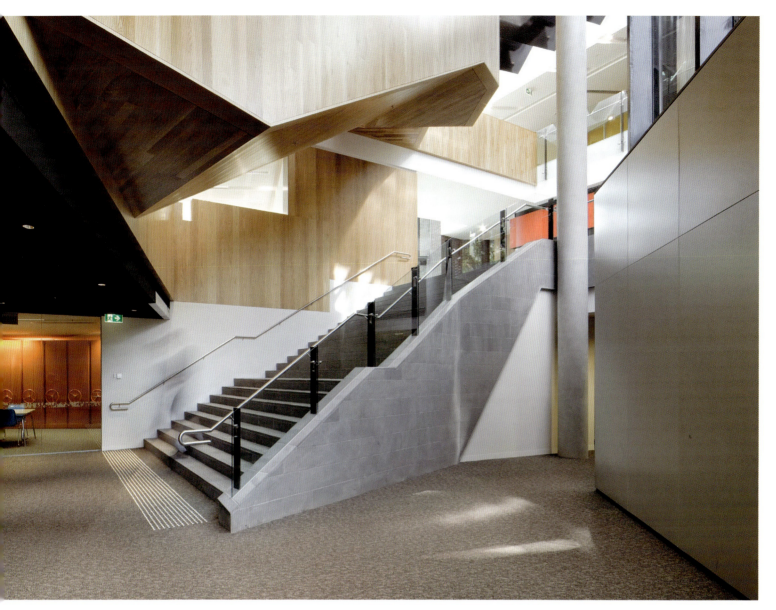

SECONDARY SCHOOLS

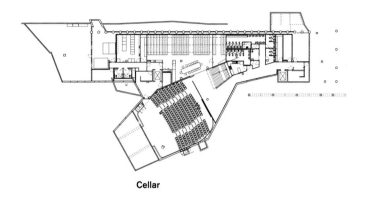
Cellar

View north

View south

View west

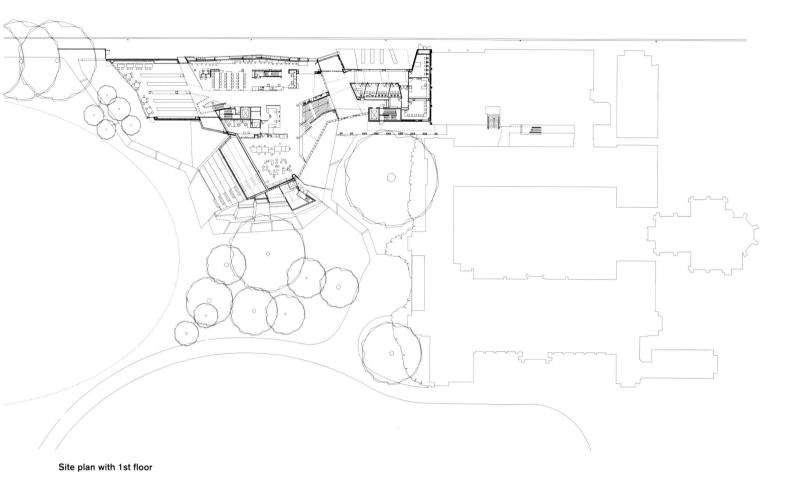
Site plan with 1st floor

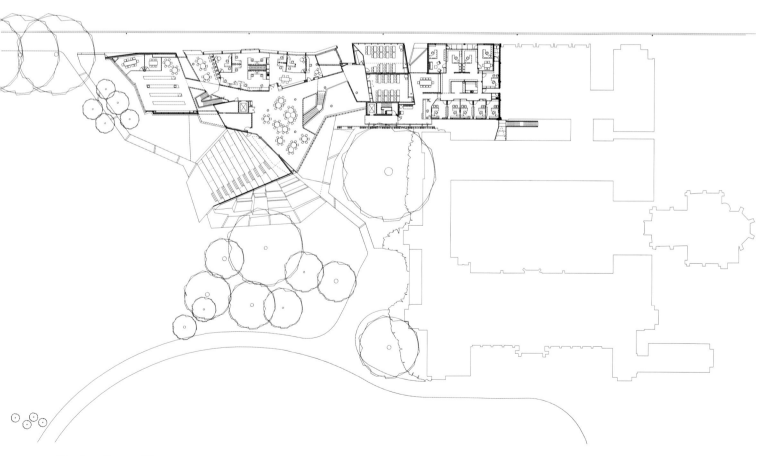
Site plan with ground floor

A. P. Møller School
Schleswig

Architect: C. F. Møller Architects
Staff: Mads Møller, Julian Weyer, Karl Asbjørn Knudsen Jan Pedersen, Dorthe Bækbz Jensen, Nicolaj Fentz, Thomas Wölke, Henrik Sebstrup
Structural design: Rambøll
BSE Planning: Rambøll
Landscape architecture: Kessler.Krämer

Planning and construction phase: 2006–2008

School type: non-denominational school and sixth form grammar school
Number of students: 625
Grades: 7–10 and 11–13
Age of students: 11–18 years

Plot size: 110,000 square metres
Built-up area: 7,300 square metres
Gross floor space: 15,000 square metres
Gross volume: 86,500 cubic metres
Useful area: 13,960 square metres
Type of energy supply: district heating and solar energy

Awards: RIBA (Royal Institute of British Architects) Award 2010, Worldwide Brick Award 2010

The A. P. Møller Foundation of Arnold Marsk Mc-Kinney-Møller and his wife, Chastine, one of the wealthiest private foundations in Denmark, bought a charming piece of landscape in Schleswig and built a new Danish comprehensive school with a preparatory high school level. It is used by the Danish school system for southern Schleswig. The architecture of the A. P. Møller School is based on a simple, clear and uncomplicated idea. The main entrance, atrium and auditorium are arranged with a view of the Holmer Noor landscape and the silhouette of Schleswig. The yellow brick façade with console cornice and ribbon windows embedded in deep niches is a well thought out interplay of transparency and mass. It admits much daylight while providing protection from the weather. The location and design of the school are determined by the relation of the property to the city of Schleswig and to the Schlei fjord. The core of the school is the atrium, where the canteen and science centre are located. It functions like a natural part of the urban squares, streets, sidewalks and balconies with places to read and relax. With the urban feel of the media centre, the atrium offers opportunities for music and theatre performances, and exhibitions. All rooms for the sciences are located on the ground floor, where the classrooms also have a direct access to the common room and the outside. A large stairway, also an invitation to learn or linger, leads to the first floor, which houses the classrooms of the secondary school. The preparatory high school is located above on the 2nd floor. The principle of two schools under one roof separates the age groups and unifies the functional use for everyone. The timeless architecture of the school is directed toward an open class management, where the whole school constitutes a teaching milieu for individual work, group work and plenary session. The inner openness and organisation of the school embodies a modern democratic education in a diverse teaching environment. By closely grouping the traditional classrooms around the atrium and the common activities, different forms of teaching can be freely conducted in the daily work while guaranteeing a high degree of interdisciplinary collaboration.

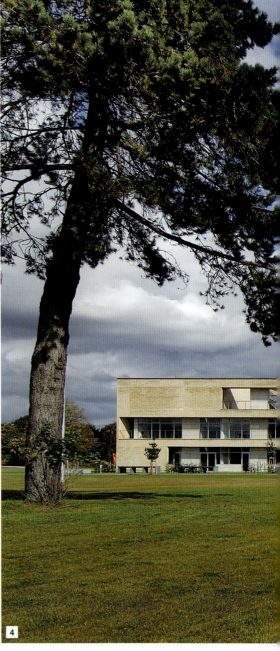

Two large inner building sections with common areas, together with a canteen, event hall and knowledge centre on three levels and a sports and multi-function hall with three playing fields, comprise the building complex. The multi-functional hall with its dark grey stone façade extends to the entryway of the main building, which radiates warmth and openness with large ribbon windows and light-coloured clinkers. Auditoriums and sports halls are located beneath the large slanted copper roof designed with the same metal profile ceiling and skylights so that it is perceived as a continuous room.

The interior design generates a bright, Nordic impression with high quality material despite the subdued design. The yellow brick construction is also found inside: brick walls frame the auditorium and sports hall. Light coloured wood panelling, wood block paving and a warm-toned linoleum flooring as well as Bornholme granite are used in the ballroom and main entrance. The Danish-Icelandic artist Olafur Eliasson set a tone in the auditorium with his sculpture Tellurium, representing the planets of the solar system as illuminated objects.

The acoustics throughout the building were created to accommodate the requirements of flexible usability for all spaces. Several ceiling constructions were designed for the school building. In the ballroom the walls and ceilings in the ballroom are equipped with acoustic panelling. For the rest of the rooms C. F. Møller developed a system that combined a quiet and acoustically optimal design which incorporates all fixtures, like illumination, ventilation, sensors, beamers etc., in an elegant track.

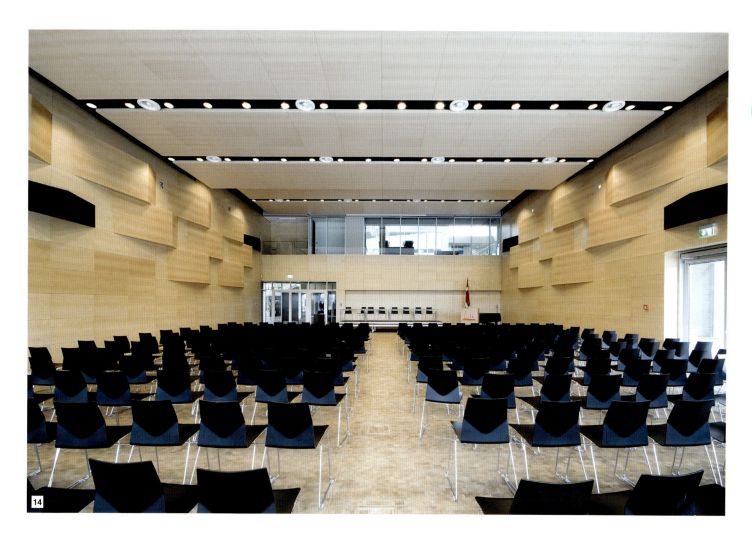

Longitudinal section

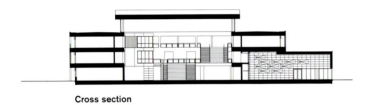
Cross section

Visualization

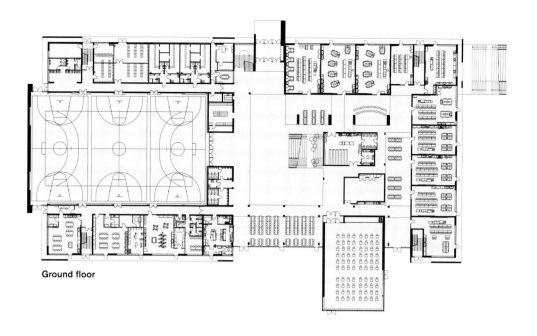
Ground floor

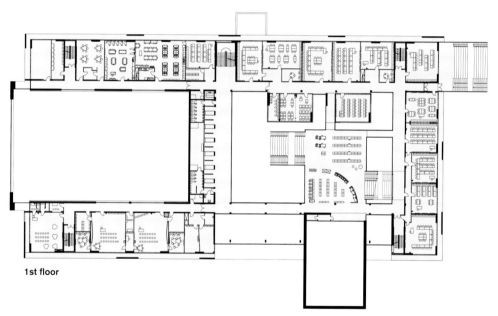
1st floor

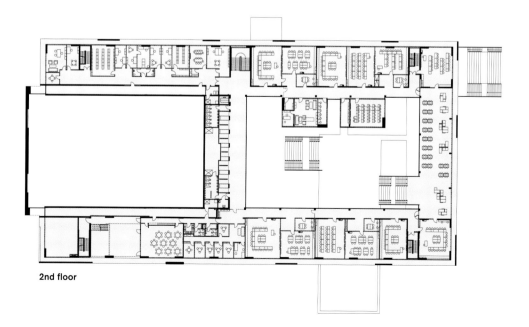
2nd floor

New School Contiweg
Vienna

Architect: Atelier Heiss
(Christian Heiss, Michael Thomas, Thomas Mayer)
Staff: Georg Pamperl, Andrea Braun, Vinzenz Dreher,
Manuela Gruber, Petra Hendrich, Petra Kogler, André Romao,
Penny Rüttimann, Adina Tomi, Jean Marie Welbes
Structural design: Brand & Partner
BSE Planning: Vasko & Partner

Planning and construction phase: 2008–2010

School type: academic upper secondary school
Number of students: 900
Grades: 5–12
Age of students: 10–18 years
Average class size: 25 students
Number of classes: 36 classes

Plot size: 20,000 square metres
Built-up area: 5,030 square metres
Gross volume: 55,700 cubic metres
Useful area: 11,000 square metres
Type of energy supply: district heating
Construction costs: 24.2 million euros

The New School on Contiweg in Hirschstetten, an eastern suburb of Vienna, is a facility planned with two horizontally emphasized structures, with a total of 36 classrooms for the Federal Academic Secondary School and preparatory high school, and the experimental Vienna Grammar School. From a distance, beginning with the three storey glazed atrium with the school library floating over it like a tree house, this is architecture that is anything but smug. The school is handicap accessible throughout, from the parking lot to the playing fields. The teaching program is based on a general transfer of knowledge as the cornerstone of a personality development designed to provide a clear orientation for the student as a mature individual entering life. No one should be denied this perspective because of a physical handicap. The new school construction is an architectural surprise which sets a standard going far beyond its immediate environs, down to the level of detail. The identity-creating leaf-shapes appearing in all different functional variants crop up over the entire property, from the planted area in front of the school to the window openings in the façade and the wall elements in the halls, to the sport facilities behind the school. Inside the school along the halls this decorative motif, in addition to other details designed for handicapped persons, like stair markings, threshold-less accesses, contrasting doors and window glass protection, operates as an especially useful tactile orientation element for visually handicapped children. In addition to the spatial organisation, the arrangement of the rooms provides a clear orientation and change of pace in the school routine. While the classrooms face the gardens and the landscape, the specialized educational facilities like the workshops open up to the courtyard, which like the greened interior of the library roof, correspond to the monastic *Hortus conclusus*, in English, "enclosed garden". Walkways in the atrium provide access between the two class areas. A flight of stairs and seating steps proceed gently through a courtyard designed with stage and terrace elements into a landscape with the outdoor sports facilities. The school in its entirety is truly a work of art.

Two horizontally emphasized classroom sections and an intervening strip consisting of a forecourt, atrium, flight of stairs and open space form the school complex. The glazed south side of the atrium and the string roof extension with library are visible from a distance. Lens shapes entwining the façade also extend into the building interior as a design leitmotif. By crossing the courtyard, one reaches the surrounding landscape with the outdoor sports facility.

Footbridges in the atrium connect both wings of classrooms of the new school with each other. The standard classes enjoy a view of the gardens and the landscape of Hirschstettes, while the special education rooms face the courtyard. From the school library, ruling over the three storey glazed atrium, lens-shaped windows provide a good view of the surroundings. The green covered underside of the roof creates a relaxed atmosphere for reading and learning.

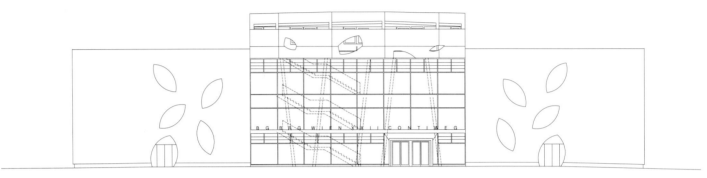
View

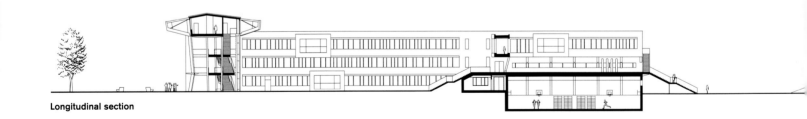
Longitudinal section

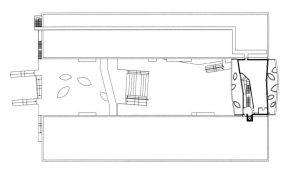
Attic

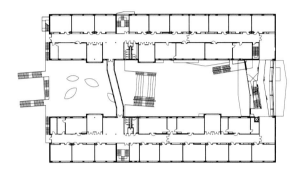
2nd floor

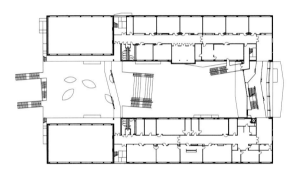
1st floor

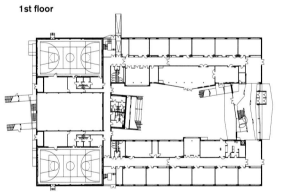
Ground floor

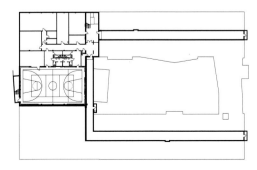
Cellar

Gjerdrum Grammar School
Gjerdrum

Architect: Kristin Jarmund Arkitekter
Staff: Kristin Jarmund, Geir Messel, Line Strand, Francis Brekke, Arild Eriksen, Nora Müller, Karin Anton
Structural design: BraCon
BSE Planning: GK Norge, Romerike Elektro

Planning and construction phase: 2007–2009

School type: Middle school
Number of students: 320
Grades: 8–10
Age of students: 13–15 years
Average class size: approx. 25 students
Number of classes: 12 classes

Plot size: 30,000 square metres
Gross floor space: 3,900 square metres
Useful area: 2,745 square metres
Type of energy supply: electric heating, district heating
Construction costs: 20.7 million euros

Awards: Statens Byggeskikkspris 2010
(Norwegian Government Architecture Prize)

This school is a perfect fit with the urban and rural landscape of the 6,240 inhabitant town of Gjerdrum in Norway. It is important to imagine the gently slanted surroundings with the mountains in the south in order to understand this building in the context of the thinly settled landscape. The compact construction on the trapezoidal floor plan, with its narrow, light-green ribbon façades opening up wide from the windows, and its wooden slat covered glass towers, is composed like an architectonic interpretation of the richly forested rural-urban foothill landscape. The architectural design of the school building is fitted into the cultivated landscape. The transition from inside to outside is as seamless as the spatial allocation itself, which follows the principle of individual houses within one house. Workshops, specialist rooms, auditoriums, a canteen and other rooms for the administration are grouped around a central circular, partially roofed-over courtyard. With the aid of a well thought out spatial arrangement, the architects have created a special school atmosphere. Administrative rooms and the canteen are located directly next to the entryway while the specialist rooms are located in the rear of the building. The atrium operates as the place of meeting and communication in the core of the school house, while one corner of the building is used to teach each of the three age groups. A staff room and an auditorium are directly connected with the classrooms. The connection between open, large areas and closed rooms makes it possible to separate the various school areas and to use them for evening events. Seating steps protruding from the slanted south façade can be used as bleachers for the sports events or for teaching outside. In coordination with the spatial structure the interior design of the school and its grounds are determined by an interplay of colours and materials which supports orientation and which optically refers to the landscape and the urban surroundings.

The main entrance of the school leads to a courtyard that provides access to the canteen and rooms for the administration. The vertical glass towers with wooden slats provide a stark contrast with the rest of the building. They represent the three classes and enable the visitor from outside to understand how the school interior is organized. The south façade is oriented to the function of the adjacent sports field: in addition to sports competitions, the seating steps and a floodlight unit make the field also attractive for learning outdoors.

Different use units expressed as individual concrete cores were strung together so that the space allocation program fulfilled all desires. The library is a plus for the canteen and a service zone connected to the courtyard houses the toilets and washrooms and the wardrobe. The form of these rooms accommodates the round atrium. Wash areas located outside the toilets and wardrobes ensure that dirt from the street does not reach the teaching rooms.

7

8

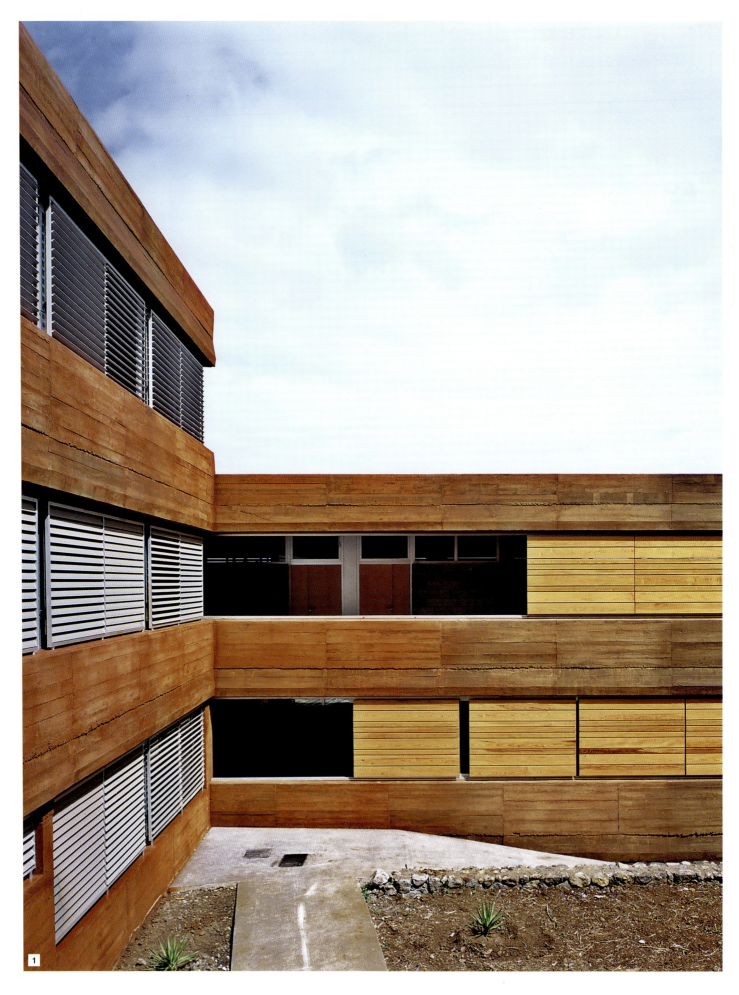

Rafael-Arozarena Preparatory High School
La Orotava, Teneriffa

Architect: AMP arquitectos
Staff: Rafael Hernández Hernández, Andrés Pedreño Vega
Structural design: Arcal
BSE Planning: CITE Diaz y Aguiar

Planning and construction phase: 2004 (completion date)

School type: preparatory high school
Number of students: 690
Grades: 7–10 (compulsory secondary school);
11–12 (baccalaureate)
Age of students: 12–18 years
Number of classes: 38 classes

Plot size: 13,450 square metres
Built-up area: 3,170 square metres
Gross floor space: 7,500 square metres
Gross volume: 20,000 cubic metres
Useful area: 6,700 square metres
Type of energy supply: electricity
Construction costs: 3.4 million euros

With the new preparatory high school in the municipal environs of the picturesque town of La Orotrova in the north of Tenerife in the valley with the same name, the architects AMP arquitectos have implanted a structure of brute dimensions, a construction jutting out into the valley like a gigantic cliff. At the same time they have shown with this building how magnificently modern architecture can harmonize with nature and an almost unspoiled urban architectural inheritance. The street access from all sides and the two circular traffic junctions surrounding the school grounds also contribute to an effect which from an aerial perspective creates the impression of a castle enclosure, in the middle of which the school rises at an altitude of 345 to 365 metres. The free-standing basement level is supported by pillars of a superimposed building structure shaped by ribbon windows. A huge alcove catches the eye within an ensemble in shimmering colours ranging from pastel green to reddish brown washed concrete structures. The colours allow the school complex to merge with the urban cultural landscape layers of La Orotava. The natural stone walls and pathways of the former agricultural terraces contribute to this fusion in the building and the overall design. This chromatic theme continues in the building interior. Disembarking from the bus and walking up a gently rising ramp, the students enter the main entrance directly from the only ground level street access which connects the school with the largest student commuter belt. Right next to the entrance is the library, which thanks to the custodian's office on the ground floor, where the rooms for the school administration are also located, can be easily used after school hours. The school activity occurs for the most part on the two floors directly beneath the entryway: the multi-purpose classrooms are oriented towards the southeast of the settlement boundary of La Orotava, with the specialist classrooms distributed in the open areas. The science, chemistry and biology labs are located on the lower level as well as a computer room on one side and a language lab on the other. The gymnasium set into the cliff is at the north end of the school grounds. This keeps free the inspiring view from the upper terrace of the school over the valley and the Atlantic Ocean.

The building complex fits well into the topography of northern Tenerife. In some places the landscape seems to rest on the building, and somewhere else the landscape seems to flow through the building. Open spaces, sometimes roofed over, are created for play. The volume of the gym is partially sunk in the ground, in order on the one hand to reduce the size and on the other hand to facilitate the view over the valley and the ocean.

The concrete surface is painted with a harmonious blend of pastels, which lend the otherwise massive building a liveliness. In addition, the pastel colours reflect the urban character of La Orotava and the rural areas to the south-west. Although the material which was used to build the school is artificially manufactured, it almost seems that the whole complex emerged from the surroundings. The earthy colours which reflect those surroundings continue into the interior of the school.

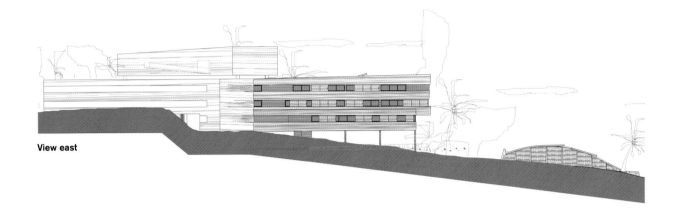
View east

View south

Longitudinal section

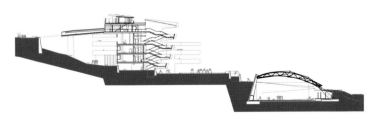
Cross section

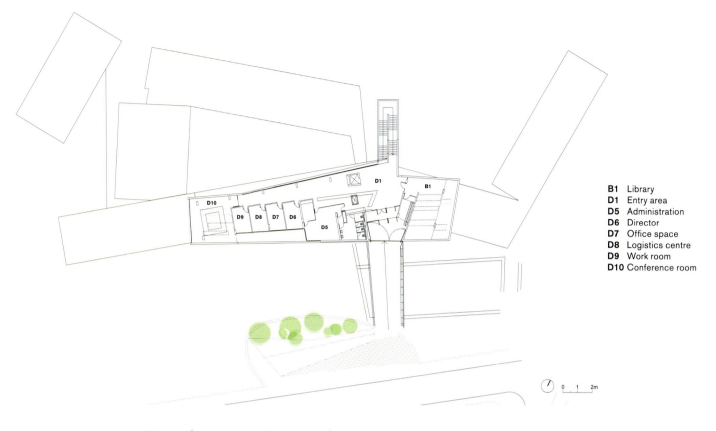

Entry level (+ 369,60 metres above sea level)

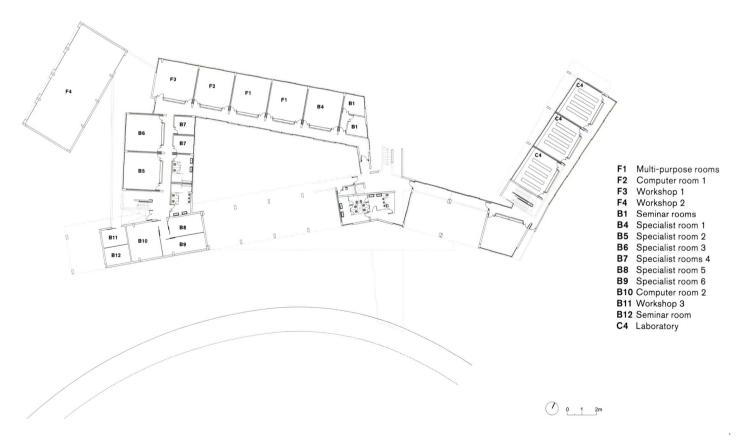

Specialist room level (+ 357,55 metres above sea level)

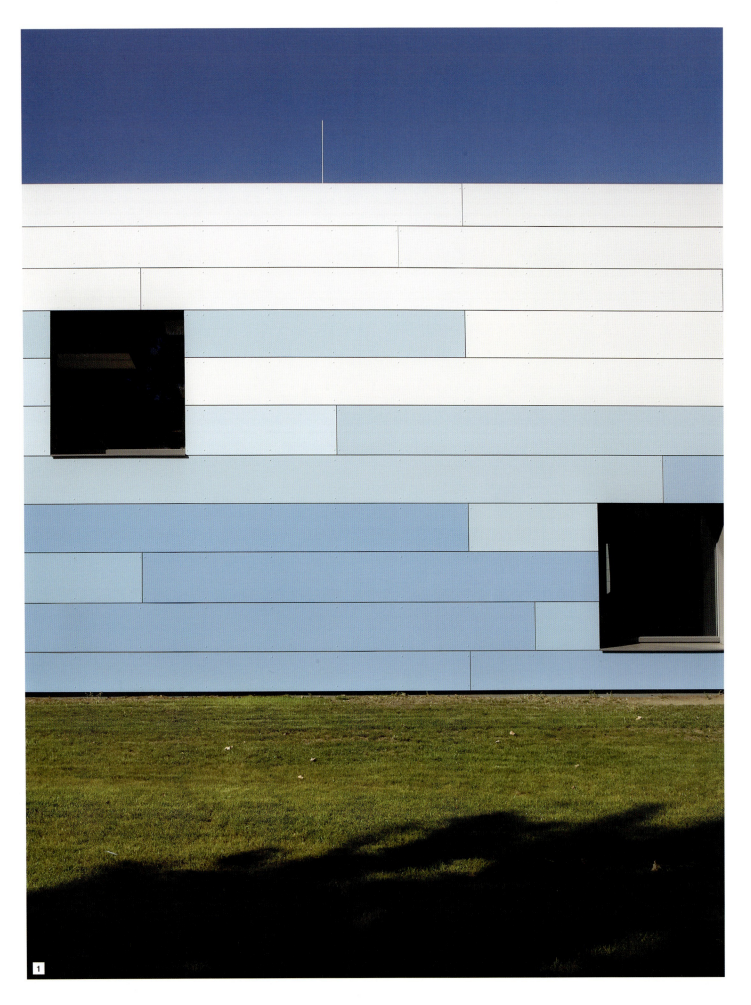

BORG and New Grammar School
Deutsch-Wagram

Architect: franz Architekten
Staff: Anna Gruber, Henning Grahn, Hannah Aufschnaiter, Christine Hax-Noske, Christian Szalay, Joe Suntinger
Structural design: Christian Petz (Vatter & Partner)
BSE Planning: BPS Engineering

Planning and construction phase: 2009–2011

School type: grammar school, Bundesoberstufenrealgymnasium or BORG (Federal Upper Secondary Academic School)
Number of students: 500
Grades: 5–12
Age of students: 10–18 years
Average class size: 25 students
Number of classes: 20 classes

Plot size: 9,650 square metres
Built-up area: 3,056 square metres
Gross floor space: 8,384 square metres
Gross volume: 42,961 cubic metres
Useful area: 7,523 square metres
Type of energy supply: ground water heat pump, photovoltaic, controlled ventilation system
Construction costs: 12.1 million euros

A square gym pokes up from the ground with blue aluminium panels and dissolves in white in the sky. With its own shades of blue the school rectangle extending along the gym competes in reverse order with the sky. The new school complex in Deutsch-Wagram In Lower Austria, not far from the capital of Vienna, together with the city office, kindergarten, the elementary and secondary school, extending along a footpath on the opposite side of the heavily travelled interstate, is the quasi nerve centre of the community. The school building planned by franz architects unites a Federal Upper Secondary Academic School (*Bundesoberstufenrealgymnasium* or BORG) and an extension of the secondary school, which as always, is a key educational opportunity. The conjunction of the two school types (BORG and New Grammar School) represented a mutual enrichment for the town. The architecture of the school is the response to a delicate piece of property which together with the park and pond are considered a valuable place for recreation for the kindergarten and grammar school and the citizens from the area. The school building comprises a broad forecourt with a striking entrance and adjacent wardrobe and auditorium. The three to four storey building fits in with the floor plan and grounds, seeming to float on a circumferential glass ring in the park. Half of the gym disappears in the earth, comprising a comparable dimension with the nearby kindergarten and elementary school. It is accessible for outside sports events with an outer stairway. The architectural fusion of a secondary school and preparatory high school follows the internal separation of standard classrooms and administration. The secondary school is located on the ground floor and the preparatory high school is on the second floor. The common areas of the sciences and art instruction are on the ground floor and in the cellar. The centrepiece of the school is the three storey library, with space for lectures and presentations. The deck chairs and seating steps on the expansive roof terrace are there for relaxation. Daylight floods the building through the two storey break rooms on the west side facing the pond and the four staircases in the east. The compact building's natural lighting, well-insulated building shell, a ventilation unit with groundwater heat recovery and photovoltaic power generation add up to an unusual passive house efficiency.

In order to establish the connection between the school block and the gym, a façade concept was developed which underscores the character of each structure. The embedded gym works its way up from the ground with light blue aluminium panels, dissolving upwards into white, while the floating school structure picks up the neutral white on the nether side of the ceiling, dissolving upwards into a sky blue. The three to four storey building fits well in the floor plan and the shape of the grounds. Mounted on a circumferential glass band, it seems to float in the sea of green.

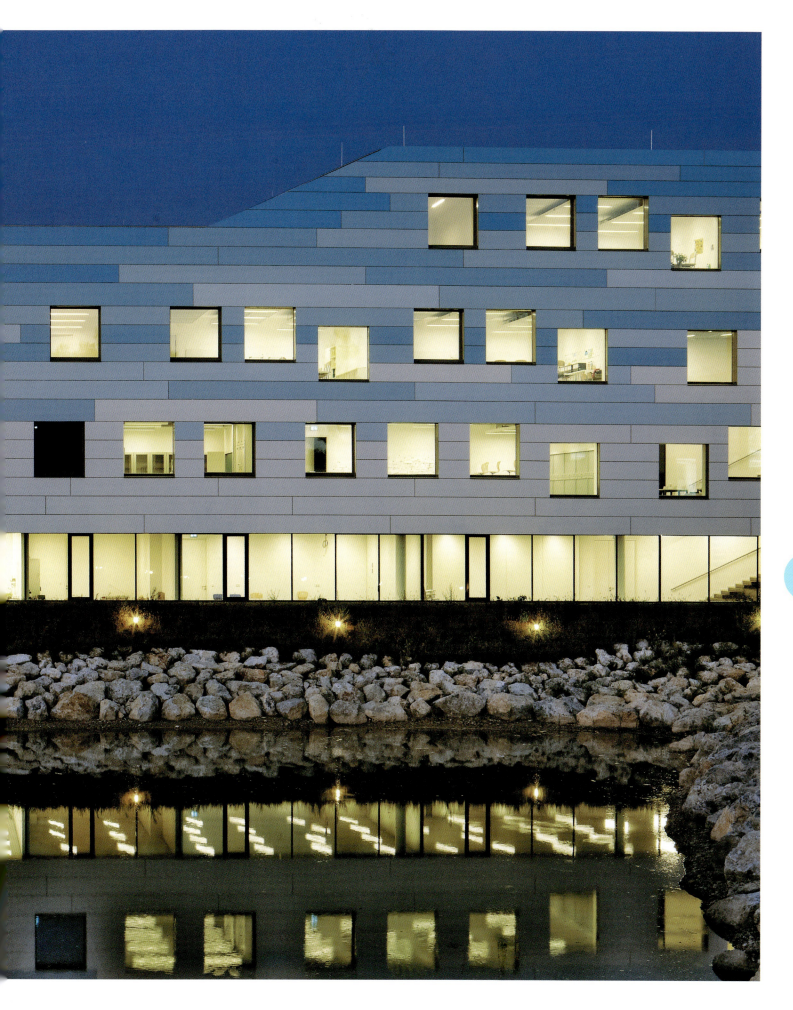

The combination of the New Grammar School and Federal Upper Secondary Academic School (*Bundesoberstufenrealgymnasium* or BORG) had to accommodate the wish list and requirements of different sponsors. The two architects Robert Diem and Erwin Stattner found the solution in the functional separation of the standard classroom and the administrative area (New Grammar School on the first floor and BORG on the second floor). The specialist rooms are jointly used, as are the workshops in the attractive cellar and the school library.

Combining the two school types made possible the use of teaching rooms which are actually not provided for in the curriculum (for instance handicrafts for the Upper Secondary Academic School or a chemistry room for the New Grammar School). The gym serves both school types. It is half embedded in the ground and lit from above and from the side. 175 windows with a standard format of 1.80 × 1.80 metres are designed to respond flexibly to the situations in different rooms like the standard classrooms, the library or the break room. Each classroom has a window with a deep alcove at seat height as a kind of mini break zone. The gym is equipped with the same square windows, creating visual contact for pedestrians with the inside and a view of the pond outside for the spectators in the bleachers.

View west

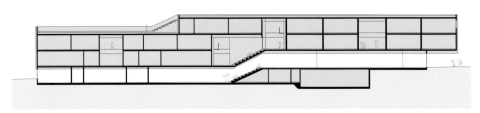

Longitudinal section

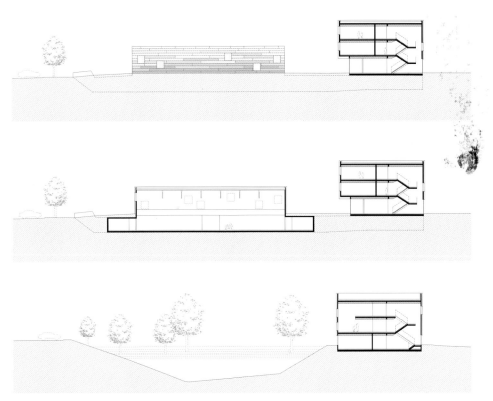

Cross sections

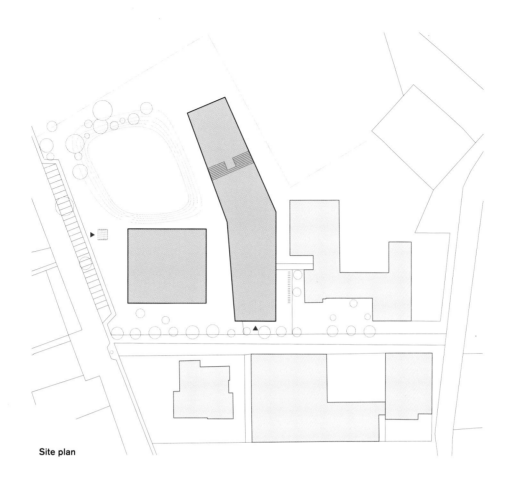

Site plan

1 Auditorium, wardrobe
2 Administration
3 Standard classrooms
4 Special education
5 Library
6 Break room
7 School kitchen
8 Roof terrace
9 Building services
10 Multi-purpose room
11 Gym
12 Equipment room
13 Wardrobes

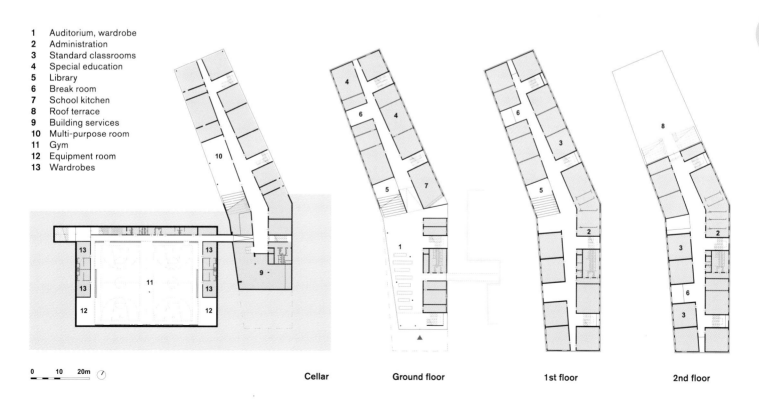

Cellar   Ground floor   1st floor   2nd floor

Floor plans

Mosfellsbær Preparatory High School
Mosfellsbær

400–500

Architect: a2f arkitektar
Staff: Aðalheiður Atladóttir, Árni Þórólfsson, Davið Friðgeirsson, Falk Krüger, Filip Nosek, Svava B. Bragadóttir
Landscape planning: Birkir Einarsson
Structural design: Almenna verkfraedistofan
BSE Planning: Almenna verkfraedistofan, Verkfræðistofa Jóhanns Indriðasonar
Acoustics and sound insulation: Efla verkfræðistofa
Interior wall design: Bryndís Bolladóttir
Planning time / construction time: 2010–2011 / 2011–2013

School type: preparatory high school
Number of students: 400–500
Grades: 11–14
Age of students: 16–20 years
Average class size: 70–80 students per specialist department

Plot size: 12,000 square metres
Built-up area: 1,820 square metres
Gross floor space: 4,100 square metres
Gross volume: 11,680 cubic metres
Useful area: 2,860 square metres
Type of energy supply: district heating
Construction costs: 7.9 million euros

With two parallel buildings, slightly displaced to each other and slanted, the new preparatory high school of the approximately 8,500 inhabitants of Mosfellsbaer, 17 kilometres north of the islands capital of Reykjavik, looks like it has been cut from the landscape. The buildings emerge from the subsurface, partially beneath and partially next to the grassy surroundings. One of the middle sections facing the square on the town side connects the two wings of the building and dramatizes the landscape view as if the school were a fissured offshoot of the mountain range surrounding the town to the east. The glazed middle section ensures that the rooms of the school on the courtyard side and the side facing the square are naturally lit. It is also the ordering principle which determines the patterns of movement in the building, connecting the school with the town in the north and the courtyard to the south. The theme of a building emerging from the landscape is the aesthetic as well as the functional leitmotif of the design, brought to a close with the greened roof. The school is organized in six departments distributed on all floors. All the public facilities, from the reception to the library, canteen, canteen, staff room and the art department are located on the ground floor. The teaching rooms of the building are made of reinforced concrete in an energy efficient and sustainable fashion as self-enclosed units. Since these are built in a lightweight construction mode, it is possible to react quickly to changes in the spatial demands: rooms can be moved, completely broken down or enlarged. Through the varied arrangement of the closed areas a multitude of niches emerges, which can be used by students to talk with one another and to work in. The spatial allowance is as inspiring as the building itself, incorporating as it does learning in an abstracted object of nature. The interior architecture is completely focused on creating the conditions for individual support of the student while doing justice to the uniqueness of each child with his or her varying demands on the learning environment. The school is always in flux, like the nature outside and the preparatory high school itself as construction task.

4

The preparatory high school is part of the landscape and the landscape is part of the school: The bevelled green covered roofs on the side of the courtyard and square conform to the topography of the surroundings. The tripartite building complex combines six faculties which are connected to each other by a glazed centre aisle, which can be used for exhibitions and joint activities. The building is naturally ventilated by sensor controlled openings located behind the curtain wall.

5

The building is based on a single colour concept. The colour design is applied to the acoustic wall elements, seating furniture, lockers and in the coloured glass. It offers a contrast to the more sober work atmosphere of the teaching areas. In addition to exposed concrete, wood and white plasterboard, linoleum and a mineral wool made of light glass laminated mat round out the material scheme.

7

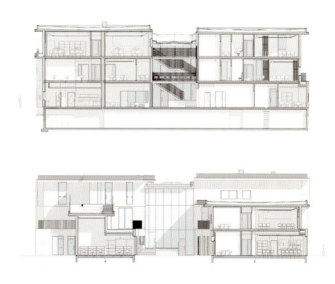

Cross sections

9

Bridges, walkways and openings in the ground support the communication between levels and introduce daylight in the lower floors. The steel construction roof over the entryway is located between the two structures and with its lateral skylights is set off from the façade. The bridges in the reception area are connecting elements and places to linger for both structures. The wood panelling of the façade continues inside the building. Acoustically active surfaces and LED illumination are integrated in the inner façade.

10

SECONDARY SCHOOLS

263

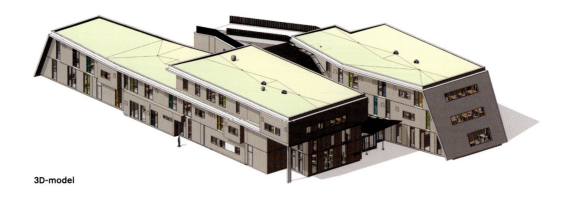
3D-model

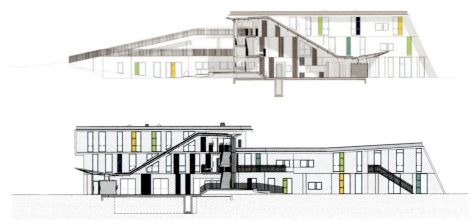
Sectional views

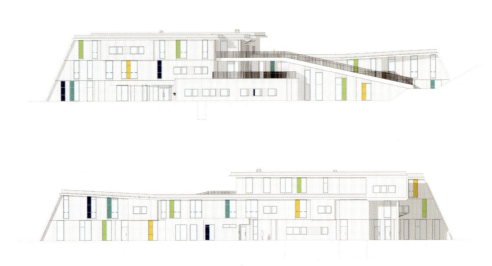
Views

Ground floor

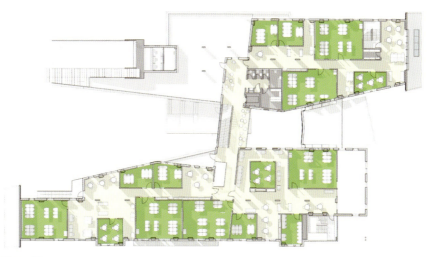
Upper floor

Attic

Råholt Secondary School
Eidsvoll

Architect: *Kristin Jarmund Arkitekter*
Staff: *Kristin Jarmund, Leif Daniel Houck, Kjell Kristian Karlsen, Per-Olav Haugen, Trine Hjelle*
Structural design: *Eiendomsprosjektering*
BSE Planning: *Giert Aasheim, SM-Engineering*

Planning and construction phase: *2004 (completion date)*

School type: *secondary school*
Number of students: *420*
Grades: *7–9*
Age of students: *13–15 years*
Average class size: *20–25 students*

Plot size: *28,800 square metres*
Built-up area: *5,625 square metres*
Gross floor space: *5,200 square metres*
Gross volume: *27,000 cubic metres*
Useful area: *4,900 square metres*
Type of energy supply: *central heating*
Construction costs: *14.2 million euros*
Awards: *Designers Saturday's Best Norwegian Interior Award 2005, National Building Quality Award (special mention)*

The Råholt Secondary School is located in a rural area in Eidsvoll in Norway, about 70 kilometres north of Oslo. The design was chosen in an architecture competition won by the Norwegian office of Kristin Jarmund Arkitekter. The one storey glass pavilion stands on a concrete pedestal seeming to float about a half metre over the grounds. A square floor plan with a side length of 75 metres is the base of the building. The entrance leads to an open atrium located in the centre of the school where students may unwind during breaks. The additional four courtyards inserted in the building volumes allow daylight to penetrate to the more inner layers of the building, providing the teaching rooms with natural illumination. The school operates as a little "city" in the interior. There are no long dark corridors. The floor plan is organized so that the transitions flow from one room to the next. A varied pattern of movement in the school building is generated by the series of open and closed rooms, open spaces and roofed over gardens and intimate squares and meeting points. The toilets and washrooms, auditoriums, staff rooms and specialist rooms are installed in the open floor plan. They define more private teaching zones and public recreation areas. A cylinder shape emerging from the floor plan surfaces is created by the circular auditoriums above the roof outside, lending the building an unmistakable appearance which is visible from afar. The auditoriums have space for a total of 120 students. But they are not just used for the usual teaching purposes. They are also suitable for film presentations, theatre performance and other events.

The glass pavilion seems to float 50 centimetres above the ground on a platform. Seen from outside as a cylinder jutting out over the roof, the circular auditorium has space for 120 students and can be used for theatre performances and film presentations.

In addition to providing natural illumination for the instruction areas, the slices in the building's volume, an atrium located in the middle and four additional courtyards also offer a varied sequence of spaces which make movement through the building a pleasant experience.

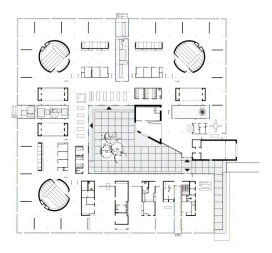

Ground floor

Toilets and washrooms, auditoriums, a staff room and specialist rooms are fixed. Other than that, priority was placed in the design of the school on the shortest possible paths and an open floor plan. The pre-set, for the most part closed rooms, like the circular lecture hall give the building its structure and at the same time provide orientation in the "city" for small children.

Floor use plan ground floor

1	School courtyard
2	Library
3	Kitchen
4	Music room
5	Atrium
6	Staff room
7	Teaching room with auditorium
8	Toilet and washroom
9	Conference room
10	Specialist rooms
11	Administration

The entrance of the square building with a lateral length of 75 metres leads to a school courtyard which provides natural illumination for the teaching rooms, while serving as a meeting point in the fresh air during breaks. Movement through the rooms is expedited by a detailed colour concept which creates a special atmosphere inside the building.

Hans von Raumer Grammar School
Dinkelsbühl

Architect: Fischer Architekten
Staff: Florian Roggatz, Sigrid Reischböck, Ralf Emmerling, Markus Seifert, Sibylle Staltmayr
Local building supervision: Stirn + Schremm
Structural design: Ingenieurbüro Herrmann
BSE Planning: Ebert Ingenieure, Planungsbüro E-Technik

Planning and construction phase: 2001–2005

School type: grammar school
Number of students: 244
Grades: 5–10
Age of students: 10–15 years
Average class size: 32 students
Number of classes: 16 classes

Plot size: 25,900 square metres
Built-up area: 2,420 square metres
Gross floor space: 4,325 square metres
Gross volume: 19,725 cubic metres
Useful area: 2,884 square metres
Type of energy supply: wood chip heating
Construction costs: 5.1 million euros
Awards: honourable mention BDA (Association of German Architects) Prize ›Gutes Bauen in Franken‹ 2006

The grammar school built in 2005 is located on the periphery of Dinkelsbühl in the immediate vicinity of the famous historical old town. Several schools from the 1960s to the 1990s which were placed in a network in the context of the 1988 State Garden Show extend along a park-like "school belt". For the time being, the Hans von Raumer Grammar School, planned by the Munich office of Fischer Architekten, is the last building block in the belt. The two storey building reacts with its angular shape to the exposed location on the edge of town: the 16 classrooms on the inner side of the two level facility orient to Segring Valley and the medieval tower of Segringen. The fine arts, housekeeping and science departments are located on the north and east side. The interconnected music and multi-purpose rooms on the ground floor and the administrative area on the 2nd floor border the central break hall. Light-coloured exposed concrete surrounds the steel and glass construction of the two storey auditorium and the adjacent teaching area with its wood-framed windows. As a climatic and spatial threshold a veranda-like area in front on the side facing the sun creates a distance to the public areas and the schoolyard. The lawned areas in front of the schoolyard provide additional distance to the teaching rooms. The materiality inside is limited almost exclusively to the reinforced concrete, larch-wood and steel used in the façades. Large area facings (hallway wardrobes and cupboards, the surfaces of the flexible partitions in the auditorium, hallway administration wall display cabinet) each in an Olympic colour coordinated with the space, fill out the materials concept. In close collaboration with the teaching staff, flexible classrooms with individual desks on casters were developed in order to create a flexible blackboard system on three sides and a uniform direct-indirect illumination for individually designed teamwork instead of the classical teacher-up-front arrangement (with a corresponding spatial conception). The energy is supplied from the nearby wood chip burning power plant.

Larch wood (floor-high windows) and white pigmented exposed concrete along with steel (sun protection construction) are the key materials of the angular building in the west of the Dinkelsbühl school centre. The L-shaped structure with a central two storey auditorium forms a courtyard which lets the gaze wander in the direction of the Segring Valley with its medieval tower. An athletics field is integrated in the schoolyard. The overhanging concrete slabs of the terrace and canopy offer a spatial and climatic buffer zone between the break areas and classrooms.

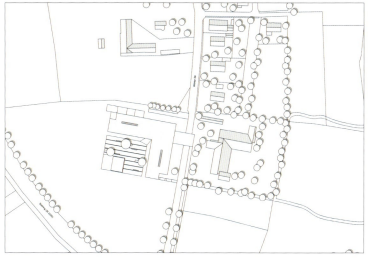

Site plan

The two storey auditorium with views into the surroundings is the spatial centre of the school building. A bridge-like walkway connects the two wings of classrooms. The materials canon of the building shell (exposed concrete, steel and larch wood) continues inside the building and is augmented by the floor surfaces (white magnesia flooring in the auditorium halls) and panelling: The different colours of the classroom walls give the access areas of the school their own identity.

The rooms designed by Fischer Architekten using the concept of the flexible developed classrooms are not rigidly determined by a single teaching situation. Instead, they offer space for individual group and team work. This flexibility is made possible with light, adjustable desks on casters, movable blackboards which can be mounted on three sides of the room and adjustable illumination, which provides direct or indirect illumination depending on the teaching situation.

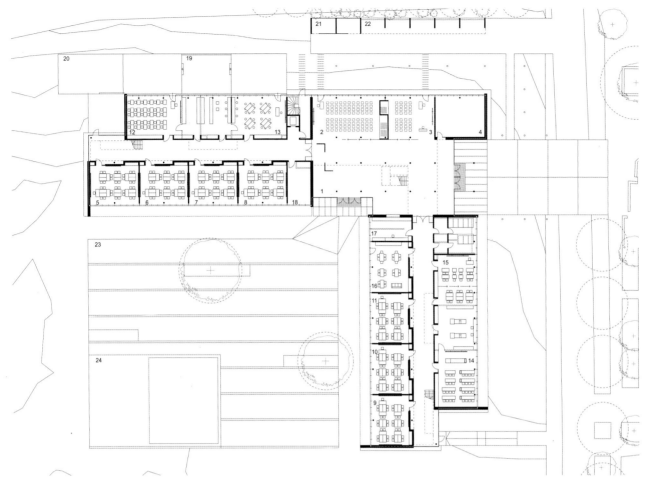

Floor plan ground floor

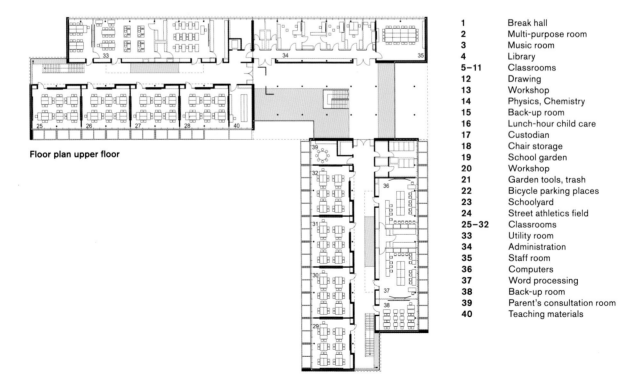

Floor plan upper floor

1	Break hall
2	Multi-purpose room
3	Music room
4	Library
5–11	Classrooms
12	Drawing
13	Workshop
14	Physics, Chemistry
15	Back-up room
16	Lunch-hour child care
17	Custodian
18	Chair storage
19	School garden
20	Workshop
21	Garden tools, trash
22	Bicycle parking places
23	Schoolyard
24	Street athletics field
25–32	Classrooms
33	Utility room
34	Administration
35	Staff room
36	Computers
37	Word processing
38	Back-up room
39	Parent's consultation room
40	Teaching materials

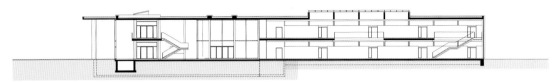
Longitudinal section

View west

View north

Cross sections

View east

Reinhold Burger School
Berlin

Architect: Numrich Albrecht Klumpp
Staff: Timo Klumpp (project director)
Structural design: Laschinski Ingenieure
BSE Planning: EST Energie System Technik

Planning and construction phase: 2006–2009

School type: integrated secondary school
Number of students: 413
Grades: 7–10
Age of students: 12–16 years
Average class size: 26 students
Number of classes: 16 classrooms

Plot size: 3,500 square metres
Built-up area: 890 square metres
Gross floor space: 3,950 square metres
Gross volume: 17,134 cubic metres
Useful area: 2,000 square metres
Type of energy supply: district heating
Construction costs: approx. 2.9 million euros

In the framework of the Berlin school reform in 2010 the secondary school, middle school and comprehensive school were combined in the new Integrated Secondary School as an all-day school. Educational reform required new spatial concepts. The Reinhold Burger School in Berlin-Pankow is one example. It was converted from a junior high school to a secondary school with an inviting design which meets contemporary spatial requirements. With its brick clinker façade the listed school building, a five storey brick building built from 1899 to 1902, documents the Blankenstein school buildings from the end of the 1800s. The building was originally free-standing on the Breite Straße side. In 1902 the Pankow Rathaus opened, whereby the north façade of the school was furnished with auditorium windows unusually high for the time. The school building receded to the second row in the block interior, with the entrance moved to *Neue Schönholzer Straße* via the schoolyard. In the course of time increased space requirements lead to two annexes and an additional expansion with a gym and classrooms. In 2008 Numrich Albrecht Klumpp Architekten took on the challenge of a renewed conversion and expansion with a canteen and break hall. Interstices and transitional spaces were viewed as strategic space potential. Today instead of the old central toilet facility in the basement, the new arrangement in the open spatial unit with a break hall and canteen provides the school with a living mid-point and an enhanced recreational quality. An expansive stairway on the entryway level conveys the height difference and provides an opportunity to sit during the breaks. From here via the two stairways on the sides the students can reach their classrooms. Hallways are now connected, with modern toilet and washrooms installed on each floor. The fire code required an additional emergency stairway on the west façade. The classrooms were renovated, acoustically tuned up and equipped with WLAN and a media facility. Specialist rooms now occupy the former location of the custodian's apartment. As the mid-point for music, theatre and school events, the auditorium was rebuilt in its historic dimension. The listed façade was also re-furbished.

The house façade had been sprayed with unauthorized graffiti before the renovation. The carefully transformed development of the spatial potentials is a process that the student can experience, with the conversion taking place during school operations. The students' participation in the development of a colour concept in the framework of the art instruction enhances their identification with school. To date it represents a successful anti-vandalism measure.

Site plan

Conversion projects require innovation. New uses, interstices and transition areas become strategic space potential. The former central toilet facility in the basement was converted into an open entryway. Today it is a lively school meeting point with a high quality of relaxation.

1 Lunch Hall
2 Kitchen
3 Foyer

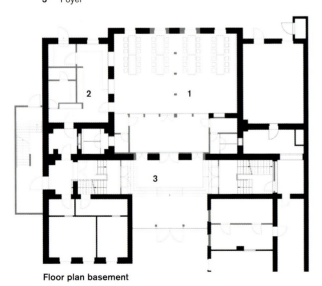

Floor plan basement

In the course of the conversion the auditorium façade with its unusually high windows was rebuilt. The event room is now the centrepiece of the school. The colour concept of the school was also used for the lateral stairways which lead to the newly designed teaching rooms.

Special Schools

Bogotá • Columbia	292
Zurich • Switzerland	300
Lausanne • Switzerland	312
Chemnitz • Germany	320
Regensburg • Germany	330

Gerardo Molina School
Bogotá

Architect: Giancarlo Mazzanti
Staff: Andrés Sarmiento, Juan Manuel Gil, Gina Amado, María Constanza Saade, Carlos Melo, Alberto Aranda, Ana María González, Jorge Gómez, Manuel Mendoza, Edgar Mazo
Structural design: Sergio Tobon

Planning and construction phase: 2004–2008

School type: pre-school, primary school, secondary school, preparatory high school
Number of students: 1,400
Grades: 1–11
Age of students: 6–18 years
Number of classes: 10 classes

Plot size: 8,000 square metres
Construction costs: approx. 3.0 million euros

Awards: Mención Bienal Colombiana de Arquitectura

Imagine the different pieces of a set of building blocks. The architect Giancarlo Mazzanti neatly sorted them out and put them all together into one school with the changing constellation of the three most frequently repeating building types. The building extends over a trapezoidal plot in a suburb of Bogotá, the capital of Columbia, like an opened chain. What looks like a piece of designer jewellery with a dark stone from an aerial perspective, is upon closer examination a single school snugly fit into the urban and topographical situation. The school is unmistakable among the teeming lower buildings on the gentle hills of the high plateau. The entire architectural shape of the ensemble comprises a long courtyard opening up to the street with two striking wing buildings. It is composed in order to engage all the senses in learning. Everything starts with motion, because the connecting links between the structures with their overhanging upper floors also determine the direction the student follows within the building. The straight connecting links ensure a straight-forward motion, while the 130 degree turned modules allow for a change in direction. These spatial modules set on a platform in opposition to each other embody not only the character of their surroundings, which Giancarlo Mazzanti draws into the school from the immediate surroundings. Together with the school courtyard they are structures belonging to a site of community life, which along with the library, auditorium, cafe and multifunctional class room in the wings is also open for events sponsored by the neighbourhood. The ground floor of the chain module houses three teaching rooms, with the staff room and specialist classrooms located above in the overhanging square structures. Built in 2008 as a community mid-point, the school is more than a construction in the spirit of the classical Modern. It much more expresses the social purpose of architecture, which together with good social infrastructure can also improve the living conditions of the less privileged citizens. With its identity creating character the architecture creates the framework for that function.

294

The strung together school complex designed by Giancarlo Mazzanti stands out from the monotone row housing in yellow and red tones and small-scale, heterogeneous multiple family dwellings built with exposed brick. With its floor level windows and the brightly coloured parapet surfaces, overhanging upper floors on the city side offer an expansive view of the surroundings, while the rear of the building, with its narrow horizontal ribbon windows is oriented to the more private school courtyard.

Section

In addition to providing an adequate supply of daylight, the wrap-around ground floor glass façade with wooden privacy screen in the form of vertical slats puts on an impressive light show by night, when the building glowing from within is used by the residents. The pre-school and multi-purpose room receives additional daylight from the circular openings which emerge from the roof of the ground floor like cylinders. Pillar-like shapes are used in this area as steel supports and as wooden elements sticking out of the ground. They give an impression of being surrounded by tree trunks.

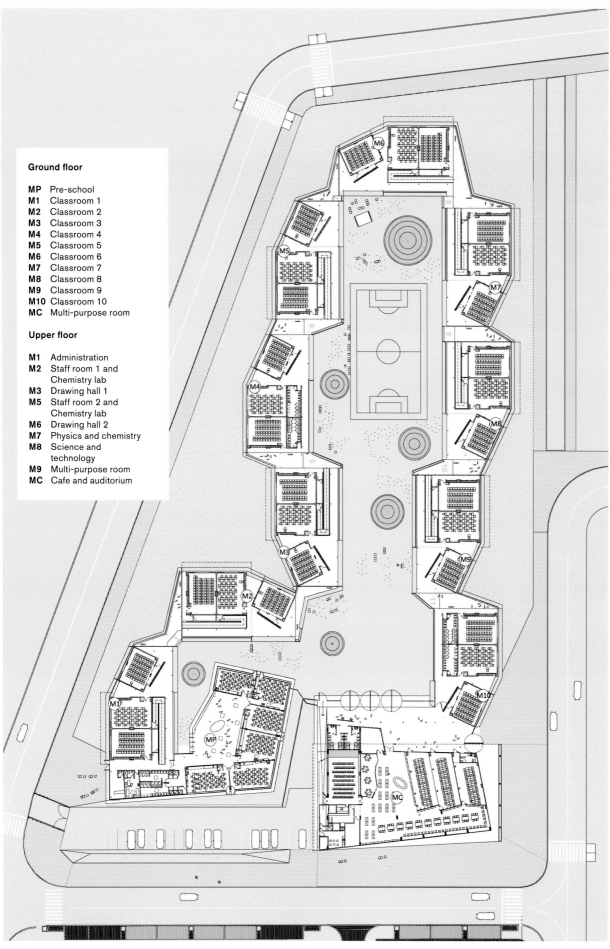

Ground floor

- **MP** Pre-school
- **M1** Classroom 1
- **M2** Classroom 2
- **M3** Classroom 3
- **M4** Classroom 4
- **M5** Classroom 5
- **M6** Classroom 6
- **M7** Classroom 7
- **M8** Classroom 8
- **M9** Classroom 9
- **M10** Classroom 10
- **MC** Multi-purpose room

Upper floor

- **M1** Administration
- **M2** Staff room 1 and Chemistry lab
- **M3** Drawing hall 1
- **M5** Staff room 2 and Chemistry lab
- **M6** Drawing hall 2
- **M7** Physics and chemistry
- **M8** Science and technology
- **M9** Multi-purpose room
- **MC** Cafe and auditorium

Floor plan ground floor

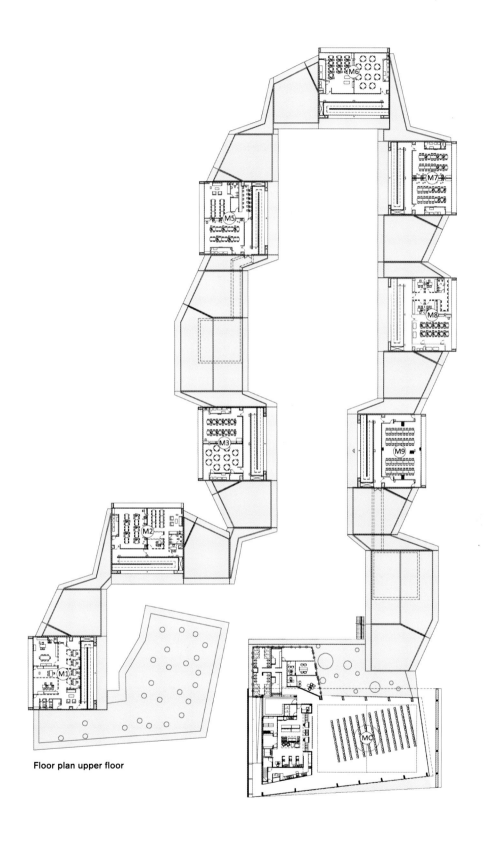

Floor plan upper floor

Leutschenbach School
Zurich

Architect: Christian Kerez
Staff: Christian Scheidegger (project director)
Structural design: Dr. Schwartz Consulting
BSE Planning: Waldhausener Haustechnik, Meili Tanner Partner

Planning and construction phase: 2002–2009

School type: primary and secondary school, kindergarten and therapeutic pedagogy
Number of students: 350
Grades: 1–6 (primary level), 7–9 (secondary level I)
Age of students: 4–16 years
Average class size: 21 students
Number of classes: 15 classes + 3 (therapeutic pedagogy)

Plot size: 16,500 square metres
Built-up area: 1,200 square metres
Gross floor space: 9,840 square metres
Gross volume: 51,000 cubic metres
Useful area: 7,430 square metres
Type of energy supply: district heating from nearby waste incinerator, mechanical ventilation unit with heat recovery
Construction costs: 32.9 million euros

Awards: European Steel Design Award 2011, Swiss Steel Construction Prize (Prix Acier) 2009, Best Swiss Building (›Goldener Hase‹) of the magazine ›Hochparterre‹ 2009

One of the largest school buildings in the area is located on the outskirts of the Swiss financial capital of Zurich. It employs a most unusual building technology which has become known well beyond the borders of Switzerland. It all started when the Zurich architect Christian Kerez refrained from the usual horizontal orientation of the functional school building, instead stacking the classroom floors on top of each other. The result is a five storey school tower made of glass held together by a steel frame joined by seemingly paper thin floor slabs. The pièce de résistance is the triple gym, whose framework is supported by just six steel tripods on the ground floor. The ground floor, surrounded by a frameless glass band, is set so far back that it creates the impression of a building floating above the ground. In other locations high buildings are erected for the thrill of the height or because there is no more space available on the plot. The school tower idea here is based on the desire to retain the breadth of the landscape together with the depth of the plot. The classrooms are located in a three storey structure with the goal of keeping the interior rooms to the smallest possible common denominator. The connecting link between this three storey structure and a framework surrounded gym is a giant glazed foyer on the fourth floor. From here all the social areas like the auditorium, library, staff room etc. can be reached. With its seven metres of height and impressive view over the roofs of Zurich, the gym is a spectacular culmination of a spatial staging present throughout the whole school. The classrooms are connected by a central stairway in the core of the building and are acoustically separated from the access area and from each other only by industrial glass. This construction allows daylight to penetrate deep into the interior of the building. At the same time the encounters of the students from the adjacent rooms can be seen in silhouette. The classrooms look more like studios, with the light pouring in and room heights of 360 centimetres. The purist design has created everything that is light, expansive and clear. The structure reflects the basic pedagogical idea of an open learning workshop.

The glass tower between the rail line and waste incinerator is a perfect building constructed from materials used which make it easy for children to grasp. From both sides of the classrooms on three floors as well as from the recreation area in the middle the completely transparent building provides a spectacular view. The escape routes designed as break areas also offer the possibility for teaching outdoors.

302

With its comparable height of seven metres and wrap-around framework the gym on the roof of a school building indeed resembles the teaching floors below it. But the school tower is not divided in two parts. It consists of several repeating access levels. In addition to the unique view from the basketball court, one has the distinct feeling of being in "seventh heaven".

SPECIAL SCHOOLS

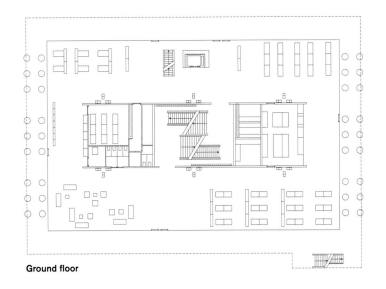

Ground floor

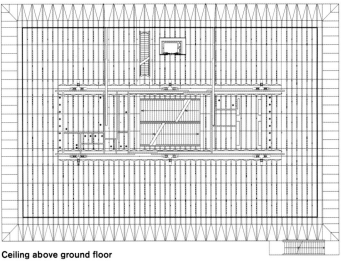

Ceiling above ground floor

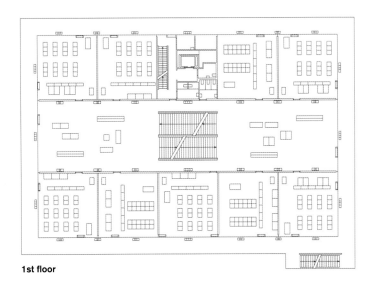

1st floor

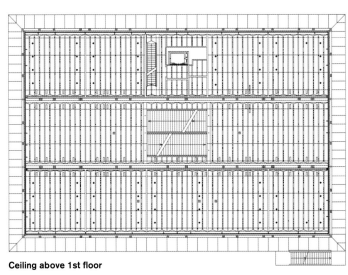

Ceiling above 1st floor

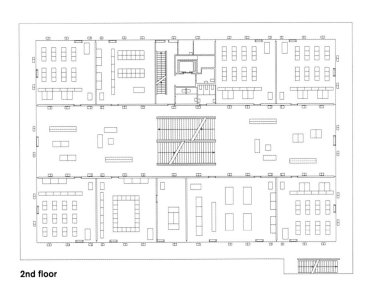

2nd floor

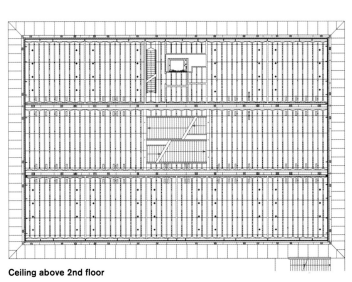

Ceiling above 2nd floor

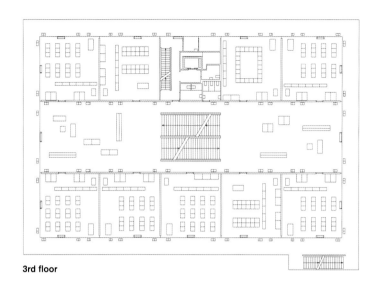
3rd floor

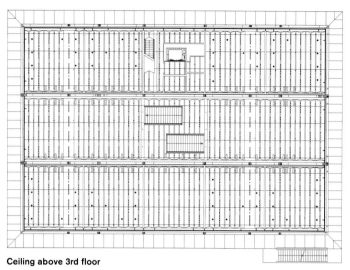
Ceiling above 3rd floor

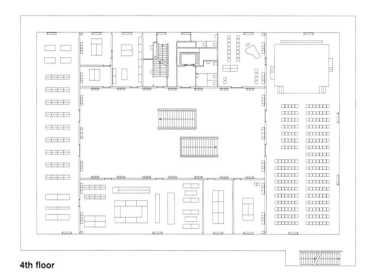
4th floor

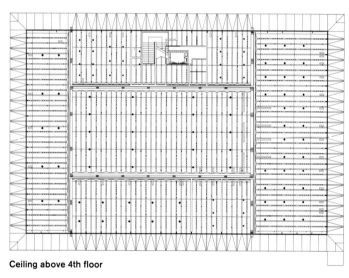
Ceiling above 4th floor

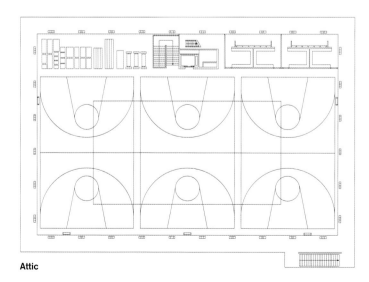
Attic

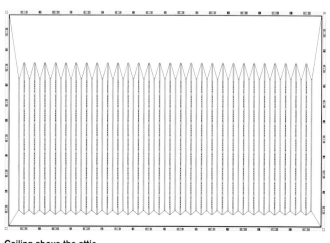
Ceiling above the attic

SPECIAL SCHOOLS

The entire weight of the building was distributed via framework elements on just six three-legged supports on the ground floor, whose construction was reduced to the absolute minimum. The fourth floor cross girders act like a kind of desktop, from which the whole façade of the three storey teaching section is suspended. The gym provides the termination with its room-high wrap-around framework.

Model photo

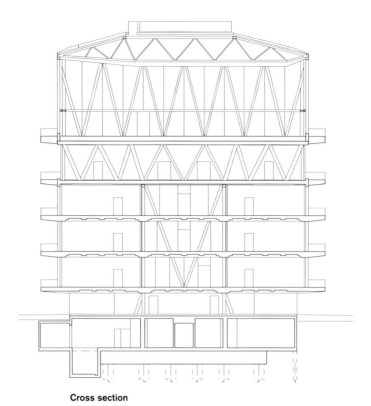

Cross section

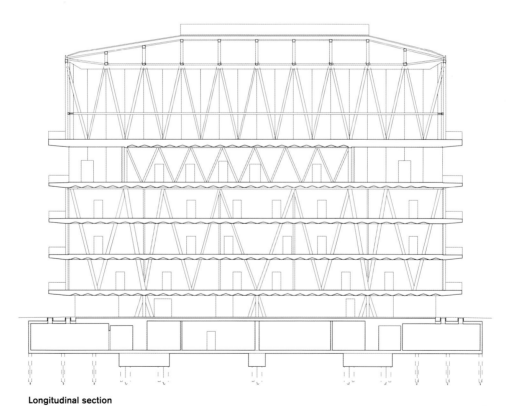

Longitudinal section

SPECIAL SCHOOLS

311

Swiss Administrative Academy
Lausanne

Architect: Geninasca & Delefortrie
Staff: Philippe von Bergen, Daniel Gobbo, Danilo Ermoli, Valérie Mathez, André Sundhoff
Structural design: INGENI Lausanne
BSE Planning: Weinmann-Energies, BETELEC

Planning and construction phase: 2007–2010

School type: Graduate School for State Administration
Number of students: 200
Number of classes: 3 classroom, 5 seminar rooms

Plot size: 6,000 square metres
Built-up area: 1,950 square metres
Gross floor space: 3,900 square metres
Gross volume: 18,840 cubic metres
Useful area: 1,950 square metres
Type of energy supply: heat pump for heating and cooling
Construction costs: approx. 13.0 million euros

With the metamorphosis of the former pharmaceutical warehouse from the 1970s into a cadre school for public administrators, the architects succeeded approximately in squaring the circle. The new tenant, the *Institut de hautes études en administration publique* (University Institute for Public Administration, or IDHEAP), gives Switzerland the capability of a university level teaching and research institute for public and state related administration. As an autonomous facility the IDHEAP, whose Switzerland-wide commission is closely connected with the *Eidgenössische Technische Hochschule* (ETH) and the University of Lausanne, especially in the post-graduate training of persons who are already employed in public or state related service. The new facility which has emerged from the skin of the old building is an osmosis between space and light. A composition of spatial depth and breadth in connection with intimate work areas has been created with the minimalistic model of monastery cells transforming the former ennui into a fascinating tension. The matter-of-fact institutional logo is a tailored fit with the broad, floor-wide white bands which optically structure the building in alternation with the ribbon windows. An elegantly polished, light ponderousness in combination with the dark, glazed ease are attributes which determine the architecture. The rooms are grouped around a green courtyard. The tasteful, interior architecture harmonizes appropriately with the noble designer furnishings, lending the building as a whole the character of a modern institute of learning. Additional daylight enters the foyer through the glass roof, to which in parallel a stairway leads to the library in the academy. The architects Laurent Geninasca and Bernard envisioned an architecture for the conversion of the warehouse which might embody a university of the future. Although the original building stood in crass contradiction to this goal, it was possible to build something that indeed looked to the future, without denying the origins of the former warehouse. The result is home to the needs of teachers, researchers and administration personnel, built according to modern ecological building principles as a model for sustainable building transformation.

The jury decided in favour of the design submitted for the competition in 2007 by Geninasca & Delefortrie not just because the architects perfectly fulfilled the requirements, but also because they made minimal interventions in the existing surroundings. The main entrance is deliberately accessible via one stair or a ramp. With a direct connection to the subway and the largest station of the bicycle rental shop Lausanne Roule, the Swiss Administration Academy is also very automobile-free accessible.

While the light suffused ground floor provides space for the "production of knowledge" as a work area for the teachers and researchers, the rooms for the "transmission of knowledge", like the lecture rooms, auditorium and library are located one floor below. The administration occupies the adjacent part of the building that was formerly used as the pharmaceutical storage for administrative purposes.

5

6

7

SPECIAL SCHOOLS

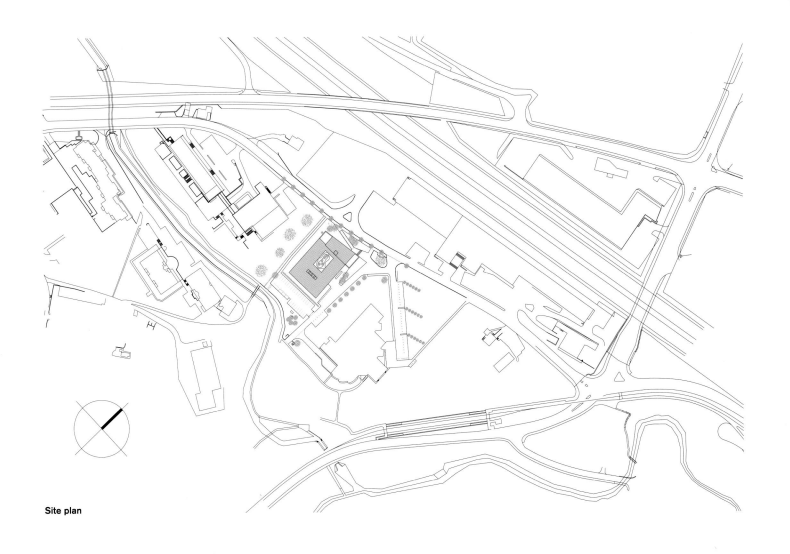
Site plan

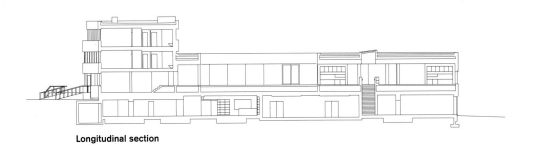
Longitudinal section

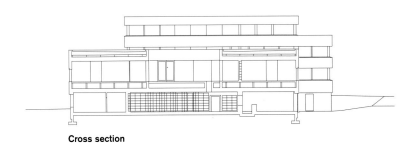
Cross section

1st floor

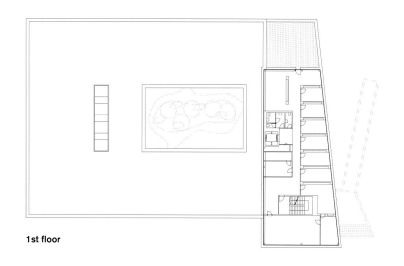

Ground floor

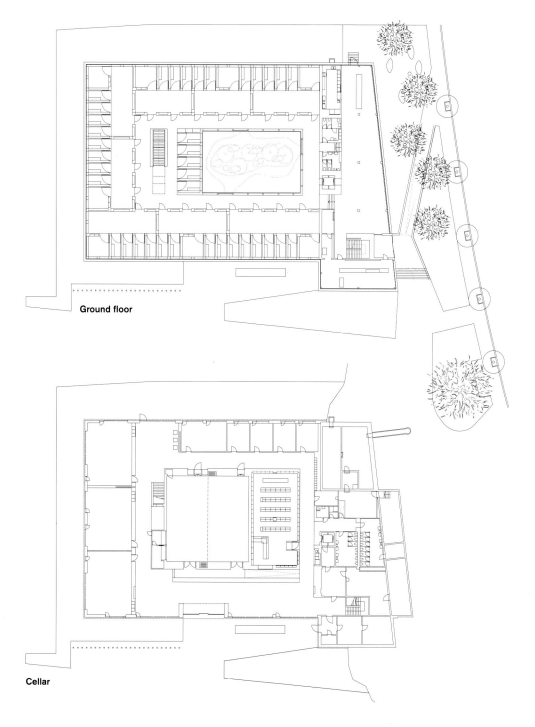

Cellar

SPECIAL SCHOOLS

State School For the Blind and Visually Handicapped
Chemnitz

Architect: bhss Architekten
Staff: Stefan Hermus (project director), Robert Laser, Gerd-Christian Wagner, Stefan Blässe, Georg Blüthner
Structural design: Henneker, Zillinger Ingenieure Leipzig
BSE Planning: Ingenieurbüro Krusche + Grünewald

Planning and construction phase: 2005–2007

School type: pre-school, primary school, grammar school, school for the advancement of learning and classes with focus on mental development (new building)
Number of students: 165
Grades: 1–12
Age of students: 5–18 years
Average class size: 5–11 students
Number of classes: 26 classes (total)

Plot size: 17.9 hectares
Built-up area: 1,115 square metres
Gross floor space: 5,996 square metres
Gross volume: 21,000 cubic metres
Useful area: 3,220 square metres
Type of energy supply: district heating
Construction costs: 9.3 million euros

More than one hundred years ago the State School for the Blind and Visually Handicapped in the north-west of Chemnitz was opened in the then modern Art Nouveau Royal Saxon State Institute for Education of the Blind and Feeble-Minded. Several buildings spreading out over 60 hectares are distributed pavilion-like on expansive park grounds in a loose pattern of buildings standing at right angles to each other, which in turn form smaller, more private spaces. The thorough renovation of the nine listed historical buildings was completed in 2010. The new building planned by bhss Architekten on the north-west end of the middle axis of the park ensemble was built to accommodate the needs of severely handicapped students and those with learning disabilities. Except for the cellar, the whole four storey building complex consisting of two asymmetrically displaced building rectangles, with an entryway at their junction, main stairway and elevator is handicapped accessible. In the north and south the two functionally separate facilities form a protected open area with their own entrances. The northern buildings on the ground floor house the therapy rooms for physiotherapy, sight training and mobility training, while the rooms for administration and various subjects are located in the southern building complex. The emergency escape balconies for the horizontal evacuation surrounding the floors also provide an open air weather-proof opportunity to relax for the severely handicapped. With the aid of these balconies the exterior soundscape, wind and odours from the surrounding parks are wafted into classrooms. The architecture of the building supports the school profile, which is focussed on the transmission of basic sensual and social abilities. As opposed to the usual practice the classrooms are oriented to the south, which is required because of the special programs. A colour concept for the visually handicapped children is designed to facilitate navigation in the school.

The functionally distinct but architecturally connected entryway structures are located at the interfaces of the two asymmetrically offset building segments. The overhanging circumferential emergency exit balconies of the southward oriented classrooms can also be used as open air recreational space. They also orient the teaching space to the surrounding park.

SPECIAL SCHOOLS

5

6

A colour concept ranging from pea green to ice blue was developed on the basis of the change in seasons. It serves to improve the orientation of the visually handicapped children in the room. Each level has accents of its own basic mood, like that radiated by the coloured wardrobes in the hallway.

The inclined access creates a connection between the group room, toilet and washroom, and classroom including the wardrobe and expedites the vertical evacuation of the students in an emergency. Underfloor heating on all floors guarantees a high quality of life for the handicapped children.

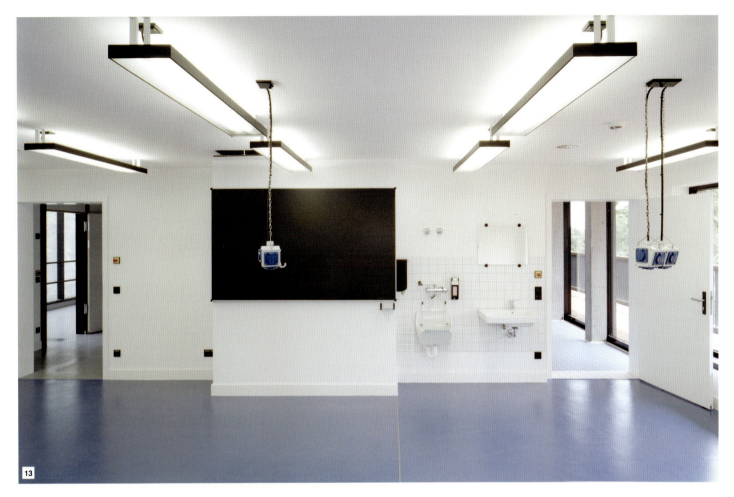

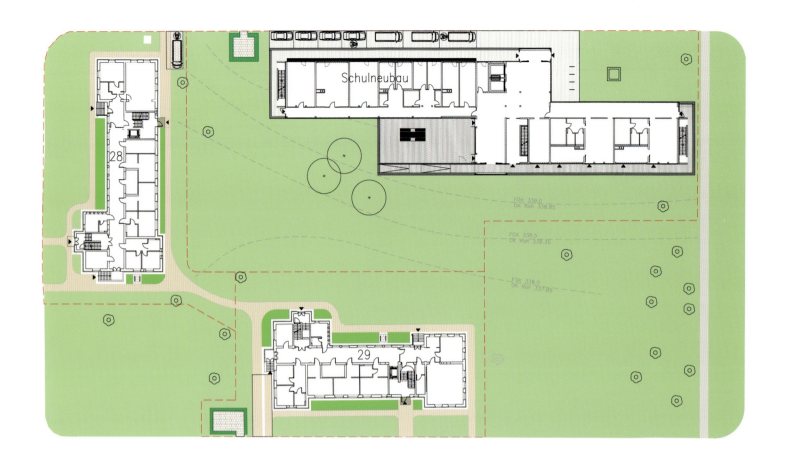

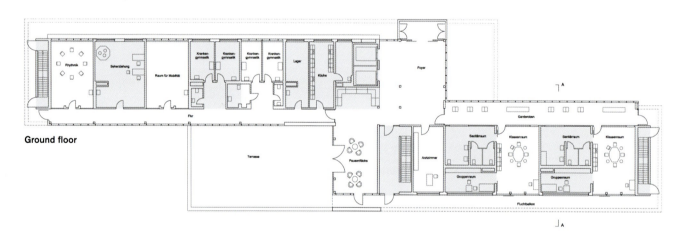

Ground floor

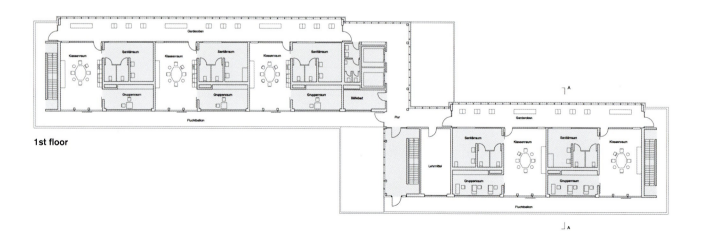

1st floor

North façade colour study

South façade

Section

School for the Blind
Regensburg

Architect: *Georg · Scheel · Wetzel Architekten*
Staff: *Martina Betzold, Florian Gayer-Lesti, Joao Concalo Pereira, Nico Kranenburg, Katharina Nailis, Katja Wemhöner*
Structural design: *ifb Frohloff Staffa Kühl Ecker, Dr. Lammel*
BSE Planning: *IB Meyer, IB Martin, REA Reinhart, Engert, Albert*

Planning and construction phase: *2000–2006*

School type: *primary school, secondary school, vocational school*
Number of students: *120*
Grades: *1–13*
Age of students: *3–21 years*
Average class size: *4–6 students*
Number of classes: *24 classes*

Plot size: *22,191 square metres*
Built-up area: *6,575 square metres*
Gross floor space: *11,800 square metres*
Gross volume: *43,000 cubic metres*
Useful area: *5,911 square metres*
Type of energy supply: *gas condensing boiler, ventilation with heat recovery*
Construction costs: *approx. 12.6 million euros*

Awards: *Nomination for the BDA (Association of German Architects) Prize Bayern 2006, Hans Schäfer Prize of the BDA, Brick Architecture Award 2007, Unipor Architecture Prize 2008, Best Architect 2008, Regensburg Architecture Prize 2009*

The Foundation Institute For the Blind in Regensburg is a facility where blind and visually handicapped children, for youth and young adults from 3 to 21 years of age, are offered different kinds of support. They can live in, are cared for around the clock and / or attend the in-house school. The foundation grounds are located on the western exit from Regensburg, in the direct vicinity of a new residential district. Nearby is the listed ensemble of Prüfening with its characteristic limestone walls surrounding the gardens. The foundation and royal house of Thurn and Taxis initiated the competition for the new building won by the firm of Georg · Scheel · Wetzel Architekten. Not satisfied with simply referring to the existing topographic situation, the architects concentrated on the special organisational-functional demands of the users. Since the severely visually impaired and multiply handicapped children are dependent on outside help and therefore need access to the different spaces without thresholds, the school areas were built on one floor. The children climb the slope in minimal steps and work their way into the intermediate courtyards in the landscape. Flat ramps ease access to the buildings. Dry walls surround the ensemble and shape the grounds into a relief, from which the building rises. Light-coloured exposed concrete and green-grey coal fired brick for the closed wall surfaces coordinate with the raw walls. A two storey connecting structure together with a free-standing building housing the gym and a therapeutic bath comprises the framework for the polygon shaped forecourt operating as the foyer of the foundation. The main entrances of the complex are located on the level of this slightly rising plateau which follows the topography of the grounds, where the children are bussed in. From there one may reach the school areas on the ground floor and the ramps leading to the large corridor, with access to the specialist rooms. The pathways are characterized by variously designed open spaces in the asymmetric construction. The main corridor opens up completely to the forecourt, while the halls of the school areas are oriented to the garden courtyards below. In addition to focusing the gradual transition into the landscape, the inner organisation comprises a simple system of orientation based on hierarchical pathways which are recognizable for the children. The natural lighting is also an aid here, as is the topography in the house: the slope assumes the role of an organizing criterion.

Three staircases were built for the access to the administration and therapy rooms on the 2nd floor – one on each end and one in the middle of the building. These are equipped with a wheelchair negotiable elevator surrounded by the staircase. A long ramp interrupted by flights of stairs defines the grounds, providing a smooth transition to the slope.

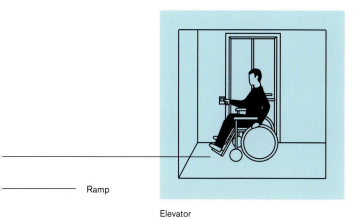

Elevator

Ramp

Ramp

Lavatory

Ramp

The thresholdless freedom of movement is organized from the school's slope location with its natural light conditions all the way inside the school. The hallways face the courtyard gardens, which with its hierarchical routing provide a simple orientation system for the visually impaired and multiply handicapped children.

In order to accommodate their needs, the transitions to all spaces were built without thresholds. In addition hand railings of various heights provide assistance for independent movement through the facility. As an enhancement of the haptic and visual experience, rods with movable coloured plastic balls were mounted in some of the walls. They are intended to encourage the children to take in their environment more playfully. Their installation, which also serves as orientation, was created by the artist Christiane Möbus.

A school which seems to have sprung up from the landscape. The elegant exterior of the building reflects the security and orientation the interior offers to the severely movement impaired student.
The handicapped accessible and thresholdless transition of the rooms was determined from the beginning by the terrain.

Design Parameters for School Buildings

Introduction	340
Space Allocation Program	344
Safety and Security	350
Access	356
Teaching Rooms	360
Meeting Rooms	370
Library	372
Staff Rooms	374
Toilets and Washrooms	376
Cafeteria and School Kitchen	380
Open Areas and Gyms	384

Ten Design Parameters for School Buildings

The following chapter is based on design studies and concrete plans for different schools. The choice of ten design parameters is intended to focus attention on the important aspects of planning, without making any claims on completeness. The intent here is to offer a road map to those architects involved in design and planning and the later users, in order to successfully work through what can be a strenuous planning phase.

What is there to design? School construction certainly has enough answers to this cardinal question of planning practice. This is not a matter of design freedom. The project location is not the issue, nor whether the contract was awarded privately or in a competition: location and the number of students are never the only criteria which the architecture has to consider. All learning facilities emerge from a conflict situation involving laws, demands and desires. The school is a most regulated building commission!

Even when the goal is clear, the course of action is seldom immediately apparent. Invitations to bid are typically laced with cross references, but it is difficult to pin down something concrete about the object in question. The same is true of the architect's contact person: the operator of the institution of learning is most often not the builder. Both of them determine at best a minor part of the rules of the game. The school supervising authority is much more important here. This entity is always a public authority, which may be national or local in scope.

In Germany the responsibility for education is primarily left to the individual states, with the federal government weighing in with legislation. And then again although many regulations are in flux, in the final analysis they are very similar. The greatest number always deal with technical norms, which are very detailed and which leave their mark on the architecture. While acoustics, ventilation, lighting are mostly left to recommendations, safety needs are binding. As a rule, the places of learning should be at least as safe for the youth as the meeting places and workplaces of adults. Therefore the specifications are much more stringent: what are the characteristics for the materials used; how should the windows or doors look and so on …

German projects are not only subject to DIN 58125. The school project is aided by the accident prevention regulations, which the legislators set up in coordination with the insurance industry. Performance parameters are an even greater constraint.

There is a long tradition concerning the space requirements for the individual student. The school supervising authority establishes them just as firmly as the size of the groups and timetable. Almost all the institutional builders have derived space programs from these factors with the aid of many rule of three formulas. Long lists separate the functional areas from each other, even if it is just the teachers' bathroom as opposed to the students' toilet, while numbers and size measure off the rooms and define the furnishings.

If taxes build the schools, the minimum requirements determine the upper funding limits, with anything more requiring state financing. In addition the public authorities systematically evaluate the actual construction costs. This advance cost control reins in the actual costs so that unreal calculations are ruled out.

In addition to these must-haves there are the project specific nice-to-haves. Almost every tender places a value on an urban developmental fit, service for the neighbourhood, integration of individuals with handicaps and the like. These wishes may have little to do with the school per se, but they often determine which design is chosen. The net result is a construction project that is loaded down like no other. The good news is all the guidelines can be fulfilled. There are very few irreconcilable situations. And stylistic proclamations are seldom heard. The designer can paint surfaces, decorate façades, distribute artwork on the site, but whether this strategy creates better schools is another question. They cannot in any case satisfy the guidelines. It is norms which by their nature address what is normal. They establish minimal standards, without ever aiming for what is maximally possible. And what is set down in black and white is compelled to ignore every development which pertains directly to learning. And that means that in the best case the essence of the school is ruled out!

This is where the real challenge starts! The architect has two approaches to pursue. The one is to attempt to optimize the school rules and regulations. The main essay in this book covers extensively the effects of design on the students and which alternatives have been tried. It can be that the designer contrives building structures that have never been seen before. The guidelines will hardly be a hindrance: safety considerations can often be addressed with straightforward construction technology and spatial aspects seldom require more than functionality.

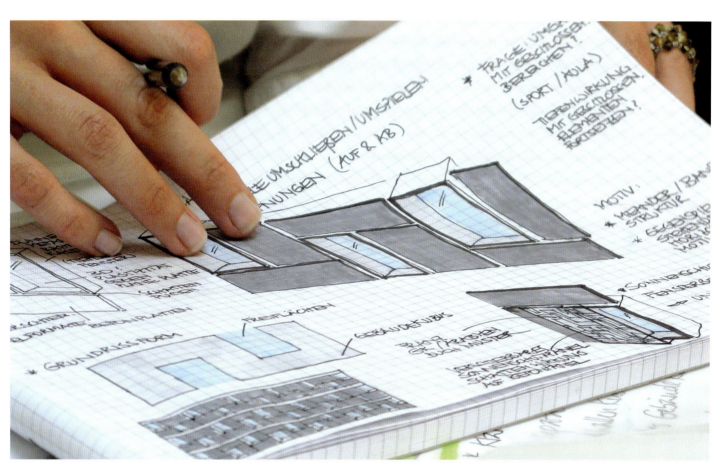

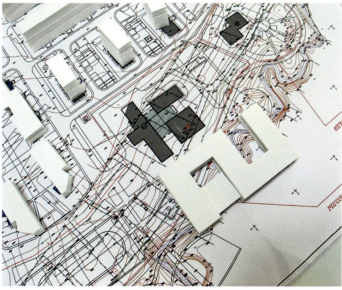

How the space allocation program takes shape
In spite of the high degree of regulations a standardized building typology like that of a school offers a great deal of design freedom. The constant focus on the required space allocation program diminishes the risk of misjudging time or concepts. Idea sketches, diagrams and work models in the early stages of the design help find the right form.

Ten Design Parameters for School Buildings

That alone rules out from the start the wildest schemes. This procedure first becomes a challenge in the context of the planning process and practice. The school rules and regulations do not work without users. The more ambitious their designs, the closer the users' connection to the designer must be. In fact, in most cases the builder is represented indirectly. Competitions take on a life of their own. During the most important phases the students and teachers are just spectators. The architects are then on their own, and are forced into a role which they cannot fulfil, namely that of teacher.

There is any easier way. The design strategy of offering more school and letting the users determine what they need is an unqualified success story. The international and historical record speaks a clear language. Without exception larger teaching spaces distinguish the leading education countries from the developing countries. Today India is striving to achieve what Switzerland had one hundred years ago. The space available for each student has been tripled since then! In addition, in Switzerland development is continuing: most of the recently completed school buildings exceed the current legally required dimensions. In some cases the goal is exceeded by one hundred percent, and the building is completed nonetheless! The constant expansion is no accident. In light of compulsory education the builders have a debt to pay. In order to stay on the safe side, they assume growth for the most important design parameters, selecting building sites which are not too tight to begin with. The exact number of students cannot at any rate be predicted. That means the school starts as a necessity with more than enough space. Which the teachers as well as the students gratefully accept. Even the financing mechanisms serve more as a channel than a brake on the desire for more space. The budget is of course a fixed sum. The approving authorities calculate every single component absolutely meticulously, so that there are no power plays on the construction site. Many current spatial reference values are relative. On the one hand, for reasons already explained, there is leeway in the space determined by the size of the construction site and number of students. On the other hand the volume control tries to hold down the operating costs, which exceed construction costs several times over the long haul. In the end only the room heights are reduced. The result is a school which comes up short, with two thirds teaching space on just as much land. More than 50 percent is seldom to be had. No class is really too small, but the circulation surfaces are disproportionately large. These proportions indicate a significant gap in the system of the space allocation program. They determine that which no school can do without.

Their thoroughly functionalistic thinking is just not capable of fathoming the problem. As a consequence when decisions are made mistakes occur. This is the grey zone where architecture thrives, where architects receive their most elegant design assignment: to maximize the learning values beyond the schedule! This book proves that it can be done, with a vengeance! Since more than four storeys are mostly not allowed, if they do not resort to a high-rise, then the architects have a free hand!

Right side
Design sketches with a space allocation plan

Space Allocation Program

No, the space allocation program does not require a model space for a program! It favours neither comb structures, clusters, courtyards, carpets, pavilions or linear structures, nor does it rule the one or the other out. In order to avoid such misunderstandings, many builders would rather speak of a standard space allocation program. As a matter of priority that means a tool that bridges the gap between pedagogy and architecture (which means not getting too bogged down in one or the other). Amorphous factors (students, learning communities or teaching rooms) are thereby assigned space requirements, from which the designer derives a form!

What the internal logic of the standard space allocation programs accomplishes can best be seen in the case of Great Britain. Step by step the required spaces are developed where the students assemble every hour in subject rooms. In order to simplify the process of calculation which the *Building Bulletin 98: Briefing Framework for Secondary School Projects Incorporating Secondary School Revisions to BB82: Area Guidelines for Schools* prescribe, the Department for Education expends no less than six dozen 8 ½ by 14 pages! The designers in Germany have no idea of this kind of diligence. The local system of fixed learning groups is much easier to calculate so that in the state school construction guidelines the result is what counts. And what counts are the lists which indicate the different functional areas and their sizes.

The finer the list is subdivided, the more space there is for didactic methods. The sequence mirrors the school timetable: basis, specialist and facultative teaching. After them come the rooms for breaks, staff and administrative rooms, followed by the auditorium and other special-use spaces. A design can neither be derived from the positions, nor can they designate a fixed room. Ultimately the reviewers calculate the surface exactly, whereby too few square metres are assigned than too many. At any rate, the jury first gets involved with the purpose of the construction plan.

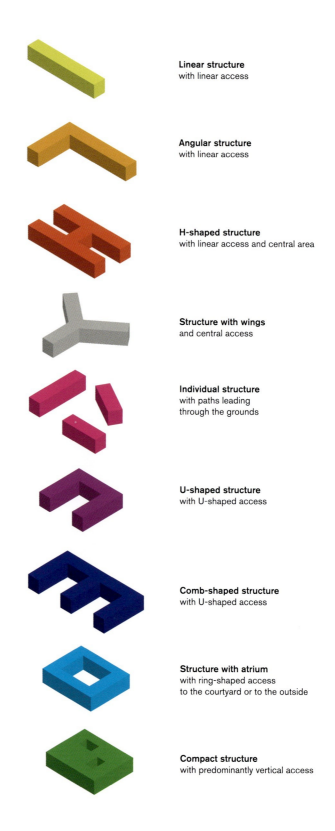

Linear structure
with linear access

Angular structure
with linear access

H-shaped structure
with linear access and central area

Structure with wings
and central access

Individual structure
with paths leading
through the grounds

U-shaped structure
with U-shaped access

Comb-shaped structure
with U-shaped access

Structure with atrium
with ring-shaped access
to the courtyard or to the outside

Compact structure
with predominantly vertical access

Space Allocation
Safety and Security
Access
Teaching Rooms
Meeting Rooms
Library
Staff Rooms
Toilets and Washrooms
Cafeteria
Open Areas

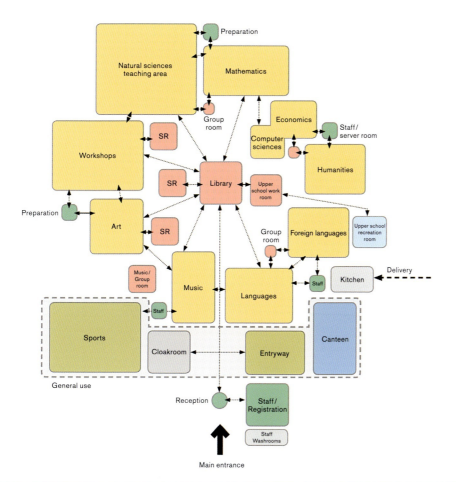

Left
Example of a space allocation program from Great Britain

Below
Example of space allocation program from Germany

The Standard Building Code (*Musterbauordnung* or MBO), is the basis for the State Building Codes (*Landesbauordnungen* or LBO). The state building codes are augmented by the School Construction Guidelines (*Schulbau-Richtlinien* or Schul-BauR) based on the Model School Construction Guidelines (*Muster-Schulbau-Richtlinie* or MSchulBauR). The model space allocation programs for the various school types involve the state's recommendations for new construction, expansion and conversion of schools.

Model program for preparatory high school 3–5 classes Regular form / All-day school							
Classes 7–12			**3 classes**		**4 classes**		**5 classes**	
Frequency (allocation): sec I 29, max. 32 / sec II 50 pup. / Class Capacity: 30 seats / room							
Organisation: Regular form / All-day school							
Male students / co-eds middle school			348		464		580	
Male students / co-eds upper class			150		200		250	
Total students / co-eds; 4 % of which with special educational support			**498**		**664**		**830**	
type	Amount of space	m²	No.	m²	No.	m²	No.	m²
AU (learning and teaching)	Standard classroom with wardrobe	65	12	780	16	1,040	20	1,300
	Group room[1]	50	4	200	5	250	6	300
	Group room[1]	40	4	160	5	200	6	240
	Student workplaces	50	2	100	3	150	4	200
	Teaching materials / technology / geography-collection incl. notebook cart*			100		120		140
	* assigned according to classes / group rooms							
	Multi-purpose room (Acting incl. podium …)	300		300		300		300
	Canteen / Cafeteria[2] at least 1.2 m²/p. (approx. 30 % participants / 2 passageways)		1	100	1	120	1	150
	Wardrobe	40		40		50		60
	Kitchen / food serving (with serving kitchen)	40		40		40		40
	Relaxation upper class		1	50	1	65	1	80
	Recreation room[3] (only in all-day operation)	45/60	3	150	4	195	5	240
	Student newspaper	35	1	35	1	35	1	35
	Amount			**1,955**		**2,455**		**2,935**

(1) Simultaneously for temporary learning groups in the framework of the special educational support (2) Where necessary in double use with multi-purpose room (3) Where necessary 1 room for school support centre

Space Allocation Program

As soon as the mass distribution and access are established, the architects can turn their attention to the building interior. If general framework conditions have been the rule until now, specific use is now the focus. Of course the analysis of the demands takes priority over the actual design. The most important specification for school buildings is the so-called model space allocation program, which is compiled on a state by state basis in the Federal Republic of Germany and which is based on the specific school type. All the model space allocation programs translate the learning mode into space requirement and subdivide the surface functionally. The tender extrapolates this square metre estimate onto the actual number of students. The result is read out consistently as an endless listing. If there are no sponsors for the project, the model space allocation program calculates benchmark values. Beyond those values "starting point" and "goal" are repeatedly compared in the course of the planning. If a preliminary draft actually diverges from the verification, the approval authorities will recheck the numbers.

Nevertheless the model space allocation program does not specify everything. It does not indicate spatial patterns, nor does it define individual rooms and of course it does not derive a linearity from the long lists. That is all left to the work of the architects. They start by ordering the long lists according to design parameters. The especially important aspects are dependent on the initial system. If tight space on the building plot requires that the biggest chunks are worked out first, the pedagogy comes out ahead by the addition of individual learning units. Basic functional areas like classrooms, break rooms, access corridors and public facilities help to organize the building. All three approaches are generally anchored in the following: For purposes of a rough building organisation the space allocation program is most often subdivided into four main programs.

A Public area (common uses)
B Teaching area (basic use)
C Service area (side rooms)
D Transition and break area (access)

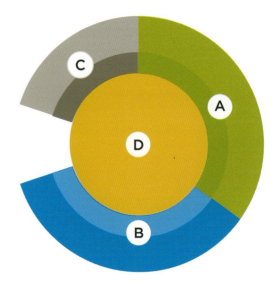

Space Allocation
Safety and Security
Access
Teaching Rooms
Meeting Rooms
Library
Staff Rooms
Toilets and Washrooms
Cafeteria
Open Areas

1

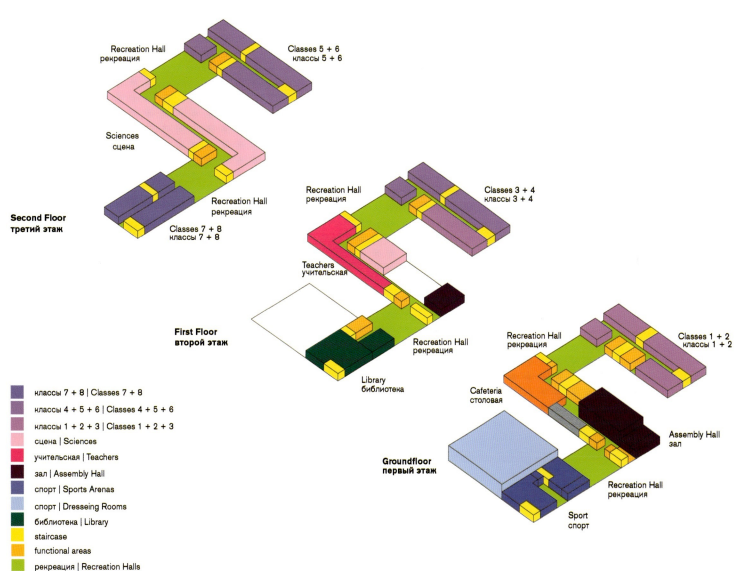

Three dimensional space allocation program
Before the first discussion about materials and construction details, a diagram with colour coding of the functional areas for checking the pre-established model program and as a decision aid is used for the next steps. This example shows the design by Meuser Architekten for a system built school in Cheboksary in the Chuvash Republic of the Russian Federation.

Space Allocation Program

In light of the turbulent ongoing debate, it may seem strange that the design is just now emerging as key in the school. This means the teaching area. In fact the reason is a many faceted discussion: different effective teaching methods have been tried, but nothing definitive has emerged. The basic message is: learning requires change. The desire to base the school on a special pedagogy is an obsession.

Even the classical concept of classes along a corridor is no solution anymore because the new forms of teaching are not addressed by special seating arrangements, even if the creatively varied seating arrangements in much school planning may suggest that. Project work, learning among different age groups, team-teaching, individual study, experiments, research or just listening to the muse are based on learning environments. They require space.

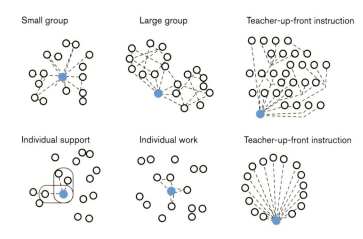

Different learning situations in the class room

The challenges facing the design of the teaching area grow with the multiplication of the forms of learning. On the one hand the space allocation programs which until now grant a fixed size to a few methods are a problem. At best, other than the traditional teacher-up-front in the classroom method, group work is considered indispensable. That means those who want their own booth for whatever reason will face an insoluble space problem. So, planners like to shift to multiple-use, as can be seen in the combinations of canteen/auditorium/foyer which have become standard. Variability has also reached an extreme in the teaching area. But use-neutral large spaces all show the same result: they overtax students and teachers because they demand all the more orientation when the learning environment changes.

The seeming contradiction between "more form" and "more space" can only be solved by a specific design: the spatial conglomerate, assembled according to a clear set of rules. In general what emerges are clusters, which roughly divide the totality of the teaching space. Generally this is done according to the age of the students, which leads to larger units. But even in an embryonic stage no entity is by any means uniform, showing instead already a middle and boundary. The classrooms establish the corners and edges. At least one out of two has a group room available. Since such a room is smaller than the classroom, niches are formed which cry out for special use, for individual work or storage. Meanwhile in the centre there is space for the big picture: it is usual to present projects here and access makes

Space Allocation
Safety and Security
Access
Teaching Rooms
Meeting Rooms

Library
Staff Rooms
Toilets and Washrooms
Cafeteria
Open Areas

1

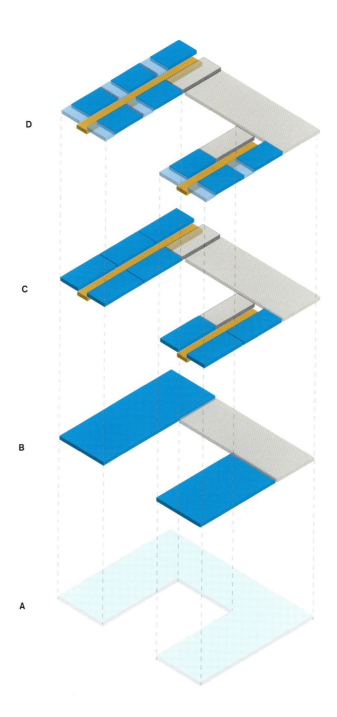

no more sense than here. The simple sketch has such an intrinsic logic at this point that the architect only has to ensure there are enough connections and terminations.

The case at hand also follows this pattern: the floors of the individual age groups pedagogically transform the tightness of the plot into something positive. There is an informal learning landscape in the middle, to which the same age group can congregate during classes as well as in the afternoon. The space is defined by three teaching blocks and a multi-purpose room. The core of each learning unit is the class room, flanked by the group room and wardrobe. Thanks to this buffer zone, noise problems among the various classes are obviated for the most part. With the aid of sliding doors two group rooms can be combined, so that the floor can also be used for team-teaching. Spaces for combined age group learning are located on the more public floors.

At the same time the cluster concept extends the basic idea of the design to organize the school according to degrees of openness. Each cluster is clearly distinguished from the main staircase: at the threshold bookshelves constitute a veritable gateway, and instead of full transparency the walls are now equipped with punch windows. They afford a large-scale view into the multi-purpose rooms and classrooms. Their actual entrance is fully glazed and can be twisted to act as a vestibule. The highest concentration is in the group rooms, which only open to the outside or to other work areas. The detail design pushes this rough division to the limit.

The presentation in the form of a functional diagram makes spatial composition easily comprehensible. This kind of representation concerning the contents of planning and design ideas simplifies communication with user groups who are not familiar with architectural terminology. In a project phase like this it is not essential to discuss the design of the interior or materials and colours. This can happen later.

Break-down of the space allocation program

A Building floor space
B Formation of clusters and function tracks
C Organization of the cluster in rooms
D Assignment of individual functions to the rooms

The individual clusters, consisting of several classrooms, group rooms and open common areas for project work, should be set up for 60 to 120 students. In the project work zones sufficient daylight and suitable room acoustics should be provided.

DESIGN PARAMETERS

Safety and Security

A latter-day Romeo wants to impress his teenage girlfriend: just before the art class begins he lights a sparkler on her drawing desk. But the sketch paper catches fire, not her heart. The class panics and the alarm goes off. The escape routes are quickly jammed, glass is broken in the turmoil. Meanwhile the fire has spread to exhibition artwork. The danger is real that the whole building will go up in flames. The school seems to be a trap! This is an imaginary horror scenario. In fact it rarely happens. The school is intrinsically a safe place, where the right response in critical situations is the subject of drills, where the students are constantly under the care of supervisors. But even the most professional supervision is not failsafe. And of course children and youth by their nature are more prone to accidents than adults.

In light of this kind of all too human unpredictability the legislators assume a good portion of the responsibility themselves. Places of learning which not only serve adults are subject to stricter regulations than the building code imposes on other recreation rooms. This is where the Federal Model School Construction Guideline (*MusterSchulbau-Richtlinie* or MschulbauR), comes into play. It subsumes all state regulations, whereby safety is set up in a much more clear fashion. It is augmented by the accident prevention regulation for schools, which the executive establishes with the insurance industry.

The latter is focussed primarily on danger avoidance and is especially involved in detailed design guidelines for windows, doors and stairs. In contrast the former is concerned with the emergency situation. In order to avoid firetraps, support structures must be able to withstand the fire long enough, while building complexes must be organized so that they can be smoothly evacuated. With increased height and size the demands are greater. Those are some general considerations.

The Model School Construction Guidelines are interested in two points in particular: they insist on more resistant constructions by classifying learning institutions one building class higher than normal residential buildings. The second pertains to evacuation: no ladders are used in schools – the fire department brings those along – each room must have two fixed escape routes which lead to ground level. In addition the building inspectors keep their eyes on the escape routes in day-to-day operations. The architects are required to safely locate the wardrobe, teaching material and presentation facilities, even if the guidelines are vague there.

All safety regulations have one thing in common: they are obligatory. Which is not to say that there are no alternatives. Instead of mindlessly implementing them, additional architectural or technical provisions are negotiable for almost every case. Especially in the case of reconstructions. Excuses for bad architecture have no place.

Conscientious designers have a blind spot: the usual rules do not foresee that dangers will be created deliberately. The case looks differently in the USA, where there is more experience with school shootings, assassinations and all kinds of school violence. The watchword there is manpower. But the architecture can also make a contribution – with sluice-like entrances and connecting passages which are easy to watch over – for safety in the school.

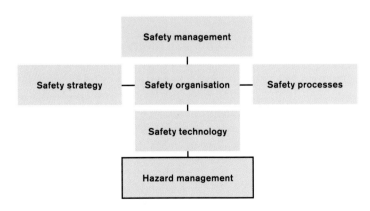

Components of safety management

Space Allocation Library
Safety and Security Staff Rooms
Access Toilets and Washrooms
Teaching Rooms Cafeteria
Meeting Rooms Open Areas

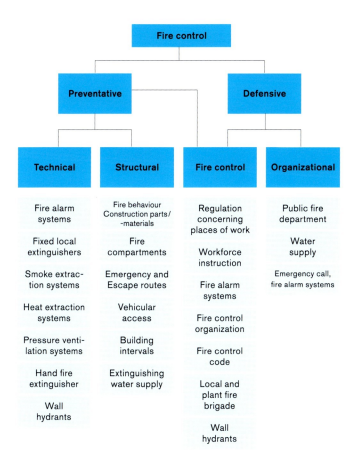

DIN EN 3501-1	DIN 4102-1	Performance requirements
A1	A1	No contribution to fire, without flammable elements, very limited fire, limited increase in temperature, no flames
A2	A2	Contribution to fire, in spite of flammable elements, very limited fire, limited increase in temperature, flames for a short time.
B	B1	Very limited contribution to fire, very limited increase in temperature, almost no spread of flame, very limited smoke emission.
C	"Adverse" B1	Limited contribution to fire, limited heat emission, very limited spread of flame, limited smoke emission.
D	"Positive" B1	Acceptable contribution to fire, acceptable heat emission, limited spread of flame, limited smoke emission.
E	B2	Acceptable fire behaviour, acceptable flammability, limited spread of fire
F	B3	no performance determined

Structure and organization of fire control
With each area of responsibility and the relevant measures

Designation of building material classes
According to the new European and existing German norms

New abbreviation in the building law	Wording of the building law	Previous designation DIN	New designation DIN EN
FB	fire-proof	F90	REI-90
HFH (new)	highly fire retardant (new)	Not available	REI-60
FH	fire retardant	F30	REI-30

Designation of the fire resistance classes
Comparing the building law with the DIN (German norms)

Formula for minimum size: 1,20 metres per 200 persons	
Exits from teaching rooms	0.90 m
Required hallways	1.50 m
Required stairs	1.20 m

Minimal widths of escape routes according to Model School Construction Guidelines 2009
Muster-Schulbau-Richtlinie 2009

Safety and Security

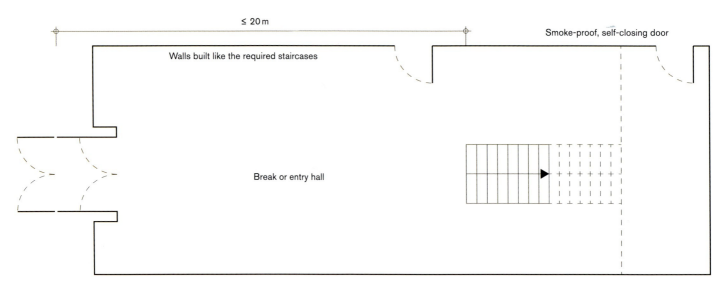

Escape routes through the halls
Emergency routes which lead through break areas or entry halls represent particular demands on the walls, which must be executed to conform with the fire resistance class, like the required stairwells. Doors which lead to the halls must be smoke-proof and self-closing. The distance from the lower stair of a flight of stairs in the hall to the exit may be at most 20 metres. In specific cases an adjustment with the local building authorities is required.

Required widths of corridors and escape routes
Every building user group has different needs regarding the movement area. In the case of the corridors this is especially evident. The rule of thumb is: transit widths, through which two wheelchairs can pass with ease in two way traffic, are sufficient in order to declare that corridor as an escape route.

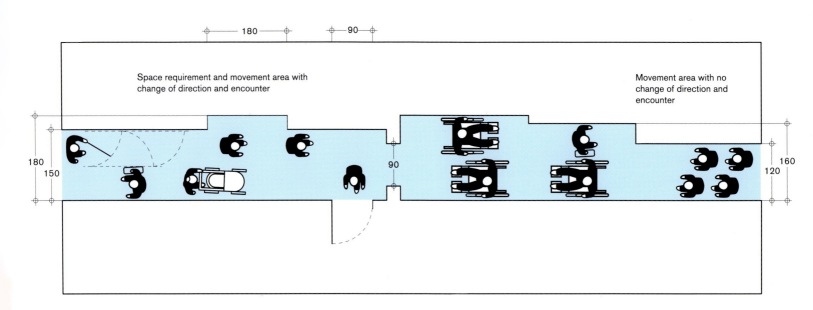

Space Allocation
Safety and Security
Access
Teaching Rooms
Meeting Rooms
Library
Staff Rooms
Toilets and Washrooms
Cafeteria
Open Areas

Signage and First Aid
In the *American International School* in Vienna the brightly coloured pictograms in speech bubbles (design: Tina Frank Design) have quickly proven their popularity in the area of safety management.

Signage and escape route marking
The guidance and orientation system of the *Hochschule für Technik und Wirtschaft* (design: polyform, *Büro für Grafik- und Produktdesign*) in Berlin combine an easily legible signage with escape route information.

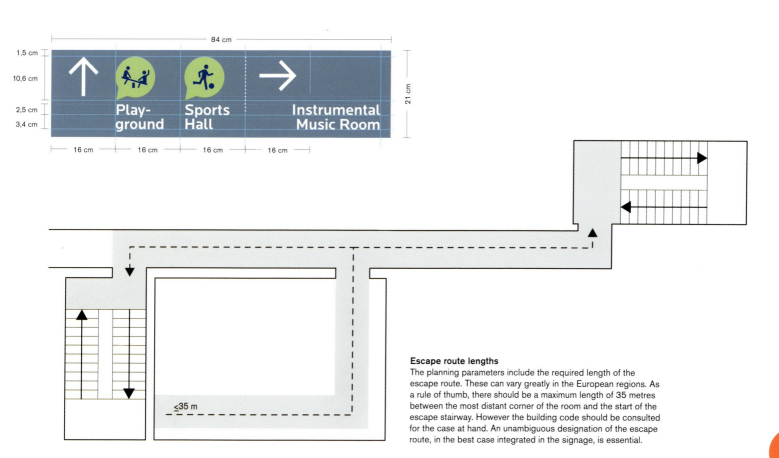

Escape route lengths
The planning parameters include the required length of the escape route. These can vary greatly in the European regions. As a rule of thumb, there should be a maximum length of 35 metres between the most distant corner of the room and the start of the escape stairway. However the building code should be consulted for the case at hand. An unambiguous designation of the escape route, in the best case integrated in the signage, is essential.

Safety and Security

Escape routes

No other safety standard than fire control so heavily influences school planning! Neither equipment nor design sophistication are enough for fire control. The demands begin with the land itself and the building: the fire department needs lots of space! The preliminary draft should already contain those escape routes that have access on every floor. The procedure is always the same: since even small deviations can sometimes seriously compromise the project, the architect first investigates which safety regulations pertain exactly to their designs. In general the rules for school construction are stricter than for other buildings (which is expressed in special regulations and their application). Of course, the provisions vary depending on location, especially in the Federal Republic of Germany, where building regulations are determined by the states.

Still, the most important factors remain: the preliminary draft is influenced above all by fire compartments and escape routes. The stipulations concerning the number and size are in part absolute and in part the guidelines are relative to the person to be rescued. The tender keeps ready the appropriate variable, whereby the official number of users is of course just one of the working hypotheses. In the final analysis in the case of the finished design it is the people who count.

On this basis the worst case scenario can be played out: evacuation of a fully occupied building that is completely on fire! The scenario, which the architect must attach to the building application, is subject to examination during the approval procedure by the academic supervision. The multi-function zones which are especially favoured by the schools come under close scrutiny. These are supposed to function simultaneously as escape routes and recreation rooms. If safe material and furniture is not available, the fire department very often has only one choice: additional safety provisions or limitation of use!

Related literature
Meuser, Philipp / Pogade, Daniela:
*Construction and Design Manual.
Wayfinding and Signage*, Berlin 2010.

Space Allocation Library
Safety and Security Staff Rooms
Access Toilets and Washrooms
Teaching Rooms Cafeteria
Meeting Rooms Open Areas

As a basis of negotiation plans like those in the present school example suffice. The property depth of 64 metres determines the division of the building in two fire compartments: the smaller one is the wing in the park, while the larger one encompasses the rest of the property up to the street. Just there is where the greatest load factor is located: when the pre-schoolers and the 4th grade occupy the specialist classrooms, the rest of the age group rooms are fully occupied and the remaining teaching staff is in the staff rooms. The main access is by no means a safe haven, because it is open to all the upper floors. Therefore four escape stairs were reserved, ventilated with smoke and heat extraction roof flaps, leading smoke-free outside. The ground floor has an additional five exits to the outside. The two more narrow escape stairs fulfil the minimum dimensions of 1,20 metres per 200 persons. For reasons pertaining to the floor plan, the two larger escape stairs measure 2,00 metres. The model school construction guideline requires doors for every teaching room which are easy to open to their full width from the inside and which open in the direction of the first emergency route. In addition, for every teaching room two or more escape routes independent of each other are guaranteed.

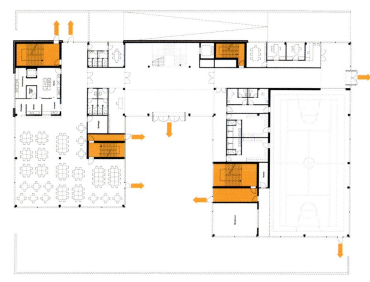

Position of escape stairs and exits

The latter must lead within a maximum of 35 metres and at the same level to the required stairs or to the outside. There is one special challenge associated with this general requirement: the cluster concept, which gathers several classrooms around a central common area. In order to furnish this access area without hindrances, an additional, independent emergency route is needed. That means the classes are connected to each other with doors, which makes possible the decentralized access to the emergency stairs.

Escape routes (independent of common area)

Access

In order to bring a fire under control, fire compartments and fire walls are indispensable. The model school construction guidelines require them at least every 60 metres. Walls should be fitted with doors which must be smoke-proof, fire retardant and self-closing, with adjacent windows at more than 2.5 metres intervals. As long as the interior walls are fire-proof, multi-storey hallways are permitted. However unlike the actual outer rooms they should be used to evacuate the upper floors.

As a rule the access provides the escape route. Every recreation room should have two such accesses, which may be up to 35 metres long. The length is derived from the furthermost workplace to the outside or to the staircase. A measurement is made of the linear distance within the classes along the middle axis. If the hallways bend, the maximum distance is shortened. For one-way escape hallways, there are only 10 metres available.

Even more complex conditions prevail for the width of the escape route. The usage must first be determined: at least 1.20 metres per 200 users. Jumps of 60 centimetres should be strived for. Secondly, the mass must increase continually in order to avoid bottlenecks. Protrusions are permitted only beyond the transitions so that the main path can be recognized. The entrances to the classrooms mark the minimum. They should be more than 90 centimetres. With conference rooms the width should be more than 1,20 metres. Required hallways must have free access of at least 1,50 metres, without being narrowed by wardrobes, fixtures or doors opening into the hall. The stairs mark the maximum. They should measure unobstructed at most 2,40 metres.

Standards are set for the building layout in connection with conventional class sizes: if the school is one or two storeys high, a maximum of twelve classes per floor comprise the design unit. If there are three storeys, eight classrooms per floor are allowed, at four storeys, six are allowed, and so on, always with the stipulation that the access is two-hip, with only those stairs which are required.

Secure glass railing

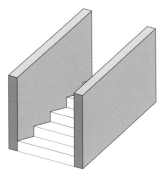

Solid parapet railings

Glass railing with steel construction

Column banister vertical

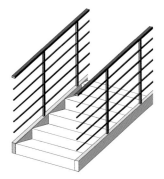

Horizontal column banister

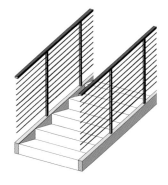

Horizontal railing with steel cable under tension

Different railing constructions

Space Allocation
Safety and Security
Access
Teaching Rooms
Meeting Rooms

Library
Staff Rooms
Toilets and Washrooms
Cafeteria
Open Areas

3

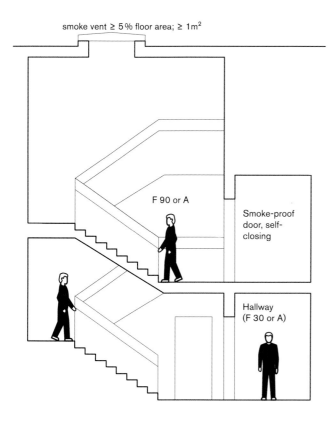

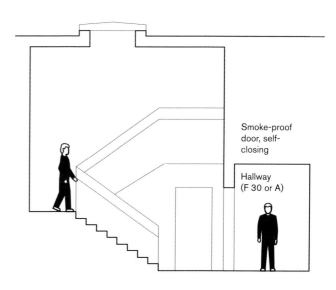

Emergency stairwell with central smoke ventilation windows (Construction parts: F 90, building material class: A)

Hallway (Construction parts: F 30, Building Material Class: A)

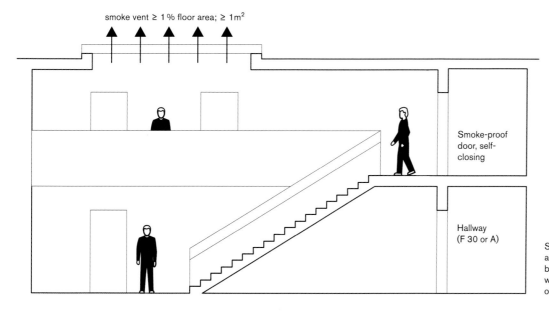

Stairway halls require a self-closing and smoke-proof door to the adjacent building sections. The smoke ventilation windows must be larger than one percent of the floor area, but at least be 1,00 m².

Access

Stairs are the creative spaces within the school, almost as much as hallways. However the regulations governing them are even more extensive, especially when they are needed as escape routes.

If a stair ends in a recreation area, the nether side of the stairs have to be padded against head injuries with a clearance of two metres. Handrails on each side are required, with no open ends and which do not permit sliding. Sharp edges and constructions which can cause the person negotiating the stairs to get caught should be avoided. Hemisphere shapes have proven effective. The recommendations for parapets should be observed. Treads and risers must be closed. The front edge must at least be slip-proof. An upper gradient limit of six percent is the norm for ramps and with stairs, the tread and double incline should add up to 59 to 65 centimetres. No step may be higher than 17 centimetres or deeper than 28 centimetres. In a curved stairway the minimum is 23 centimetres; beyond 1.25 metres the maximum is limited to 40 centimetres.

Winding staircases which serve at the same time as escape routes are not permitted. Their passable width is limited to 2.40 metres. They require above all a non-flammable staircase. All entrances and exits require landings and self-closing and smoke-proof doors. These should ideally be located on the façade, because the escape routes must lead directly outside. Their containment must at least be fire retardant and made mostly of non-flammable construction materials. Depending on the size of the building there can be even stricter requirements.

Parapets which develop into interior walls provide the greatest safety, but are not yet required. There is not one regulation which prohibits open stairways. Thanks to this loophole vertical access becomes a matter of spatial art.

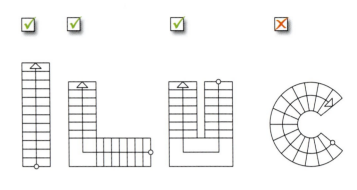

Directions of movement for emergency staircase
Emergency routes must be so constructed so that the users in an emergency can easily find their orientation and not be distracted by the form of the stairs. Spiral staircases as escape routes are therefore not allowed. In the case of older buildings they most often require a request for exemption from the local regulations.

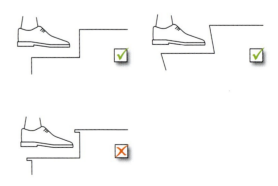

Handicapped accessible design of steps
The design of a step in schools is the construction task with the highest aesthetical demands. It can quickly become a barrier because of small details in day-to-day operation as well as in the case of an evacuation of the building.

Space Allocation   Library
Safety and Security   Staff Rooms
Access   Toilets and Washrooms
Teaching Rooms   Cafeteria
Meeting Rooms   Open Areas

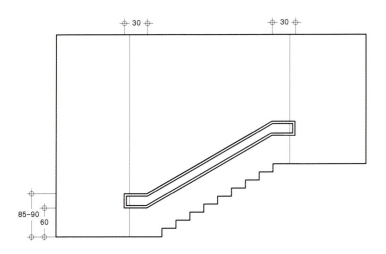

Handicapped accessible marking of handrails
With stairs in corners it is possible to wrap the railing around the corner. This draws attention to the stairs in the hallway.

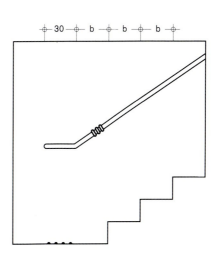

Handicapped accessible marking of stairs
Stand out markings on the floor and on the railing assist in the early recognition of stairs and reduce the danger of falling.

Handicapped-accessible railings which can be gripped

Railings which may be partially gripped in a slot in the wall

Railings which may not be gripped in a slot in the wall

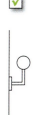     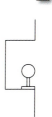

Design of stairway railings
Railings which cannot be properly gripped are of no assistance in the case of a fall. The optimal construction is a round or oval cross section with a thickness of between three and 4.5 centimetres fastened from underneath.

Teaching Rooms

Around 30 students, each with just under two square metres space, a blackboard, a desk and a chair. Those are the standard guidelines for the basic German school. The height of the seminar room should be at least 2.7 metres. When the sun only shines from one side, the width is limited to 7.2 metres. And no pupil should be more than nine metres from the teacher.

The absolute numbers may differ somewhat in other countries, but the general set-up is the same. The dimensions are designed to create the optimal conditions for the sight and hearing of the teachers. The proportions encourage natural illumination and ventilation, which is demonstrably crucial to the learning success. If medium-hard mineral materials like plaster, aerated concrete or brick cover the walls, then everything is acoustically ok. If it is perfect for teacher-up-front instruction, the basic framework does not just work according to pattern. Architects like to demonstrate this matter-of-factly by outfitting their plans with different seating arrangements. Additional didactic methods may be added: for instance, with somewhat smaller group rooms (for those in Germany about 50 square metres may be reserved) between two seminar rooms – or in front, which is an arrangement preferred and practiced in many different ways by the northern Europeans. There are more choices to be made with the furnishings, which are subject to greatly varying regulations: what is contemporary, what is a central computing room or a fixed distribution of desktops? Does each seminar need a sink or even its own washroom? And where should all the school materials be stowed, from the pupils' coats or the teachers' visual aids?

The greatest challenge is the time which the student spends in the seminar room. The usual system of fixed classes cries out for a living space, not a stripped down teaching cell! The regulations are nowhere to be found here. The pupils have no one else to rely on for domestic furnishings other than the designers!

From a stationary lectern to a loose arrangement of chairs
A corresponding rethinking of the teaching rooms is needed in light of the emergence of a new learning culture in the 21st century. New pedagogical concepts are distinguished by different learning and teaching situations. With flexible furnishings and learning landscapes, group work, individual teaching and combined teaching units can be accommodated according to need.

Above: Flexible arrangement of chairs with desk pads
Below: Historical classroom in the Museum Senftenberg

Space Allocation   Library
Safety and Security   Staff Rooms
Access   Toilets and Washrooms
Teaching Rooms   Cafeteria
Meeting Rooms   Open Areas

4

Class room perspective

Class room longitudinal section

DESIGN PARAMETERS

361

Teaching Rooms

For classrooms that are both healthy and conducive to learning the following factors are important:

Acoustics
Current research shows that noise and bad room acoustics can severely impede teaching and learning. Today classrooms can be designed to optimize the acoustic relationships for teachers and students. The DIN 18041 norm, *Hörsamkeit in kleinen und mittleren Räumen* (Audibility in Small and Medium Sized Spaces), contains specifications regarding the amount of allowable noise and number of sound-absorbing surfaces in the room, in order to reduce the period of reverberation to 0.4 to 0.6 seconds. However in many cases these values are not achieved.

Colour scheme
Colour is an important factor in the design of the rooms. The effect of individual colours is dependent on intensity, contrast, and size of the surfaces to be designed, and the interaction with other colours. In addition, the selection of the materials and the surfaces as well as the purpose of the object exerts an influence on the colour. The effect of colour has a close relationship with illumination and is therefore dependent on the light planning in the room. Everything must be well coordinated.

Furnishing
Modern teaching rooms can accommodate different learning and teaching situations by quickly converting the furniture in the room. Group work, individual attention and shared teaching units are available according to need. A flexible learning landscape allows for the implementation of different educational concepts. Therefore, in the selection of the furniture, next to maintaining ergonomic requirements, attention should be paid that the pieces can be easily and quickly moved, to place them in different constellations in the room. That can be done with furniture equipped with casters.

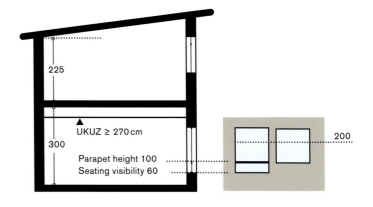

Room dimensions
The clear height of the classroom should be at least three metres and should not drop more than 30 centimetres because of individual construction elements, like beams. With slanted ceilings the unobstructed room height must be at least 2.25 metres.

Illumination
In order not to compromise the lines of sight when sitting, solid parapets should only reach a height of 60 centimetres. The shell dimension of the window openings must maintain a proportion to the surface area of the classrooms of at least 1:8. Safety glass is required at a height up to two metres.

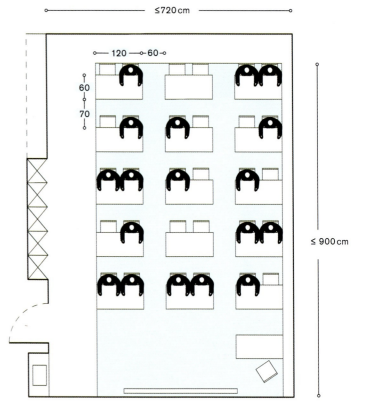

Space Allocation Library
Safety and Security Staff Rooms
Access Toilets and Washrooms
Teaching Rooms Cafeteria
Meeting Rooms Open Areas

4

Size of the classroom
Reference value: a space requirement of 1.9 to two square metres per student workplace has been calculated. The classroom size should not be more than 32 students.

Blackboard
The distance between the blackboard and the furthermost workplace should not be more than nine metres.

Fixtures
Every teaching room must have a washbasin, storage space and a closet that can be locked for teaching material

Wardrobe
The wardrobe for the student should be accessible from the hallway and should have hooks and a shelf for bicycle helmets and umbrellas.

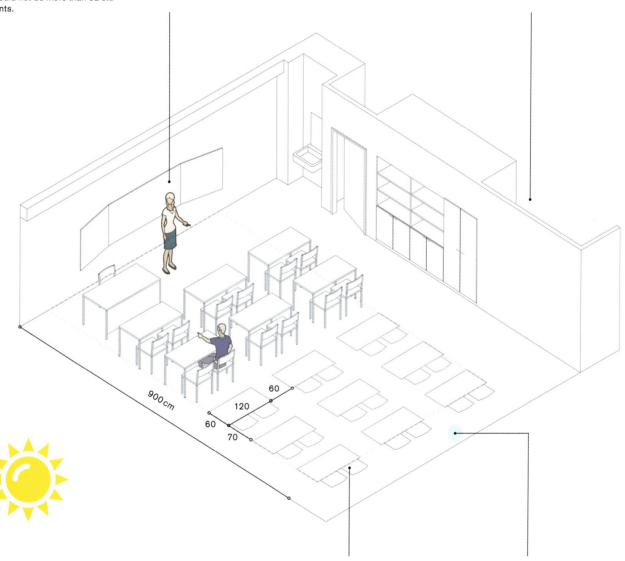

Orientation
If the room receives natural light only from one side, the recommended room depth should be no more than 7.20 metres and should ideally face east. With classrooms which are oriented to the south adequate sun protection is required.

Room acoustics
Suitable room acoustic measures like the installation of sound absorption areas provide minimal reverberation periods. The goal is good speech intelligibility in the room, which exerts a positive influence on the concentration of the students.

Desk arrangement
In regular teaching rooms the distance between the desks must be at least 70 centimetres with an aisle width of at least 60 centimetres.

Media
Projectors, which should operate as quietly as possible, should have a place for a stand to put the projector. For slide shows the room must be able to be darkened.

DESIGN PARAMETERS

363

Teaching Rooms

**CHECK LIST
Sitting**

- The soles of the feet touch the ground when sitting.
- The thighs lie perpendicularly on the chair seat.
- The angle between shank and thigh is about 90°.
- The backs of the knees do not touch the forward edge of the chair seat.
- The thighs can move freely when sitting.
- The backrest supports the shoulder blades when sitting in a listening position.
- The backrest props up the back at the edge of the pelvis while writing.
- The elbow crooks are at the level of the desktop.
- The lower arm lie on the desktop, the shoulders are relaxed.
- Dynamic sitting is the goal.
- The connection between a wrong sitting position and back problems should be regularly addressed.

Desirable features:

- The desktop is adjustable up to 16°.
- The surface coating is non-slip or the desk has a small edging.
- The adjustable desktop has a perpendicular shelf or a storage tray.
- The chair has a lumbar support with a fixed pelvis support.
- The angle between the seat and backrest is about 100°.
- The seat is tilted slightly forward.
- The chair has a flat slightly arch seating surface.

**CHECK LIST
Computer workplace**

- The optimal illumination for computer use is at the window facing the north side.
- Sufficient circulation areas and storage space devices like printers, scanners etc. should be provided.
- The teaching rooms should be naturally illuminated and ventilated.
- An optimal protection against glare reflection must be provided by blinds, slats or filter blinds.
- Potentials for stumbling like cable glands are to be avoided. Cable must be installed with wall or under flooring ducts.
- The furniture should be height adjustable in order to accommodate the different sizes of the students.
- The desks should be at least 80 centimetres wide with unlimited freedom of movement for the legs.
  Primary school height: 64 centimetres,
  Secondary school height: 82 centimetres
- The seating height of desks in specialist rooms equipped with computers should be adjustable from 38 to 50 centimetres.
- The view of the monitor should be parallel to the windows.
- While the distance between the individual rows of chairs should be at least 100 centimetres, 120 centimetres is better, so that the teacher can reach the individual workplaces between the rows.

Desks and chairs
Most tasks in school are accomplished in a sitting position, so the furniture should be adjustable according to the body height of the children.

Computer monitor workplaces
Teaching should be able to be followed from each computer workplace. That means correcting seating posture is necessary in order to avoid impairment of health.

Space Allocation
Safety and Security
Access
Teaching Rooms
Meeting Rooms

Library
Staff Rooms
Toilets and Washrooms
Cafeteria
Open Areas

4

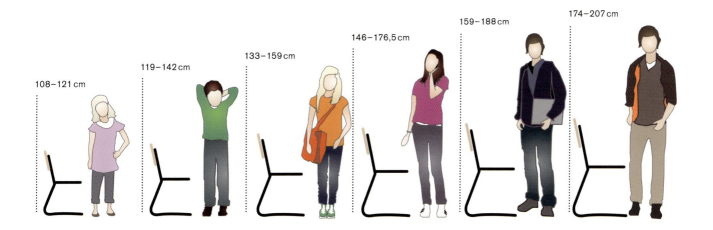

Grade 1	Grade 1–4	Grade 2–7	Grade 5–13	Grade 7–13	Grade 9–13
Seating height: 31 cm Desk height: 53 cm	Seating height: 35 cm Desk height: 59 cm	Seating height: 38 cm Desk height: 64 cm	Seating height: 43 cm Desk height: 71 cm	Seating height: 46 cm Desk height: 76 cm	Seating height: 51 cm Desk height: 82 cm

Body height:
According to DIN ISO 5970:1981-01, average body height refers to the seat and desk heights.

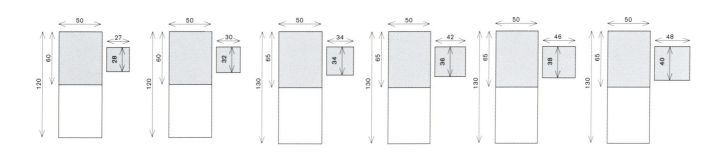

In DIN EN 1729-1:2006-09 Furniture – Chairs and desks for Learning Institutions – Part 1: Functional Dimensions *(Stühle und Tische für Bildungseinrichtungen – Teil 1: Funktionsmaße)* Safety requirements for chairs and desks in schools providing general education are established.

Teaching Rooms

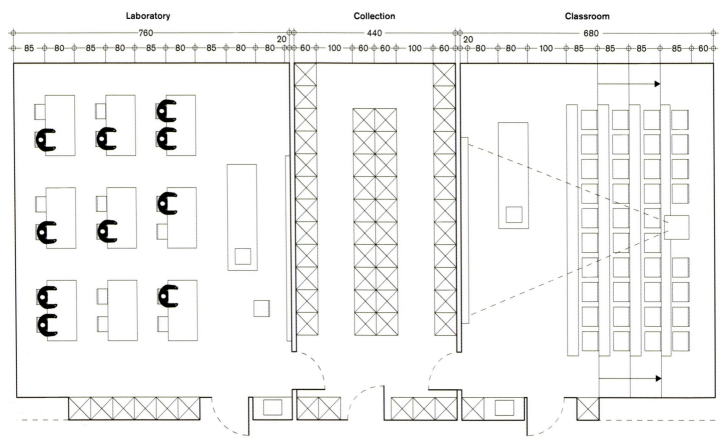

Science teaching area

When science teaching areas are planned as combined practice and instruction rooms, the highest possible utilization is reached.

A centrally located storage and exhibition area, for example for diverse biological collections, enhances the teaching concept.

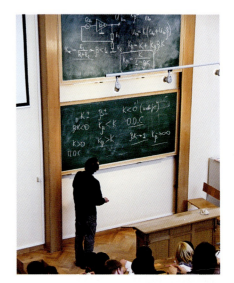

A teaching room for the transferring of knowledge is important. It can be planned as a lecture hall which can be darkened for presentations.

Space Allocation   Library
Safety and Security   Staff Rooms
Access   Toilets and Washrooms
Teaching Rooms   Cafeteria
Meeting Rooms   Open Areas

4

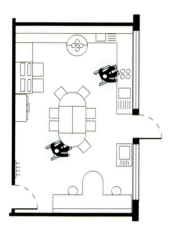

Teaching kitchen
If the teaching kitchen is to be used after the housekeeping instruction, computer workplaces are a good addition in order to use the room during breaks.

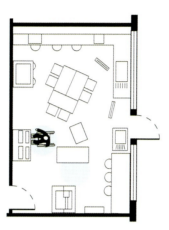

Specialist room for biology
In order to conduct research and do experiments in biology, a sink is just as important as a washbasin with paper towels and a soap dispenser.

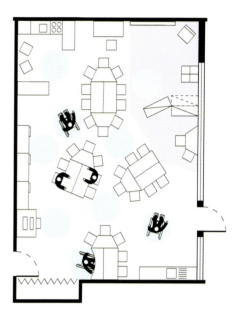

Learning landscape
A room which is not primarily arranged for teacher-up-front instruction, but which can also be used for learning, experimenting or cooking, is called a learning landscape. Flexible shelving providing storage space creates individual areas for retreat.

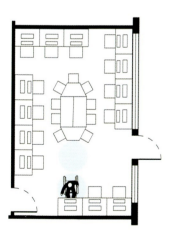

Computer work room with common area
Individual desks line the wall around a conference table which is also suitable for group work.

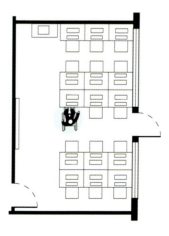

Computer work room
The individual workplaces are oriented in on one direction in order to project presentations on the walls.

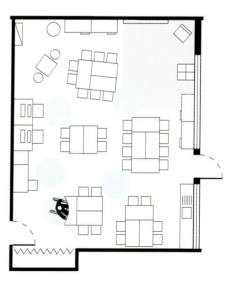

Learning landscape
The classroom accommodates the user. Easy to move furniture simplifies the quick transformation from individual to group work.

Teaching Rooms

The significance of the specialist room is heavily dependent on the type of school and system, which is why no general specifications can be given. But the value of the specialist room in the course of the educational career cannot be denied: while the teacher-up-front method with the required teaching material is enough for the small children, those who want to enter a profession immediately need individual, hands-on experience. The specialist room is mandatory beginning in the middle school, also in Germany. The disciplines that use such rooms are even more egocentric than the rooms themselves. Each one requires a burgeoning amount of equipment which dominates the design. The demands can at best be alluded to here. In general, specialist rooms are larger than those used for general instruction. In Germany the sciences take up at least 2.5 square metres per student. When demonstrations augment the lecture, another two square metres are needed. The simple lecture hall is tightly calculated at about 60 square metres, with room just for folding desks. Practice rooms exceed that by at least one sixth. In addition preparation areas are needed which are almost as large and which as a rule are located inside or between two teaching units. Music rooms sometimes need practice booths of six and eight square metres. A training workshop is comprised of the minimum areas which the individual machine parts need. Quality instead of quantity determines the location within the school complex: artwork gains from natural light which comes in directly from the north. Workshop noise and music emit a noise level which should not interfere with other teaching activity. Technology and the sciences are particularly prone to fire, which is why their spaces are equipped with two exits which lead directly outside. The multitude of requirements often leads to additional sections which combine all the specialist rooms. The following sequence of layers has been established in the stacks of floors: while the workshop noise is banished to the cellar, biology, chemistry and physics are located on the ground floor. Music is in the middle and art rules supreme from the top floor. As a rule, the whole package spills over onto the street, in order to advertise the special competence of the school to the world.

Workroom with media
Specialist rooms which are important for specific teaching purposes, like this workroom in the State School For the Blind and Visually Handicapped, Chemnitz (design: bhss Architekten), must accommodate the needs of the students and teachers. Sufficient supply of electricity and toilets and washrooms as needed should be given special emphasis.

Class room with integrated kitchen
In the planning of single-use areas like utility rooms or teaching kitchens (In this example the State School For the Blind and Visually Handicapped, Chemnitz; design: bhss Architekten) it should be borne in mind that these rooms are not empty after the instruction is finished. A connection between the class room and the integrated kitchen is one solution.

Space Allocation
Safety and Security
Access
Teaching Rooms
Meeting Rooms
Library
Staff Rooms
Toilets and Washrooms
Cafeteria
Open Areas

4

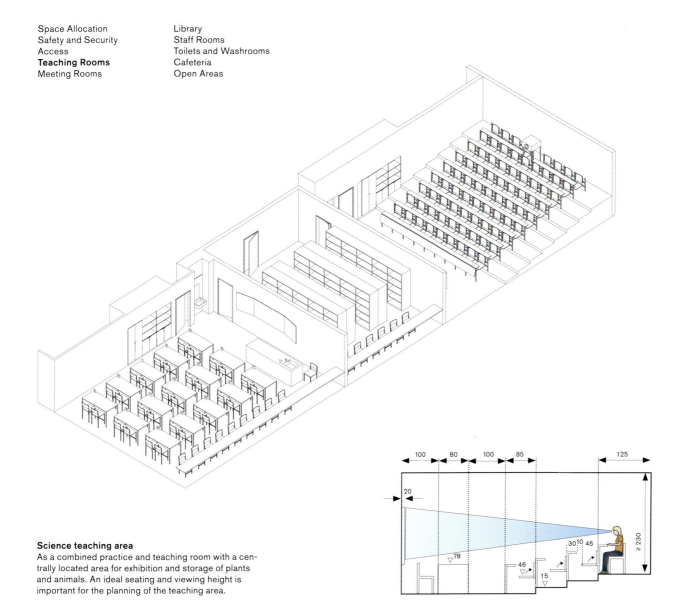

Science teaching area
As a combined practice and teaching room with a centrally located area for exhibition and storage of plants and animals. An ideal seating and viewing height is important for the planning of the teaching area.

Workroom with media
For certain specialist rooms – like the workroom of the Dinkelsbühl Secondary School (design: Fischer Architekten) – it is necessary to provide sufficient electricity, for instance with a ceiling outlet, so that devices can be used during teaching.

Utility room with kitchen
In the planning of certain specialist rooms, like the utility room with teaching kitchen (shown here the Dinkelsbühl Secondary School; design: Fischer Architekten) sufficient ventilation must be provided. A ventilation hood and illumination are integrated in the ceiling here.

Meeting Rooms

Hallway or festival theatre? There is no other school building block with so many design possibilities than the auditorium. Its construction is very project specific, and how! If extracurricular activities are planned and the budget is fat, chances are good. In German guidelines a meeting involving at least the entire school is desirable, but a place to hold such a meeting is not often specified.

Often enough the space allocation programs create the necessary leeway. The internal break areas are already there, for which each student receives almost a half square metre. Also the so-called multi-purpose rooms, which in the mid-sized schools have at least three digit surface areas. The main stairway, the foyer, hallways and a specialized room for music or theatre, plus the cafeteria can be involved. In order to compress all that, equipment and the acoustics face a major challenge. The interweaving of the different functionalities, use frequencies and escape routes can never be perfect. But the agora, as a true point of crystallisation, is the compensation!

Handicapped-accessible in the auditorium
Space for wheelchairs should be provided at different intervals from the stage. Floor space that can be accessed from the back as well as from the front must be at least 130 centimetres deep and at least 90 centimetres wide. The aisle in front of the parking space must be at least 150 centimetres deep. Floor spaces with side access (chair on the aisle side) must be at least 150 centimetres deep and 90 centimetres wide. The circulation area accessible from the side must be at least 90 centimetres wide.

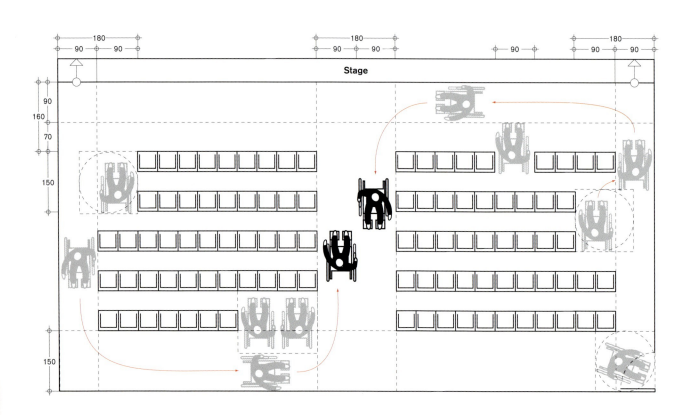

Space Allocation
Safety and Security
Access
Teaching Rooms
Meeting Rooms

Library
Staff Rooms
Toilets and Washrooms
Cafeteria
Open Areas

5

1
In rooms with theatre seating (shown here the Reinhold Burger Grammar School, planning and construction management: Numrich Albrecht Klumpp) space for wheelchairs is reserved. Space on the side facing the aisle is ideal for threshold-less access. Seating for an escort person next to the person in a wheelchair person must be provided. In addition the wheelchair user needs space equivalent to two seats back to back for sufficient manoeuvrability.

2
Darkened event rooms (shown here, Råholt School, designed by Kristin Jarmund Arkitekter) must have sufficient safety lighting. Independent of the safety lighting, the exits, aisles and steps should be recognizable in the dark. The construction components used, insulation material, dropped ceilings, panelling, floor covering and doors must observe the requirements of the fire code.

3
Especially suited for films and other presentations, the Swiss Administration Academy (design by Geninasca & Delefortrie) has a large, round lighting fixture which can illuminate the event room with a special mood. The doors open in the direction of the escape route and can be easily opened to their full width. The exits of the auditorium are also prominently marked.

4
Natural materials, from floor to ceiling, lend the space of the A. P. Møller School (design by C. F. Møller Architects) a light and cheerful ambiance. Seating can be individually arranged according to the type of event. Seating arrangements which offer solutions for different events are one option. A movable lectern transforms the auditorium into a room for podium discussions or screenings.

DESIGN PARAMETERS

Library

Does the school need one? The guidelines do not give a clear answer. But where studies are being conducted, the square metre figures can easily become three digit. In practice the library ends up with a few bookshelves and a check-out counter. In light of the constantly exploding universe of knowledge that is a bad joke!

Main libraries, which are faced with a similar dilemma, have already responded a long time ago: by shifting the storage of books into modern media, electronically accessing the information world and providing equipment and the right ambience for the processing of that information. The student more often prefers to do homework in the library, although the pedagogical supervision which the educational service can offer is missing. From that standpoint cooperation between the school and municipal libraries would be ideal.

If that doesn't happen, then there is the minimum model: the unused book storage is commandeered by other school spaces. The just as unsatisfactory computer booths share the same fate, as well as out-of-the way break rooms, not to mention special care stations. Altogether a learning pool would accumulate, which could truly support the teaching. This is where the designers can really show their stuff!

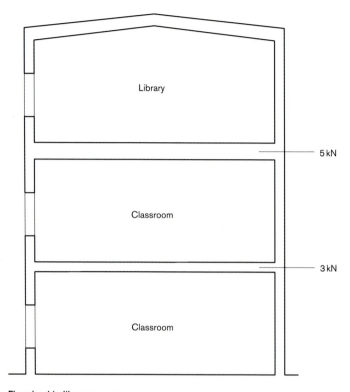

Floor load in library rooms
For rooms which are used to store books, in contrast to teaching rooms (3 kN) an increased floor load of 5 kN is required.

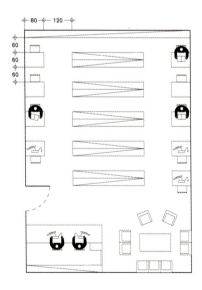

Small school library with media centre (cm)

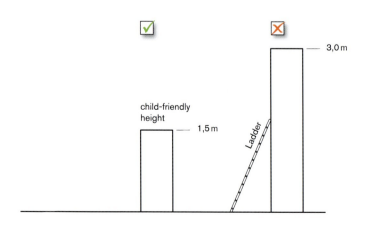

Plan with children in mind – avoid accidents!
A ladder standing around can cause an accident. Therefore it is important to consider heights of the various fixtures like shelving in the design.

Space Allocation
Safety and Security
Access
Teaching Rooms
Meeting Rooms

Library
Staff Rooms
Toilets and Washrooms
Cafeteria
Open Areas

6

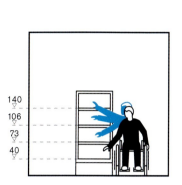 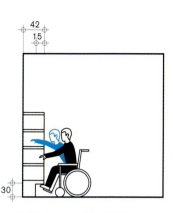 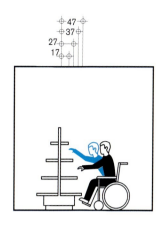 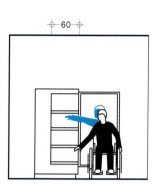

The grip height of a person sitting in a wheelchair is between 40 and 140 centimetres. The majority of shelves are placed at this height. Care should also be taken that the shelves are not too deep. In order for the wheelchair to fit underneath the installation approximately 40 centimetres of depth are needed.

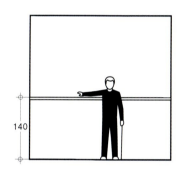 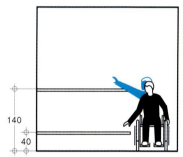

Strict attention must be paid in the mounting and dimensioning of items of furniture that a reasonable grip height in a zone between 40 and 140 centimetres be provided for standing as well as sitting persons.

The library as place of retreat
Sound absorbing materials, curtains and carpets like those in the Hampden Gurney School in London (design: BDP) enhance the atmosphere of the library as a place of retreat, a place to read and enjoy the quiet.

Library as an open common area
The location of the school library and a separate entrance of the Brede School Antares in Leusden in Holland (design: RAU Architects) help make this facility one that the residents also gladly use after school hours.

Staff Rooms

It should be clear that teachers need a break in order to teach effectively. But school opinions vary as to where and how to facilitate that task. As long as space allocation programs require a per capita calculation from the architects, they have the choice … in Germany the staff room is traditionally assigned to the administration tract, which makes up about ten percent of the school. Of course the school direction, secretarial pool, custodian and out-patient care all need their cubby-holes. In the battle for individual space the staff in small schools often comes up short. And even in larger schools each teacher ends up with at best three square metres, seldom more than a desk. And the colleague is usually sitting there, too.

In the specialist class system the space is the same but the method is much more professional, especially in the Anglo-Saxon realm. There, every teacher has his or her class room, and every faculty has a space for preparation. Relaxation rooms are docked on both areas, and occasionally in tandem with a break area. The teachers can go about business here without interruption in their capacities as contact and supervisory persons.

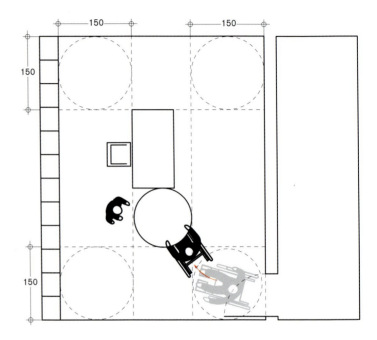

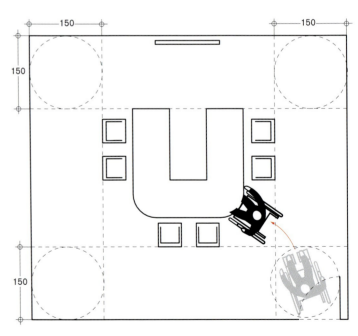

Handicapped accessible planning of faculty rooms (cm)
In the planning of faculty and conference rooms care the manoeuvring area in transit areas and in front of items of furniture like shelves and cabinets should be at least 150 square centimetres. In addition the writing desk and conference table should be high enough to accommodate a wheelchair. These distances are not just important for the users of wheelchairs. They are also help parents who want to bring along their baby carriage to a discussion with the teachers.

Space Allocation
Safety and Security
Access
Teaching Rooms
Meeting Rooms

Library
Staff Rooms
Toilets and Washrooms
Cafeteria
Open Areas

1
A staff room should aid in the preparation of classes, make conferences happen, as well as facilitating parent-teacher discussions. In order to fulfil all these functions, in addition to adequate shelf space, the room should have movable furniture for different purposes.

2
For conference situations it is important that the room can be darkened, for instance for beamer presentations on the wall. This can be accomplished simply with the aid of curtains or blinds. Sufficient ceiling and floor outlets should be available to connect the equipment.

3
The goal of the planning of a teachers' room is to create an atmosphere for rest and work. A carpet can contribute to the spread of sound, not just when students knock on the doors during their breaks, but also when several teachers are working at the same time in the room.

4
Individual work desks can be combined to create a conference situation. A monitor is mounted on the wall to call up information and make presentations. The selection of colours for the floor and walls is restrained. Only the colours of the chairs stand out here.

Toilets and Washrooms

It's amazing what can happen when nature calls! Especially the school planners, who are concerned with emancipation, like to ask that question. To the extent that there are guidelines for toilets and washrooms, they try to at least provide a handicapped equipped toilet for visitors who need them.

In contrast the separation by sex is approached more designer-friendly than operational: women have the same per capita square metres as men, but always have less toilets. Since women constitute the clear majority of teachers, their needs quickly accumulate!

The requirements for the distribution throughout the school are much more pragmatic. Central distribution is passé. The students should be able to relieve themselves where they tend to congregate: toilets are installed in the schoolyard at ground floor level, and at a maximum distance of 40 metres away from the teaching area. The class toilet so popular with teachers, which share two service units user-neutrally, is only relevant for day-cares as a rule. And something happens more often at any rate to the smaller children when nature calls.

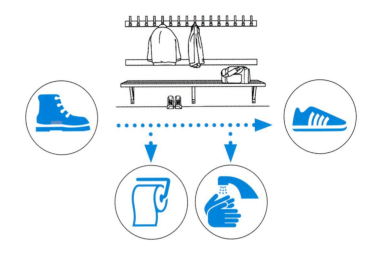

Cloakrooms and side rooms
In order to keep the floor in the gym and school clean, a dressing room is important to act as a buffer between the toilets and washrooms and the sports areas.

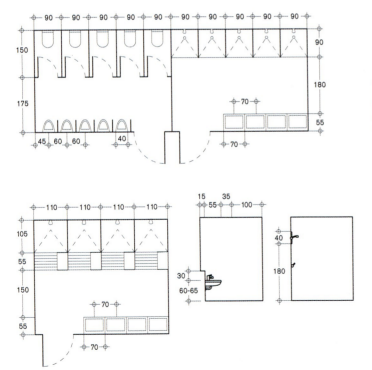

Lavatory with adjacent washroom
At intervals of 90 centimetres five toilets are placed in a row. Across from them are the urinals. A washroom adjoins the toilet facility.

Shower facility with washbasin
In order to accommodate the traffic after gymnastics a reasonable amount of space is needed for the shower stalls. In addition slip-proof floors should be installed.

Space Allocation   Library
Safety and Security   Staff Rooms
Access   **Toilets and Washrooms**
Teaching Rooms   Cafeteria
Meeting Rooms   Open Areas

1
Doors opening outwards mean that the stall can be longer than with toilet doors that swing inwards. If additional urinals are needed, a minimum distance of 205 centimetres is needed between the toilets and the urinals.

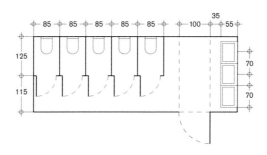

2
If additional storage space is needed, like a set of shelves across from the toilet area, these can be installed at an interval of 190 centimetres. The same principle applies to additional toilets. Attention should be paid to the number of washstands.

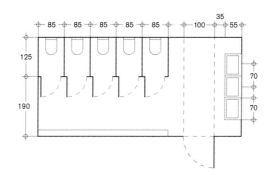
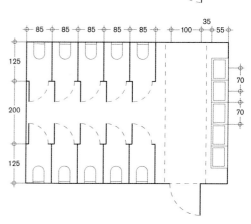

3
If space allows, the stall doors can also be designed to open inwards. In this configuration the toilet partition is 25 centimetres longer, providing more space directly in front of the toilet. The space in front of the stalls is the same.

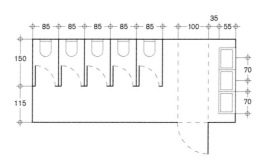

4
As a consequence of the stall doors opening outwards, the required space in front of the storage spaces and the toilets across the way is less, reduced to 155 and 125 centimetres respectively.

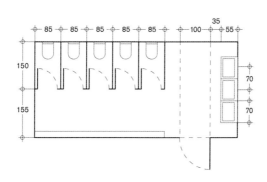
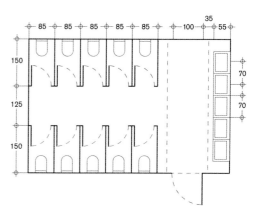

Toilets and Washrooms

Lavatory installation	Lavatory	Urinals
for 40 boys	1	2
for 40 girls	2	–
for 15 teachers	1	1
for 10 female teachers	1	–

Reference values for lavatories
For female students and teachers a washbasin is required for every two toilets. For male students and teachers one wash basin per toilet is needed. In addition for every toilet facility there should be at least one handicapped accessible toilet.

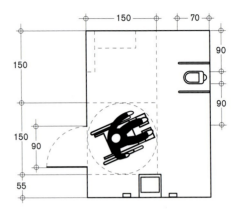

Standard values for handicap accessible toilets
For a handicapped access of the toilet facilities an area of wheelchair manoeuvrability from 1.50 cm × 1.50 cm in front of the toilet and the washbasin is needed.

Wash basins do not need to be in a room with the lavatory. They can be located in a hallway in front of the lavatories as they are here in the Råholt School designed by Kristin Jarmund Arkitekter.

Careful planning and collaboration between the architect and the engineer contributes to the functionality, hygiene and comfort of the sanitary facilities.

Space Allocation
Safety and Security
Access
Teaching Rooms
Meeting Rooms

Library
Staff Rooms
Toilets and Washrooms
Cafeteria
Open Areas

8

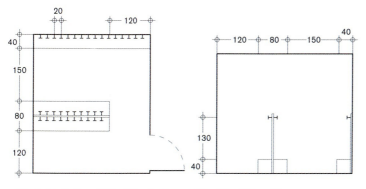 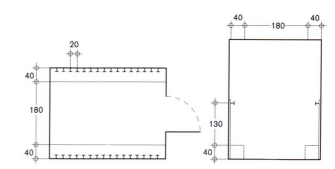

Wardrobe (in the middle of the room or on the side of the wall)

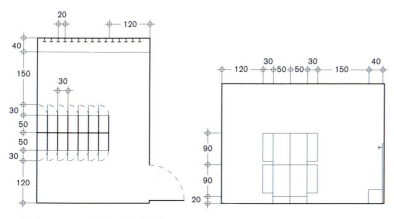 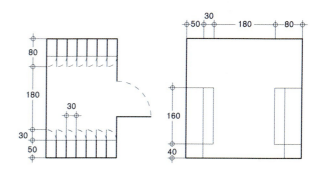

Lockers, accessible from both sides
(in the middle of the room or mounted on the side of the wall)

Lockers for the storage of clothing can be mounted in the middle of the room or mounted on the side of the wall. Movable benches aid in changing clothes before and after sports.

The wardrobes of the State School for the Blind and Visually Handicapped in Chemnitz (design: bhss Architekten) are placed in front of the classes so that the students have access at any time to their possessions.

DESIGN PARAMETERS

379

Cafeteria and School Kitchen

Joint catering is considered indispensable for all-day schools. Student cooking would make sense from every standpoint, but it only works in small groups, which seldom are full class strength in number, even if teaching kitchens are available.

Normally it is the most efficient when the food is prepared off campus. In the school a room to warm and distribute the food is sufficient, generally measuring between 35 and 60 square metres. The caterer may have specific requirements.

If the food is distributed, the choices are greater. Simple dining halls, which require at least one square metre per student, and where the students eat in up to three shifts, are the best solution.

The alternative is to distribute the food through the whole building (eating is only expressly forbidden in certain specialist rooms). That generates surface area advantages and design possibilities which create identity for the school.

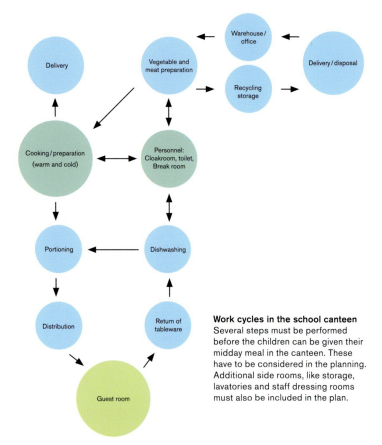

Work cycles in the school canteen
Several steps must be performed before the children can be given their midday meal in the canteen. These have to be considered in the planning. Additional side rooms, like storage, lavatories and staff dressing rooms must also be included in the plan.

Making room for the School Kitchen & Co
The school kitchen with adjacent dining room is part of the space allocation program for all-day schools. That means many school building must be adapted to have that capability. The refurbished canteen of the Wilhelm von Humboldt School with two dining halls and an intermediate gallery offers a view onto the courtyard.

Materials in the food area
In the conversion of the former heating and coal cellar lasting five years in Berlin-Pankow into a canteen, the Berlin firm of Architekten Numrich Albrecht Klumpp used a design employing exposed concrete in combination with wood slats with a filigree effect as a ceiling construction.

Space Allocation   Library
Safety and Security   Staff Rooms
Access   Toilets and Washrooms
Teaching Rooms   **Cafeteria**
Meeting Rooms   Open Areas

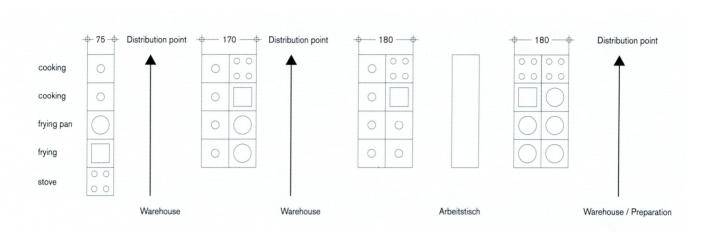

Work flow from warehouse to counter

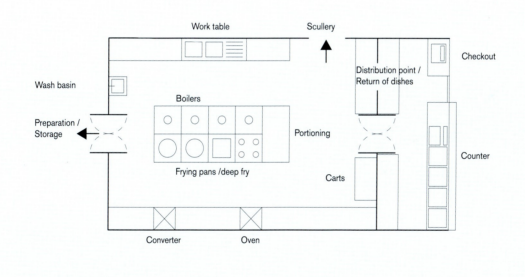

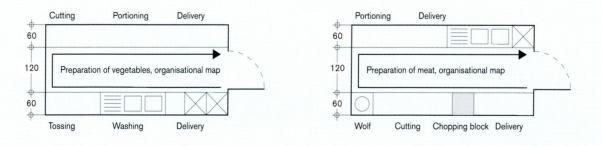

Organization of the school kitchen

Cafeteria and School Kitchen

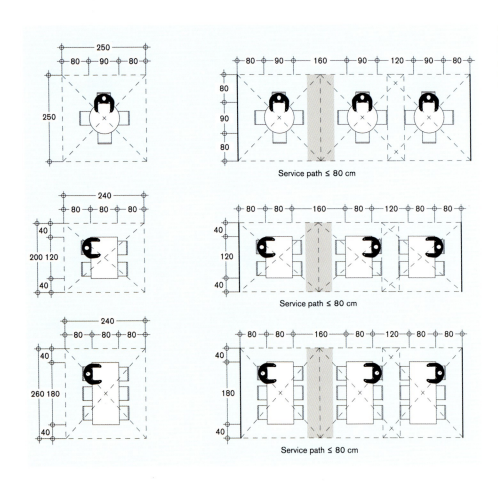

Depending on the size and shape of the desk and the type of chair arrangement, different minimal distances apply in order to guarantee the smooth preparation of the food. For the size of the table it is important how many people are seated and how much space a table can occupy in a given room.

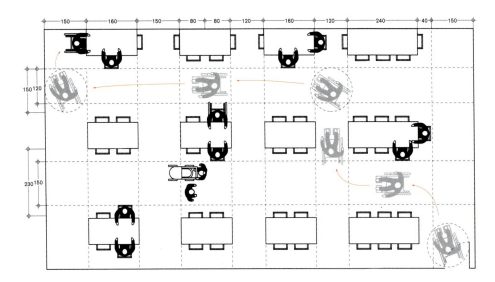

A visit to the restaurant, even for persons without handicaps, can be trying because of the densely packed chairs. For a wheelchair user a clear width of 120 centimetres between persons sitting at adjacent tables is required. At the unoccupied ends of the table 150 centimetres of transit space should be guaranteed.

Space Allocation
Safety and Security
Access
Teaching Rooms
Meeting Rooms

Library
Staff Rooms
Toilets and Washrooms
Cafeteria
Open Areas

The arrangement of the tables in small rooms is especially critical because with a well thought-out plan much space can be saved. For instance with a diagonal arrangement a reduction of the space requirement of 1.84 square metres is possible. With three adjacent tables for four persons the space saved is 5.36 square metres.

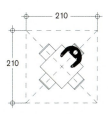
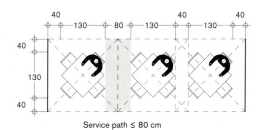
Service path ≤ 80 cm

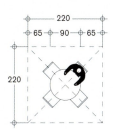
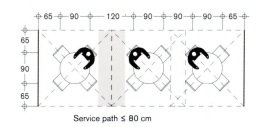
Service path ≤ 80 cm

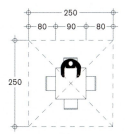
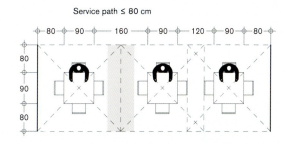
Service path ≤ 80 cm

Canteen of the Carl von Linné School in Berlin
The listed school complex, a relic from the 1970s, was renovated while still in operation by Numrich Albrecht Klumpp Architekten.

After the conversion of the school for physically handicapped children from 2003 to 2013, 400 students now have a large canteen to use. The bright and cheerful dining hall is handicapped accessible.

The newly created canteen is also used for school events. With larger numbers of visitors the yellow folding walls can be opened to the hallways in order to provide more space.

Open Areas and Gyms

Schools always use their open spaces for sports and games, for reflection and to learn from nature. German guidelines assign an average of five square metres per student for such activity (in total at least several hundred). That certainly is enough for an enclosed school garden along with an open air classroom. In addition some playground equipment can be installed, with the required safety intervals.

The playing fields are a little more critical where the surfaces are cordoned off. Their format pushes everything else to the side-lines. When everyone takes care of themselves first, then freedom in the open spaces is inevitably lost.

This is where planning can help: the individual interest groups have to take a step back. Experience shows that egomaniacs will use everything to get their way. Architecture can help avoid cardinal errors and keep the space intervals to the street to a minimum. The green landscaping accomplishes the most: It is a reminder that the open space is there!

Above
Seesaws
Equipment like swings, seesaws, slides or gymnastic bars belong in a movement-friendly schoolyard. They provide opportunities to move during the breaks and lay the basis for concentration in class.

Below
Monkey bars with slide
Balance can be learned with multi-piece equipment like certain kinds of monkey bars. In addition coordination and motor skills can be acquired. And the children's creativity benefits too.

Space Allocation
Safety and Security
Access
Teaching Rooms
Meeting Rooms
Library
Staff Rooms
Toilets and Washrooms
Cafeteria
Open Areas

10

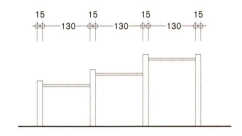

Horizontal bars (cm)

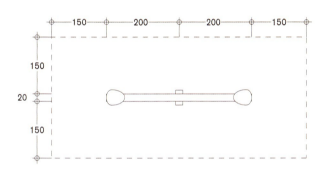

Seesaws (cm)

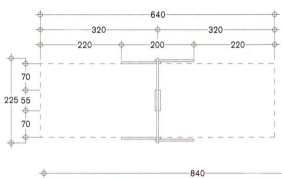

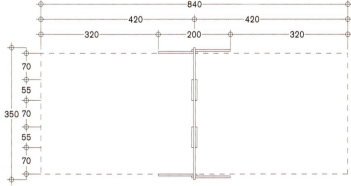

One and two person swings (cm)

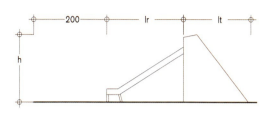

Height (h)	Slide length (sl)	Stair length (stl)
125	260	130
150	300	150
175	340	175
200	385	200
225	430	225
250	470	250
300	560	300

Slide: heights and lengths (cm)

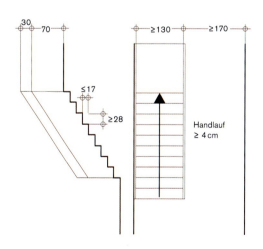

Slide: stairs and railing (cm)

DESIGN PARAMETERS

385

Open Areas and Gyms

Sports and games also take place inside. Especially when the weather is inclement or the gymnastics training involves certain equipment, gymnasiums are an indispensable addition to every school. Three basic types are recognized according to the requirements of DIN 18032, Gymnasiums Halls, Rooms for Sports and Multiple-use (*Sporthallen – Hallen und Räume für Sport und Mehrzwecknutzung*): individual – (15 × 27 metres, clear height of 5.5 metres), double – (22 × 45 metres, clear height of 7.0 metres) and triple (27 × 45 metres, clear height of 7.0 metres).

Gyms should of course be illuminated. Costs increase the more glass is used, not only for the ball-impact proof glass surfaces needed, but also for glare protection and cleaning, and costs are greater the more windows are used. Natural ventilation must also be provided.

Individuals with special needs must be considered in the planning of gyms and their side rooms (cloakrooms, equipment, teachers' rooms and washrooms and toilets etc.) If all areas for sports instruction are on one level, then these goals are easy to fulfil. It becomes more difficult when the areas are distributed over several floors. Careful planning is also important here.

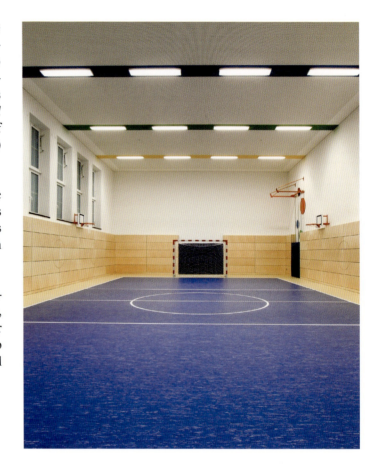

School Scheffelberg in Zwickau
After the conversion of the listed school ensemble from the 1950s by architectural office G & J Kretzschmar coloured ceiling stripes were used to define the renovated gym. They recall the historical connection of the existing building. The effect is enhanced by the bright impact walls made of birch veneer which define the dominant blue playing surfaces of the gym.

Space Allocation
Safety and Security
Access
Teaching Rooms
Meeting Rooms
Library
Staff Rooms
Toilets and Washrooms
Cafeteria
Open Areas

The access and transition area of the historical staircase in the gym of the school was transformed into a tunnel to underscore the theme of the location. The floor stylized as a running track continues the theme. In addition this area sets off the newly created sports instruction area from to the stairway.

The geometric form of the circle, the idea of which is based on an old tossing game in the wall area of the existing building, is continued as a pin board element and signage in the staircase. One reaches the toilet and washroom area for boys and girls via the stairs which lead to the 2nd floor. A gymnastics room and staff room are also located there.

Index

A

Access 48ff., 54, 344ff., 356ff.
Access gate 52
Administrative area 52f., 344f., 374
All day care 29, 36, 40, 47, 52, 54, 354, 380
Athenaeum 27, 183
Auditorium 14ff., 18ff., 28, 30, 37, 44, 48, 51, 54f., 344, 348, 370f.

B

Ballroom 54
Blackboard 363
Break room 32, 346, 380
Building material classes 351, 357
Building organization 346
Building process 46

C

Cafeteria 380ff.
Campus 15, 20, 26, 32
Canteen 48, 54f., 345, 348, 380, 383
Chair 41, 360, 364
Class pavilion 6, 21, 34, 344
Classroom 36, 349, 360ff.
Cloakroom 13, 376, 380, 386, 379
Cluster 47, 50, 344, 348f., 355
Colour scheme 36, 362
Common area 7, 20, 47f., 54, 345, 349, 355, 367
Communication area 50ff.
Community school 27ff.
Comprehensive school 46, 23, 37, 51
Computer 32, 42, 44, 364, 367, 372
Conference area 24, 48, 52f., 367, 374f.

D

Design parameters 7, 340ff.
Design requirements 46
Desk 6, 38, 40ff., 360, 363ff., 382
Desk height 41, 364f.
Dining hall 18, 127, 145, 380
District school 46
Doors 48f., 349ff., 356, 358, 371, 377

E

Eligibility criteria 46, 340
Emergency stairway 355, 357
Ergonomy 7, 41, 362
Escape route 350, 352ff., 358, 370
Escape route marking 353
Event hall 55, 370f.

F

Fire control 50, 351, 354, 371
Fire resistance classes 351
Fixtures 356, 363, 372
Floor space requirements 344
Foyer 27, 30, 48, 370, 348
Functional diagram 7, 349
Furniture 6, 38, 40ff., 64, 362ff., 375, 382

G

Grammar school 17, 19
Group area 36, 40, 48f., 345, 348f.
Group size 340
Gymnasium 48, 386f.

H

Hand railing 359, 385
Handicapped accessible 7, 349, 370, 374, 378, 383
Handrails 356

I

Illumination 34, 36, 360, 362
Individual 40, 48f., 52f., 348, 367
Information storage medium 11
Interactive electronic blackboard 42

J

Joint specialist room 50
Laboratory school 23ff.

L

Laptop cabinet module 42
Lavatory 376, 378, 380
Learning groups 50, 345
Learning landscape 7, 34ff., 40, 44, 47, 51, 349, 360, 362, 367
Library 2ff., 28ff., 54, 127, 372f.
Locker 379

M

Main staircase 349, 370
Media centre 40f., 372
Media utilization 6f., 12, 32, 40, 42, 44, 363, 368f., 372
Meeting room 54, 340, 370f.
Model space allocation program 46, 50, 344ff.
Monastery school 12, 17, 24
Montessori School 22, 26, 30, 34ff., 40
Multimedia room 42
Multiple learning 44
Multi-purpose room 47, 53f., 345, 348f., 370, 386
Music room 54, 368, 370

N

Needs assessment 47
Non-denominational school 46

O

Open learning area 51
Open plan principle 23
Open space 13, 47, 384ff.
Open-air school 21f.
Organizational model 7, 46ff.
Orientation 353, 358, 363

P

Partition 23, 25f., 48, 55, 377
Pavilion school 21f., 34
Pedagogy 20, 22, 34, 36, 46f., 344, 346
Performance requirements 351
Physical training 14
Preparatory high school 13f., 20, 25, 30, 36f., 55, 345
Progressive school 20f., 34
Public facilities 346, 370ff.
Public square 14, 25, 27

Q

Quality criteria 7, 46
Quiet area 50, 54

R

Recreation area 50, 54, 354, 356, 358
Regional school 46
Retreat area 40ff., 52, 367
Riser 358
Room acoustics 20, 36, 340, 349, 362f., 370
Room dimension 362f., 386
Room height 46, 342, 362f.
Room module 26

S

Safety and Security 350ff., 354, 362, 365, 371, 384
School construction debate 47
School funding 46, 340
School kitchen 101, 369, 380
School timetable 340, 344
Schoolyard 21, 37, 44, 376, 384
Seating height 41, 364f.
Seating posture 41, 362, 364f.
Secondary school 46, 369
Service area 346
Shower 376
Side room 49, 346, 376, 380, 386
Signage 353f.
Single purpose 47
Smart Sync 42

Smoke ventilation windows 357
Space allocation program 18, 26, 27, 33, 46, 340ff., 346ff., 370, 374, 380
Spatial organization 37, 47ff.
Specialist room 50, 367ff.
Specialist room for biology 367
Specialty area 36, 48, 50
Sports field 14, 21, 30, 34, 384f.
Stairs 350ff., 358f.
Stairway hall 357
Stairwell 358
Standard surface value 46
Step 358

T

Tablet 6, 42, 44
Tandem class 49
Teacher's area 7, 26f., 36, 48, 52, 374f.
Teacher-up-front 47
Teaching kitchen 367, 369, 380
Teaching materials 42, 345
Teaching room 346, 360ff.
Team area 47, 48, 50ff.
Team-Teaching 348f.
Temple of Knowledge 11ff.
Theatre seating 371
Think Tanks 51
Toilet and washroom area 50f., 376ff., 387

U

Usage requirement 46, 48
Utility room 369

V

Ventilation 36, 340
Wardrobe 25, 345, 349f., 356, 363, 379
Warehouse 25, 50f., 345, 366, 372, 381
Washbasin 363, 367, 376, 378
Work place 32, 40, 42, 44, 48f., 345, 348f. 363f., 367ff., 372

Illustration Credits

The ordering of the illustrations follows the page number and the illustration number (in brackets). The list of illustrations contains unnamed graphics, plans and photographs by the authors and the relevant architectural firms. Unless indicated otherwise the technical drawings beginning on page 338 were created by DOM publishers.

p. 2	VS Vereinigte Spezialmöbelfabriken GmbH & Co. KG	p. 144–149	photos: Straßgütl, Nina/www.ninastrg.de (1–8)
p. 11	photo: Villgratter, Stefanie	p. 150–157	photos: Verme, Miguel (1–4)
p. 12	Arnold, Dieter: *Lexikon der ägyptischen Baukunst,* Düsseldorf 2000, p. 264.	p. 162–169	photos: Mørk, Adam (1–10)
p. 13	Deutsches Archäologisches Institut	p. 172–179	photos: Young, Nigel/Foster+Partners (1–12)
p. 14	Von Corven, O./Tolzmann, Don Heinrich et al.: *The memory of mankind. The story of libraries since the dawn of history,* New Castle 2001 (above left); Reisch, Emil/Wilberg, Wilhelm/Keil, Josef et al.: *Forschungen in Ephesos, vol. 3,* Vienna 1923, p. 128 (above right).	p. 182–187	photos: Rob 't Hart Fotografie (1–8)
		p. 190–195	photos: Vulkers, Ben (1–4)
		p. 198–203	photos: Southwood, Dave (1–6)
		p. 206–211	photos: Snape, Diana (1, 5); Mein, Trevor (2–3); Hyatt, Peter (4, 6)
		p. 214–221	photos: Henriksen, Poul Ib (1, 4–5, 7–9, 13); Weyer, Julian (2–3, 6, 10–12, 14)
p. 15	Intorcetta, Prospero/Couplet, Philippe et al.: *Life and works of confucius,* not stated 1687.	p. 224–229	photos: Burgstaller, Peter (1–9)
p. 16	photo: Boerschmann, Ernst	p. 232–237	photos: Stokmo, Rune (1, 2, 3, 4, 5); Grønli, Espen (6–8)
p. 17	photo: iStockphoto/Spiro, Peter	p. 238–243	photos: De Guzman, Miguel (1, 2, 4–10); AMP arquitectos (3)
p. 18	drawing: Neuffer, Johann Christoph/Source: *Illustrissimi Wirtembergici Ducalis Novi Collegii Quod Tubingae qua situm, qua studia qua exercitia Accurata delineatio (Fragment),* not stated 1606/1608.	p. 246–253	photos: Rastl, Lisa
		p. 256–263	photos: Andersen, Magnús/a2f arkitektar ehf, (1, 2, 4–10); Arason, Vilhjálmur Ari (3)
		p. 266–271	photos: Wiik, Stian (1, 3–7); Maning, Per (2)
p. 19	drawing: Conz, Karl Philipp/source: Schukraft, Harald: *Kleine Geschichte des Hauses Württemberg,* Tübingen 2006, p. 175.	p. 274–281	photos: Braun, Zooey (1, 2, 4–14); Forkel, August (3)
		p. 284–289	photos: Straßgütl, Nina/www.ninastrg.de (1–5, 7); Lintner, Linus (6)
p. 20	Müller, Thomas/Schneider, Romana: *Das Klassenzimmer vom Ende des 19. Jahrhunderts bis heute,* Tübingen 2010, p. 120.	p. 292–297	photos: El Equipo De Mazzanti (1); Sergio Gómez (2–7)
		p. 300–307	photos: Pfammatter, Dario (1–12); Mair, Walter (13)
p. 21	drawing: Tomokiyo, Masako/source: Gropius, Walter: *Schema zum Aufbau der Lehre am Bauhaus,* 1922, published in: Gropius, Walter et al.: *Staatliches Bauhaus Weimar 1919–1923,* Weimar 1923.	p. 312–317	photos: Jantscher, Thomas (1–7)
		p. 322–327	photos: Laser, Robert (1, 5, 9); Junghans, Steffen (2, 6–8, 10–14); Hermus, Stefan (3, 4)
		p. 330–337	photos: Müller, Stefan (1–7)
p. 22	Lods, Marcel: Section du Plan. Wiederaufbauplanung für Mainz. 1946–1948. Freiluftschule/Source: Müller/Schneider, p. 139.	p. 341–343	design: Tobolla, Jennifer
		p. 341–343	design: Tobolla, Jennifer
		p. 348	Hausmann, Frank/Pfaff, Florence: *Das offene Klassenzimmer,* Fachhochschule Aachen, Aachen 2004.
p. 23	Bundesarchiv Picture 102-15782, photo: Pahl, Georg	p. 349	design: Tobolla, Jennifer
p. 24	Müller/Schneider, p. 149.	p. 350	Verband für Sicherheitstechnik e.V.: *Handbuch Gefahrenmanagement-Systeme (GMS). Wirtschaftliche Fragestellungen – Nutzungsanforderungen – Lösungskonzeptionen,* not stated.
p. 25	Bielefeld Marketing GmbH, photo: Freitag, Susanne		
p. 26	photo: flickr/SEIER+SEIER		
p. 28	photos: Knjasewa, Irina (above left); Knoch, Peter (above right)		
p. 29	Venturi, Robert: *Complexity and Contradiction in Architecture,* New York 1996 (above left); *Schulbetriebsgebäude. Bauliche Hülle für veränderbare Unterrichtsformen,* in: werk 8/1971; Modell: ARB-Arbeitsgruppe; photo: Burkhard, Balthasar (above right)	p. 351	Pottgiesser, Uta/Wiewiorra, Carsten: *Handbuch and Planungshilfe. Raumbildender Ausbau,* Berlin 2013, p. 55.
		p. 353	photos: Grabner, Wolf-Dieter (above left); polyform, Büro für Grafik and Produktdesign (above right)
		p. 354–355	design: Tobolla, Jennifer
p. 30	photo: Rohmer, Marlies	p. 356	Pottgiesser/Wiewiorra, p. 218.
p. 31	Müller/Schneider, p. 236.	p. 359	photos: Mitchell, Dean (left and middle); Meuser, Philipp (right)
p. 32	photo: Rob 't Hart Fotografie	p. 360	Illustration: Castilla, Carlos (above); photo: Praefcke, Andreas (below)
p. 33	Learning & Teaching Development/York St John University (above left); VS Vereinigte Spezialmöbelfabriken GmbH & Co. KG (above right)	p. 361	design: Tobolla, Jennifer
		p. 364	Deutsche Gesetzliche Unfallversicherung: *GUV-SI 8011. Richtig sitzen in der Schule. Mindestanforderungen an Tische und Stühle in allgemeinbildenden Schulen,* Berlin 2008.
p. 35	drawing: Voltz, Johann Michael/source: Müller/Schneider, p. 11 (1823); Müller/Schneider, p. 30 (1904); ibid., p. 123 (1928); ibid., p. 37 (1929); ibid., p. 142 (1935); ibid., p. 147 (1939); ibid., p. 21 (1948); p. 175 (1954); Neutra, Raymond (1926); photo: MYDECK GmbH (2012)	p. 366	photos: Can Stock Photo/sayuri_ao (left); iStockphoto/nano (middle); Can Stock Photo/photostocker (right)
		p. 368	photos: Junghans, Steffen
p. 36	Roth, Alfred: *Das neue Schulhaus,* Zurich 1950 (Fig. 2).	p. 369	photos: Braun, Zooey
p. 37	Bauwelt 15/2013, p. 19 (Fig. 4); Bauwelt 15/2013, p. 22 (Fig. 5); Müller/Schneider, p. 46 (Fig. 6).	p. 370	photo: Meuser, Philipp
		p. 371	photos: Lintner, Linus (1); Wiik, Stian (2); Jantscher, Thomas (3); Weyer, Julian (4)
p. 38–45	VS Vereinigte Spezialmöbelfabriken GmbH & Co. KG		
p. 48–55	Montag Stiftungen	p. 373	photos: Hamilton Knight, Martine (left); Vulkers, Ben (right)
p. 60–65	photos: Van der Meer, Alexander (1, 3–7); Rohmer, Marlies (2)	p. 375	iStockphoto/arcady_31 (1); iStockphoto/montiannoowong (2), iStockphoto/titlezpix (3); iStockphoto/frazaz (4)
p. 60–65	photos: Van der Meer, Alexander (1, 3–7); Rohmer, Marlies (2)		
p. 68–73	photos: Hamilton Knight, Martine (1–7)	p. 378	photos: Stian Wiik (left); iStockphoto/xyno (right)
p. 76–81	photos: Kroth, Andrea (1–7)	p. 379	photos: Can Stock Photo/edarchinyan (left); Junghans, Steffen (right)
p. 84–89	photos: Hörbst, Kurt (1–8)		
p. 92–105	photos: Pluchinotta, Fausto (1–9)	p. 380	photos: Straßgütl, Nina/www.ninastrg.de
p. 108–113	photos: Spengler · Wiescholek (1–7)	p. 383	photos: Lintner, Linus
p. 116–123	photos: Vulkers, Ben (1–6)	p. 384	photos: Can Stock Photo/kungverylucky (above), Can Stock Photo/WDGPhoto (below)
p. 126–131	photos: Schinko, Michael (1–4); Junghans, Steffen (5–10)		
p. 136–141	photos: Weber, Jens (1–7)	p. 386–387	photos: Kretzschmar, Jörn

Notes

The *Deutsche Nationalbibliothek* lists this publication in the *Deutsche Nationalbibliografie*; detailed bibliographical data may be found in the internet at *http://dnb.d-nb.de*.

ISBN 978-3-86922-038-3 (English)
ISBN 978-3-86922-037-6 (German)

© 2014 by DOM publishers, Berlin
www.dom-publishers.com

This work is protected by copyright. Any use beyond the limits of the copyright laws without the permission of the publisher is prohibited and liable to prosecution. This applies in particular to reproductions, translations, and microfilming, as well as storing and processing in electronic systems. The naming of the authors has been made to the best of our knowledge and conscience.

Final Editing
Stefanie Villgratter

Editorial Assistance
Annabelle Eicker
Ansgar Oswald
Jennifer Tobolla

Technical Drawings
Jessica Findeisen
Martin Kragh
Fabio Schillaci

Translation
Geoffrey Steinherz

Design
Nicole Wolf

Printing
Tiger Printing (Hong Kong) Co., Ltd.
www.tigerprinting.hk